Walkabout

Walkabout

JOHN ARTHUR

This book is dedicated to all the people
in the world who get all the horrible jobs and
never get recognised

John & Sue

Best Wishes

John Arthur x

September 2014

arthurboyd@aol.com

© John Arthur, 2014

Published by John Arthur Boyd Publishing

A CIP catalogue record for this book is available from the British Library.

ISBN 978-0-9928013-0-4

Book layout and design by Clare Brayshaw

Cover design by Bruce Argue

Prepared and printed by:

York Publishing Services Ltd
64 Hallfield Road
Layerthorpe
York YO31 7ZQ

Tel: 01904 431213

Website: www.yps-publishing.co.uk

Contents

SHETLANDS
ISLANDS

ORKNEY ISLANDS

THURSO

GLASGOW

NEWCASTLE

LIVERPOOL

BOSTON

TAUNTON

PLYMOUTH

DOVER

Introduction

This is a story about a farmer's travels around the outside of the UK walking and using public transport, taken over three and a half years, returning home after each chapter. After many years of foreign travel I thought it would be interesting to discover my own country, and at least I could speak the same language, or that's what I thought until reaching Scotland!

Also I was becoming more useless on the farm and quickly being superseded by the younger generation and would not be missed. I had no intention of writing a book, and thought it would be a pity just to leave the diaries stacked in the attic after meeting so many interesting people and listening to some of their fascinating stories.

I would also like to give a big thank you to Martin Porter and Valerie Hoad and all the other people who have helped me putting this in to the Queen's English.

A lot of this is written with tongue in cheek, so please do not take offence!

CHAPTER ONE

Dover To Arundel

It was autumn on the farm and time to start ploughing. The fields are large and the seagulls were gobbling up the worms that had been exposed by the plough, and even the odd mouse. When the gulls were disturbed they took off like a huge sheet being waved in the air, but they soon returned. Going up and down the field my mind started to turn to my travels.

After years of foreign travel and being frustrated at my inability to speak a foreign language, I thought it would be great to discover my own country. I also felt that as I was becoming more and more useless on the farm I wouldn't be greatly missed. I could go round Britain clockwise, keeping roughly to the coastline, using public transport as well as walking. This way I would educate myself and meet other people. I could do it over several years, always returning to the last place I'd visited. At the time it was certainly not my intention to write a book about my travels.

I made Valerie, my partner a very early morning cup of tea, threw a rucksack over my back, and had the feeling that she was going to survive very well without me for a few days.

We're lucky in Lenham as we have a really cheerful station master who makes a big effort to clean and decorate the place with flowers. It's just what the early commuters need to cheer them on their way. Now, with my £9.40 ticket in my pocket I was actually on my way to Dover.

Dover seemed to be full of immigrants and low-income families, who were fat and covered in tattoos, stuffing themselves with chips in McDonald's before 10.30am.

I caught a bus, the first of over two hundred I would eventually use on my 'walkabout'. A nice smiley 'breath-of-fresh-air' lady driver dropped me off at the first footbridge that crosses the A20 to Shakespeare Cliffs.

Wow, what a walk that was with no barriers or fencing – I felt I was living right on the edge! However, it didn't last long before fencing and paths took over.

As it was a warm October day and there was nobody about I took off my shirt – all the way to Folkestone I only met one young man with his dog – but I should have kept it on when going through the prickly gorse bushes.

The Saxon Shore Way is a real beauty spot, but sadly it was littered with beer cans, empty water bottles, fag and crisp packets, as well as plastic bags hanging in the blackthorn bushes. How ugly the National Cycle Network signs are – it's a pity they didn't provide more rubbish bins instead. One particularly nice part was spotting the large snails basking in the humid air after stuffing themselves on sea-kale. The last thing I'd expected to see here was a woodpecker, keeping company with a few magpies and crows. A cat, hunting a mouse, took no notice of me.

At Capel-le-Ferne, I came across the Christopher Foxley-Norris Memorial Wall, which is a monument to all the airmen who flew in the Battle of Britain. There were three Boyds on it: AD; AH; and RF. It made me realise how lucky we are to have our freedom.

As I walked down the hill into Folkestone, my knees weren't feeling that good. I passed a Martello Tower where there was a kestrel sitting on the top – maybe this had been its home before the builders had moved in.

I had ham and chips in a dead-end seaside pavilion, which even advertised itself as a venue for weddings. The food sat in my stomach like a dead hedgehog.

As I walked further into Folkestone the wind was so strong that the rubbish overtook me, and it was so quiet that I wondered if the whole place had been struck by the Black Death. I bought a throwaway camera – a tough looking coloured man who'd bought cigarettes chucked the wrapper on the ground. I said nothing. *'Coward!'*

I decided to walk part of the Hythe Military Canal, which was built in 1804 to keep the Napoleonic soldiers out of Romney Marsh. At one time there were 15,000 troops stationed in Hythe. What a tribute the canal is to the men who dug it out by hand.

'What's in it?' I asked a fisherman.

'Everything,' came the reply. I was not sure that fishing was his main preoccupation as there was a large bottle of whisky beside him.

This stretch of the water buzzed with wildlife in one form or another. The light was fading and so I turned off and walked into Hythe. I suddenly realised how unfit I was. I found one of my hated brown B&B signs. I followed it and ended up at 'Dolly Dream' or something like that. I arrived at the little bungalow showing a 'Vacancies' sign. When I knocked on the door the lady said she was full – she probably didn't like the sight of me – and recommended a pub in Hythe. *Thank you, Ma'am!*

The bar was full of construction workers. I nearly dropped down dead when the barmaid told me the room would cost £54. A worker said that the pub up the road the rooms were £49. He said he tended to get pissed so slept in his car. I offered £40, thinking I was so tired I would pay the full price if need be. The barmaid said that she would speak to her boss who was in the shower.

The place stank of fried food and the carpets were well past their sell-by date. Nicotine stained the ceiling and the air fans seemed to have been blocked for years. At least the bathroom was brand new, although it wasn't quite finished. However, I was happy that there was hot and cold running water.

After that disgusting lunch I'd had earlier, I went for the prawn cocktail. It was like eating Kleenex tissues, but most of the rest of the food was edible. One thing about the pub was its love of dogs – they were everywhere.

DYMCHURCH TO WINCHELSEA

At breakfast it seemed there were just four of us, including a German couple – here to visit gardens. They had paid 240 euros to come over. The other man said, 'Do you know how much it cost me? One euro. My son works on the Eurostar.' *Clever little man!*

I handed my keys to the phone-bound lady who didn't even look up, and I went out to get some fresh air.

It was a damp misty morning but great for a 'walkabout'. I got on the bus and bought my £4.50 'all-day' ticket. We passed some really scruffy farm buildings – not a good advertisement for us farmers – and then we passed Littlestone Golf Course which made me chuckle at the thought of all the awful golf I'd played there. Passing fellow farmer, Mr Robert Thompson, on a tractor and trailer taking more seed wheat to the field, I wondered who the mug was – him, still drilling; or the chap on the bus? I think it was probably the man on the bus.

Arriving at Lydd, a garrison town since the 19th century, I remembered my Spanish lessons here. I attended six out of the ten lessons and then realised languages were not for me, so I did a runner.

I found the footpath to Camber and now the boot was on the other foot. I was no longer a farmer, but a rambler and these farmers hadn't done a good job marking the footpaths. I was dreading bumping into Mr Balcombe, a farmer I knew, because the family didn't suffer fools lightly. Luckily, he never spotted me, and I moved on to the next farm scaring off hundreds of swans that were eating his forward crop of oilseed rape.

I startled a marsh harrier that was eating a dead sheep and round the corner there was a small field of wild bird food, grown specifically to feed the birds in winter. It was a sight to behold as every kind of seed-eating bird imaginable flew up out of it.

There was a lady walking towards me in the lonely distance, but taking one look at me, she turned around and went back!

What messy people some farmers are. There were plastic fertiliser bags all over the place; gates with more string than metal; old pallets scattered around; and a dead sheep in a ditch.

I had a 'meal' of baked potatoes and chicken curry in Camber.

'Is everything OK?'

'Why do I lie, and why don't I tell her it's a load of shit?'

Even the seagulls didn't eat the chips.

'Why buy a caravan...?

1. 24-hour security

2. Move within a week

3. Only £200 per week

4. On-site facilities

5. 100 reasons not to buy a caravan

I am a snob.'

It's funny the difference between Camber caravan area and 'up-your-jumper' Rye, with its antique shops and its attempts at being a non-tourist harbour.

I went into the tourist information shop and a farming friend, Helen Langrishe was doing a tourist promotion plug on TV, saying how wonderful Rye and Romney Marsh are.

I boarded the bus for Winchelsea and there were loads of school children flirting with each other. An empty fag packet suddenly went flying out of the window. We drove past Camber Castle and soon I was dropped off on the edge of lovely Winchelsea.

I walked back into the town past the beautiful church, which is a real gem with its stained glass windows. Spike Milligan is buried here and the Gaelic inscription on his headstone translates as:

'I told you I was ill!'

1918-2002. Love from your children, Laura, Sean, Sile and Jane.

However, since my visit the headstone was later removed after the death of his wife Shelagh in 2011.

I booked into the local pub, which was run by a manager who looked at me as though I had spoiled his day by walking in.

I found my room with the stale urine still splattered on the loo, but I was too tired to look elsewhere, so I had a shower and went down for my evening meal.

There was a steady trickle of locals coming in and blaming the council for their lack of business because they were not allowed to put up signs. They weren't even allowed to advertise the pub! I said, 'I like it without signs and that is exactly the reason why I came to Winchelsea. Lenham village could learn a thing or two from here!' That went down like a dead duck and was the end of the conversation for the evening. I had a mediocre meal and called it a day.

Before leaving the next morning for Eastbourne, I left a note on the loo seat saying: 'Try harder. This is not my piss!' I told the boss that his loos were dirty.

His reply was: 'They shouldn't be.'

I got the hell out of it.

I jumped off the bus at Guestling and did a triangular walk passing Avalon House, Three Acres, Honeysuckle Cottage, Sweet Briar, Stream Farm, Woodlands, The Green, Well Cottage, The Glebe, Apple Cross and... wait for it... The Cottage! There was no shortage of acorns and chestnuts around this cosy little hamlet.

Arriving at Hastings, I discovered that it was 'Hastings Week Classic Car Show' and they were all lined up with their shining examples, swapping stories about their precious cars.

Behind the car park is the last remaining real Hastings: with fishermen, trawlers, nets, winches, lobster pots, and old Marshall tractors, in various states of repair – they were used to pull the boats out of the sea.

I've never known a fisherman who wants to talk to you – regarding tourists as a nuisance that they have to bear.

I asked, 'How's the fishing industry?'

'Has been better, has been worse.' *'What a stupid answer!'*

When walking the streets I managed to step in someone's sick from the night before. There were the usual crappy tourist shops selling junk.

I caught the wrong bus to Eastbourne and landed up at Tesco.

PEVENSEY CASTLE

This dates back 1700 years; it was a Roman fort to start with and then it was refortified by the Normans after William the Conqueror landed here in 1066. A great medieval castle was built within the Roman walls. Having fallen into disrepair in the late Middle Ages its defences have been renewed twice: once to defend itself against the Spanish Armada in 1588, and then again in the Second World War.

Getting off the bus at the seafront I thought I was the youngest man in town, but I was wrong – I stepped off with another sad old backpacker. We were both in our late fifties. We were standing on the kerb waiting to cross the road when suddenly we were covered in water. There were no puddles and it wasn't raining. A car full of youngsters had whizzed by and then it clicked...

Their car had been caught by red lights. I said to my friend, 'Fuck 'em!' and I ran after them. Just as I reached them the lights went green but they got stuck again. They had no idea I was after them until I banged on the roof. All the windows went up but they forgot about the sun roof! I peered in and the two girls in the back had a huge toy water gun. *'Hello girls. Having a bit of fun are you? You know you never want to fuck someone up unless you know you can get away with it, and you haven't, have you?'*

I gave the sunroof a tap, and said, 'Don't do it again!' There was a hell of a bang and it shattered, sending glass all over the girls. They screamed and the boys jumped out. I couldn't believe it had broken so easily. *'I think I'm in trouble.'*

'What's your game, mate? Stop hassling us.'

They were looking for a policeman, but the good news for me was that there's never one when you want one! Now they would have to clear that lot up and buy a new sun roof – and you know what? It started to rain! I slipped into a side street.

Eastbourne Pier is a feat of engineering; it seems a pity that piers such as this are not treated with a bit more respect rather than just selling rubbish food and being turned into tatty amusement arcades.

I booked into the Langham Hotel for £40 per night. The

room was tiny and had no sea view and I felt like a rabbit in a warren, but at least it was clean and warm.

I wandered along to the Queen's Hotel, built in the 1890s, with its high ceilings. The clientele were elderly and from up north. The only young person was a waitress from Saskatchewan who had worked here for seven months and now felt it was time to move on. I asked her what she liked about the UK, but she couldn't find an answer.

I went back to my hotel and had dinner, served up in record time on a wobbly table, by a girl from Poland. I tried to explain in my best Polish that we have a dear friend who lives in Sosnowiec.

She replied, 'Yes, Poland does get a lot of snow.'

After breakfast, I left a note in my room saying how clean it was and went to find the bus to Beachy Head. I met Ruby on the bus, a smiling man from Indonesia. He worked in London as a printer and was having a day off. He was the kind of person who makes you feel glad to be alive. We chatted and laughed so much we missed the stop for Beachy Head, so we had to walk back. We thought it was too nice a morning to jump.

I decided to walk out to Birling Gap. There were huge tracts of rolling countryside and lovely flint walls which were all well preserved.

I had been offered a bed for the night by Karen and Dave, whom I'd met on a trip around Central America, and had arranged to meet them early evening.

I made my way to Seven Sisters Sheep Farm and wandered all around but saw no one. It was open to tourists from March to September.

I then walked on to East Dean, to the church with its fascinating swing gate that swung at both ends. I left a note congratulating the cleaning lady and whoever else keeps the church clean. A sign said: 'Do you want to join the Bible Reading Group?' *'No thanks.'*

Next, I walked on to Friston church, which looked as though it may have been a bit too well kept. *'Smug.'*

As I walked towards Brighton my bus whizzed past, much to my annoyance as this is a dangerous road to walk along and I was glad when the next bus stopped.

Two very tarty looking girls got on. I tried not to stare, wishing I was eighteen and thinking of all the happy boys they would entertain. An elderly couple also got on the bus with their dog.

'Does the dog like going on buses?'

'Don't know, never been on one before.'

We drove on past Roedean School which is huge and someone said it only had twenty British girls; the rest came from the Far East.

BRIGHTON PIER

Brighton Pier was heaving.

'Cockles, mate?'

'Bit of crab, mate?'

'No salad, mate?'

'Mate, mate, mate!'

Once again a big, black, burly security guard came up to me as I nudged a penny machine!

'Sunday night is music night' at Karen & Dave's and their friends came and played their guitars. I got to bed at midnight. We had talked 'travel' late into the evening as they were making plans for their second trip to Antarctica. They were both in good form.

I'm not always that comfortable staying with friends as I always think I'm putting them out and fear that I might mess something up.

We said our goodbyes in the morning and at 9.30am I set out for Arundel. I met Mr Darkey, in the greengrocer trade, who was off to meet a friend who had just opened up a greengrocer's shop. Mr Darkey had lost his wife several years ago and was just getting over it. He had been a cook at a big hotel in Brighton for fifteen years. He now played tennis, went horse racing and smoked too much.

The bus filled with people with learning difficulties and a chap named Herbert, who was wearing a label that said: 'Herbert Matthews is authorised to collect money for Brighton and Hove Football Club. Signed: Finance Director.'

Another member of this group, Ernest, kept addressing the driver in a big loud voice as 'Driver'. Every time the bus stopped to pick up passengers he shouted, 'ARE YOU ALL RIGHT, DRIVER?'

Another old boy of seventy-two was really hitting it off with an old lady in front of me, saying that it's not true that sailors have a girl in every port. They roared with laughter, but Herbert moved to sit next to the old lady and the conversation died.

We passed a banner made out of a sheet saying: 'Bob the Builder Rips off Old Ladies.'

We drove on through Portslade and Shoreham, where I noticed that a mobile home costs £139,000 and a small static home up to £77,000. *'Not bad for a – um – caravan.'*

ARUNDEL

I was hungry, so while Herbert went off to a café to flog raffle tickets I had breakfast.

'Nice to have polite staff for a change.'

Even here, there were more rubbish-selling shops and antique shops. I hate them but I suppose that is how they can make a living.

Arundel Castle is huge and is owned by the Duke of Norfolk. As I struggled up the slope a dear old lady whizzed past me. *'I know you're fitter than me, clever Dick!'* Some Iranians living in America sort of apologised for their nationality and wanted me to take their photograph.

In the castle there were fireplaces that could have stored a Mini, and two mangy-looking tiger mats.

I asked two lady guides if they thought women had had a good life in the olden days and before I could finish they said, 'No.'

Just up from the castle was the Cathedral of St Nicholas. They had reached the £100,000 mark of their projected £250,000 target for the repair of the organ. *'Wow.'*

I bought a card, from a lovely church lady that said: 'Lord, may I never leave a lame dog by a stile but lift it to the other side and make its life worthwhile.'

It was time to make my way home after an interesting five days. On the train I talked to a bird watcher who had been 'twitching' in the fog, but he seemed to have enjoyed it, nonetheless.

At Redhill I was greeted by a blonde American station 'master', who was good-looking and had a big smile. A schoolgirl kicked the station café door open and the station 'master' and I looked at each other if to say, 'Little madam.'

Soon afterwards we pulled in to lovely Lenham.

CHAPTER TWO

Arundel to Plymouth

I returned to my 'walkabout' by spending two days at Goodwood, playing golf with Valerie, before getting back to Arundel. Goodwood itself is a rich man's paradise that I call *'Playboy Paradise'*. It has a motor-racing circuit, an airport, golf courses, horse racing and prime shooting in beautiful countryside. When I had my little plane I used to fly in to Goodwood and always got the impression that they thought they were a little bit better than me.

Horsey people never do the countryside any favours with ugly white electric fencing, old baths and sinks and wrecked horse boxes sitting in the corners, not to mention the ragwort that nobody bothers to pull out.

I caught the train en route to Southampton and looking out of the window I could see some seriously intensive farming, including glasshouses.

At one point, we passed a football pitch completely covered with grey-leg geese grazing.

Eventually, the train rolled in to Southampton where the station seemed to be right in the middle of the city.

It was cold and everyone seemed to be doing their Christmas shopping. John Lewis seemed to dominate the whole city.

I found a hotel that resembled a prison. *'At £60 per night it's bound to be a good prison.'* Yes, it was like a prison but my room smelled of fresh paint, with the decorators just a few rooms away.

I lost my way to the restaurant and came down in the service lift which landed me outside via the emergency exit and onto waste ground. I then had to go round to the entrance again and ask at reception which floor the restaurant was on. 'Third,' came the reply, accompanied by a pitying look. The staff, however, were friendly and the food surprisingly good.

SOUTHAMPTON TO DORCHESTER

Waiting for the train to Wareham, I asked the newsagent which papers he sold most of. They were *The Sun* and *The Times* and I said to him that that seemed a good balance.

What a ride it was, with the sun just coming up on frosty ground as we went through the New Forest.

I decided to get off as this really was too good a place to miss. I stood on the platform at Brockenhurst and decided to walk to Lyndhurst. I was in the company of all the students walking to college – I felt I had the wrong coloured hair and of course I should be texting.

Lyndhurst Road is too busy for hitching. I walked the whole way, chatting to the ponies and told them that if ever they were in Kent to look us up!

There were signs saying that picking fungi is illegal.

LYNDHURST

'Christ, that seemed a long way!' I was hoping to find the New Forest Museum, but after photographing the church I walked into town and saw a little shop selling contemporary goods.

It was the guy I'd seen on television the previous February. He had been interviewed on how to set up a small business. I recognised him as soon as I saw his Ferrari picture. I asked him what he'd learned from the film and he replied, 'Nothing.' They only reported on the negative things like saying that he should've got his Ferrari from his own designed website and not a shop. I asked him if I could take his photograph and he was quite flattered.

The museum was well worth the visit.

I jumped back on the train again and decided to get off at Wareham and go to Swanage. Why I did, I don't know.

At the bus stop we were entertained by a five-year-old who was trying to conduct his mother and aunt while they sang one of his songs. He was a horrible little boy who reminded me of the advert: 'Why didn't you wear a condom?'

CORFE CASTLE

En route we passed some real marshes with rushes; fairly rare these days. Corfe Castle is a quaint little village, with its ruined castle dominating the view. In 1646 the King at the time tried to blow it up and one archway shows that there is a three metre gap from the other pillar. Then the locals pinched many chunks of stone to build houses. 'Corfe' comes from old English meaning a gap or pass: Corfe Castle was built in a gap in the Purbeck Hills between Wareham and Swanage.

I got my first lift ever on my 'walkabout' – a young heavy-smoking lady going to pick up her children. I was soon joined by a Jack Russell on my lap.

I found Swanage to be another highly interesting seaside town! *'What am I doing in this shit hole?'* I bought some dirty postcards and sent one home.

I decided Dorchester railway station is not the place to be at night, but I was soon in the High Street which looked better. I went to the Westwood House Hotel, run by the charming daughter of the owner. I knocked them down from £40 to £35 and fifty steps later I was in the top room. *'That'll teach me not to bargain so hard!'*

I ate out at a Chinese restaurant which was run by perky little Malaysian girls.

'What's the thing you like most about the UK?'

'Ta pound,' came the reply.

'And what's the worst?'

'Ta weather.'

Thinking I'd lost my notebook I walked the fifty steps up and fifty back down, only to find it in my trouser pocket.

I heard on the news that Bodmin Moor was closed because of snow and I was heading that way: I didn't sleep too well that night.

DORCHESTER TO ABBOTSBURY

This was a really special and beautiful day. I had breakfast in the conservatory which felt as though the whole world was watching me. I exchanged polite 'good mornings' with the only other couple and tucked into an English breakfast.

I visited the museum. The agricultural side was interesting and made me realise that some things on our own farm need to be looked after better.

I walked out to Maiden Hill Fort. This is the largest hill fort in Europe. I was joined by a Mr Drystick. I told him I was from Kent and he just said, 'Oh yeah,' and then said that the weather wasn't good for maidens! He seemed to walk more slowly than me and yet I couldn't keep up! It was a relief when he turned left.

This was golden plover country – my favourite bird after the cuckoo. Not only do they lay their eggs in someone else's nest, but they let them rear them while they fly away. Now that is smart.

Back to Maiden Hill Fort. Built in 600 BC, it has three dry moat-type defences built by hand. It overlooks Dorchester and is now grazed by sheep. Hill forts were used by people in the Iron Age although the idea had dawned in the Bronze Age in Europe.

As I walked into Winterborne Monkton I realised what a cold and sunless valley it was to farm in. *'Well, this farmyard looks more tired than me. The place lends itself for conversion.'*

I was nosy and looked under a lean-to and saw a Clayton & Shuttleworth Lincoln wooden cart with a water bowser. Its wheels had all sunk in the earth and it could've been there for fifty years.

St Simon and St Jude's Church had a burglar alarm and a locked door.

A buzzard with a stoat-like animal in its mouth flew off, watched by a lone rook.

I found myself back out on the busy A354, a fast road with no chance of getting a lift. I bumped into a delightful couple from New Zealand who had run out of petrol and wondered if I carried any in my rucksack!

In Weymouth I had a cold mug of chocolate served by a girl who was dead from the waist up!

Buses were few and far between so I negotiated with a taxi driver. The fare is normally £30 but as he was not busy he said that he'd do it for £10. George was a countryman at heart and not your usual fat, smoky, lazy taxi driver. He helped the local sheep farmers in the summer and had worked in Saudi for nine years in dairy units. With that money he'd bought himself a house in the village with his hygienist wife.

It was a mistake being dropped off at Portesham as it was far too neat and tidy, so I started to walk to Abbotsbury which is about two miles away. The light was fading and I failed to get a lift. I disturbed the pheasants flying to roost across the road. By the time I got to Abbotsbury it was dark.

I was drawn to this place as it had a 14th century Tithe Barn. It was an eerie town at night, with no lights – I couldn't even see the pavement – but according to the taxi driver it had hotels and pubs. I passed a pub which looked dead and then I found The Ilchester Arms, which looked more welcoming. After a pint of John Smith's I asked for a room. It was £65 but I only had allowed £40 for a room and they wouldn't take it. However, they kindly phoned the local B&B place which had one room left. I was the only one in it.

As soon as I walked through the door he pissed me off by asking me to take my boots off, and then put me in a tiny room with no bathroom. Something about this place had a 'tight-arsed' feel about it.

I decided to go back to The Ilchester Arms to eat and when I got there I saw an old shooting friend, Timmer. He hadn't changed and was still smiling and smoking. He'd had to pack up his cows after thirty years as he couldn't find a cowman. He really missed them, but they would have interfered with his lifestyle.

I put my hand where my wallet should be – NOTHING! – I tried all the other pockets and it was nowhere. Panic! I stood up and like some one-armed bandit, £500 in £50 notes fluttered to the floor. *'Phew!' (Never did get around to eating.)*

Later, a little the worse for wear, I went to bed!

It was a beautiful November Sunday morning and time to discover Abbotsbury's medieval barn.

Renovation work had been going on for some time. As it was Sunday, none of the workers were there. I managed to squeeze through the security fencing and then climbed a ladder right to the top. Incredible how they do the thatching and all from local rushes, and the carpenters had been splicing some new timber rafters with such skill. It was beautiful craftsmanship. I felt like a naughty boy up there.

This magnificent place had originally been twice as long at ninety metres. It was a clear indication of the wealth of the Benedictine Abbey. The thatched roof was 17th century and the barn is now used for various exhibitions.

I walked down to the biggest swannery in the world and saw not a single swan, probably because it was closed! The swans were at the far end. I smiled to myself as I could see where they were eating the farmer's rape crop. Anyway, this Swannery was first mentioned in 1393, but it may be older, and it provided meat for the monks throughout the medieval period. It has been owned by the Ilchester Estates since the 16th century and is the only colony of managed swans in the world. Visitors can walk past the nesting birds and their young here.

I have been back since, when it was open, at hatching time – it was full of swans and their cygnets and well worth a visit.

Nearby on the hill overlooking Abbotsbury Abbey is St Catherine's Chapel. It was built by the monks in the 14th century as a place of pilgrimage and retreat. In addition to the chapel it has a tiny oratory in the turret. The chapel is a useful pointer for ships because of its prominent position. It has a monumental silhouette despite its small size and has a carved stone tunnel vault supporting the masonry roof covering.

Chapel message
'St Catherine, watch over all the orphans of the world and give them peace and health. And watch over hate.'

J.A's message
'St Catherine, watch over the beautiful surroundings of Abbotsbury and keep it free from urban development.'

Walking back to the village I passed a very smart thatched house, with its PVC windows – *'Personally Vandalised Countryside'* – that had helped to destroy the character of the place. It was so neat and tidy and I reckoned it must have been a holiday home. *'A smug little house.'*

The local gamekeeper had stopped to buy some cigarettes and had left his keys in his Land Rover. A lady was selling vegetables outside on the pavement and had left an honesty box in place. It was good to see that England still has some trusting places left.

I hitched out of Abbotsbury and about thirty cars passed by. Then a white van stopped and I chucked my rucksack in the back.

'Where are you going?' asked the driver.

'Not sure!' He was going to Lyme Regis. 'OK, take me there then!'

Bob was a modest man and said he didn't need to work. He fished for pleasure and sailed in the summer. I plucked up courage to ask if he had won the lottery. He said he was into property and had loads of houses in the area and that his father owned ninety in Whitby. During the journey we became good mates. He invited me to join him for a beer in Lyme Regis, but after the previous night I gave it a miss.

He dropped me off on the outskirts of Lyme Regis refusing the £5 I offered him. He hated Blair and after working his bollocks off for years he was not going to do so again for that man.

It was cold and I had caught up with the snow although most of it had melted. I went into a café for a cup of tea and was served by a girl, whom I'm sure you would've had to ask to wiggle her arse if you were making love to her to make sure she was alive.

I had a couple of hours to kill, so went into a pub with a wonderful sea view. I sat and wrote *Walkabout* while the locals watched Newcastle v Everton on the television above my head.

What a way to view the countryside – from the top of a bus! The snow was hanging in the shadows of fields as the low sun refused to melt it and happy pigs were wallowing in the mud.

The fields were getting smaller and the hedges thicker. I was happy that I didn't have to farm this land.

I arrived in Exeter at 4pm on a Sunday and all the shops were open, trying to grab the last of the Christmas trade.

Out of curiosity, I popped into a hotel close to the cathedral and at £120 per night I told the man that I would think about it. The cathedral looked wonderful, floodlit.

I spent ages looking for accommodation and then asked a taxi driver to take me to a hotel. 'I don't need a palace and I don't need a dog kennel!' Jim had been taxi driving for ten years. He dropped me off outside the Travelodge.

I had a pretty shitty meal – only the Knickerbocker Glory saved a dull evening – and so to bed.

Bus stations are always good places for man-watching, and the poor come in for warmth and a brew-up. An old boy who came walking down the steps in a trilby, looked pretty fragile. He was followed by some social worker types who talked to him and slipped him a few coins. It made me feel proud to be British and to know that there's a system out there that cares for the vulnerable.

I went to the ticket office and said, 'I know it's Monday morning, but can I get a bus to Princetown on Dartmoor?'

He burst out laughing and said that the nearest was Moretonhampstead. It was the number eleven and it left in ten minutes.

The only other passenger was Mr Grumpy.

'Am I at the right bus stop for Chagford?'

'Yes, and it's late.'

Our bus driver was a little flustered as he was late, but we were off within seconds.

'Do you live round here?'

'Yes, and it's beginning to rain...'

SIGN ON BUS

'OUR STAFF ARE ENTITLED TO CARRY OUT THEIR DUTIES WITHOUT FEAR OF ASSAULT. OUR VEHICLES ARE FITTED WITH ALARMS WHICH STAFF CAN USE IN AN EMERGENCY. WE WILL PRESS FOR THE STRONGEST PENALTIES FOR ANYONE WHO ASSAULTS A MEMBER OF STAFF OR CAUSES WILFUL DAMAGE TO OUR VEHICLES.'

Unfortunately, Ron, the driver, had to reverse when meeting a diesel lorry and left part of his bumper in a farmer's gateway. I congratulated him on his driving but got no response. Mr Grumpy was out of the bus and enjoying every moment of the adventure. Needless to say, the driver was not. Driving buses in these narrow lanes must be a nightmare.

We passed the entrance to Drogo Castle and I got Ron to drop me off. I asked him to pick me up if he saw me hitching later on and he said he was on this route all day, so that would be OK.

The sign on the drive said: 'CLOSED', so at least I knew there wouldn't be many tourists. As I walked up the drive there were a couple of chaps discretely setting up traps.

'What are you trapping?' I asked.

'Grey squirrels.'

'Good, I've seen the damage they've done to our own trees.'

They seemed quite surprised at my response as they were probably thinking I was an anti.

Jim, the head gardener, talked enthusiastically about the estate and the views they had made and their plans for the future. He gave me tips on hedge planting and how to clip yew not too tightly, and that it's best done from July to September. These were the sort of people I wanted to meet and I felt good on the way down the drive. The closed castle at this time of year looked pretty uninviting.

Back on the road it was so quiet and I could hear the stream flowing. There was just an occasional car – only one in forty minutes. There were ancient hedges and crumbling stone walls with huge trees growing out of their tops. There was high deer fencing, but I was not sure if it was to keep them in or out. Even though it was raining it was a beautiful walk.

Like a dream come true, suddenly and in the middle of nowhere was a pub. It was run by a young couple from Cambridge. I had a half in front of the log fire and chatted to Ronald – a bit of a stuffy gent who was rather wrapped up in himself. Through cunning conversation I surmised he was a shooting type so asked about the number of pheasants. Soon I was hearing all his *boring* shooting stories.

Again there was nobody to pick this pretty boy up. And it was raining! What the hell!

Hooray for Ron, who doesn't worry about official stops and was glad to get me back on his bus.

'I got some stick from the other drivers about the bumper, but none of them want this route' he said.

We passed through Chagford, dropping off one passenger and then went on to Moretonhampstead.

Company rules say you should not talk to the driver but he was in full flow. I asked what Stagecoach was like to work for.

'Bastards! Horrible people to work for. Only interested in money.' Ron had collapsed one day after work because of a dodgy clutch pedal that had affected his leg. Nothing had ever been done about it, but in spite of the fact that it wasn't his fault, because he'd had to take five days off work, they deducted £80 from his wages.

On another occasion, he'd given a teenage girl a late night lift home for free as she had no money. He got reprimanded for that, but I told him that had she been murdered he would never have forgiven himself. He said he'd enjoyed our chat and we parted with a smile and wishes for good luck.

MORETONHAMPSTEAD TO PRINCETOWN

Grumpy had told me not to take risks in this lonely moorland area, but there were no buses so I decided to walk. About twenty cars later, Cherry and Linda screeched to a halt and I clambered into the back. I was comfortable among the sleeping bags and clutter and we laughed and chuckled all the way to Princetown. Linda was down from Yorkshire looking for work; any work as long as it paid. They were big camping buddies and every time we passed a flat piece of Dartmoor they said, 'That would be a good place to pitch a tent.'

The prison looked extra gloomy and it was getting dark and snowing. I gave the girls a fiver, which they reluctantly accepted.

I went into the local store and said to the shopkeeper that it seemed a pretty lonely place. He said he got 500,000 visitors in the summer! A young lad at the bus shelter told me that it would be two hours before the next bus.

I popped into the local museum. Sir Arthur Conan Doyle stayed here when he wrote *The Hound of the Baskervilles*. I asked once again how long till the next bus. I was told thirty minutes, so my young friend at the bus station had been a bit wrong.

Waiting for the bus I met Gordon, a quiet man with a grey beard. Gordon was a warden for Dartmoor Council and had three mates who kept the paths and bridleways open. He had worked here for twenty years having meant to stay only three months! He used to work in the local library, but working in the open he found he got fewer colds. We chatted all the way to Tavistock.

I caught another bus to Plymouth and tucked up in The Jack Rabbit Travelodge, where I rang Lynn, a friend of ours who lived in Plymouth. We had a meal and poor Lynn had to listen to all my boring stories about my 'walkabout'. Later in the year she helped me type it up.

After breakfast I caught the bus into Plymouth. There were loads of scruffy schoolboys who boarded; one with hair sticking out of his baseball cap and he was spitting before boarding. He annoyed me as he tried to use a false bus pass, but the driver didn't stand for any nonsense so the fare was paid. The driver congratulated him on his forgery and we all waited while he reported the boy to the authorities on his mobile.

It was time to get home and sitting on the train I had the pleasure of sitting opposite Mrs Strict. I said, 'Good Morning,' and she didn't stop talking till we got to Bath.

Her husband had died after being an army man all his life and they had travelled round the world. She had three marvellous boys; big tall lads and all in the armed forces.

She was off to Bath for an appointment with her consultant and every time we passed a station she would give a running commentary and say: 'Ivybridge, Totnes, Teignmouth, Dawlish, Exeter,' like a parrot who knew it all.

She told me that before he'd died, she and her husband had taken it in turns to decide where to go on holiday. One particular year it was her turn and she chose the Lake District. Harold wasn't that keen and wanted to know what there was up there to see. Then the night before the due departure date he said he wasn't going, so she replied that it didn't matter as she would go on her own. She had booked the chalet and was looking forward to it. The following morning Mrs Strict packed the car and had just turned out of the drive when she saw Harold running down the road, having changed his mind. She'd said, 'Get in and don't say a word until we get to Keswick.' *This was some bitch!'*

When they got to Lancaster she said she locked the car with Harold in it while she went to get petrol. He ended up enjoying the Lake District and wanted to go back again and even more so after going round the tank museum!

I got to know more about Mrs Strict; how her son nearly whacked the consultant when he said she didn't need a new hip, and how her son had told her to leave the room. She had her new hip within three weeks!

On the way to Dawlish I thought it would be a great way to go bird watching, so out came the binoculars.

Meanwhile, Mrs Strict continued with her running commentary... She had met Richard Branson twice, once on a Virgin train and once when flying to Florida. Apparently, he was very nice and was serving wine on the plane. On the train he realised the problems the waves could make and why the train was sometimes delayed at Dawlish, which was right on the coast.

I noticed that few people on the train looked out of the windows, but with an announcement of a delay all the mobile phones suddenly appeared for them to report to offices of their late arrival.

We passed a new building, whereupon Mrs Strict said, 'Horrible!' Then, rounding a bend to a new housing estate she exclaimed, 'Terrible!'

When she got off at Bath I felt like apologising to the other passengers!

At Bristol the atmosphere changed completely, from happy-go-lucky holidaymakers to serious business folk on their way to London. Mrs Strict was replaced by a planning consultant who was busy with maps and plans all the way and never had time to look out of the window. He looked tired and pissed off.

We arrived at the beautiful Paddington station built by Brunel and I just looked up in amazement. I caught the underground to Victoria and was soon back home in sunny Lenham.

CHAPTER THREE

Plymouth to Taunton

It was time to get to London again. It was February and it was cold and foggy. My Great Western train was ready and waiting at Paddington; clean and comfortable. I was to have an interesting journey.

I travelled with a lady called Anne and we chatted all the way to Exeter. She was working at Moorfields Eye Unit. She had worked in a kibbutz and was into healthy eating. I told her I was a farmer and grew linseed. She quickly produced a document saying how good linseed is for your arteries. She talked about organic food and I did my usual about food produced with the aid of chemicals, and asked why, if chemicals were so bad, were there so many elderly folk who refused to die?

A guy called Robin joined us and added to the humour with his lunch – sausages, pork pies and Scotch eggs. Anne was aghast! 'How can you eat such stuff?' He just said that he'd been eight stone forever.

Robin, having started with body panelling and paint spraying, now worked for a main Vauxhall repair dealership in Horsham and liked working directly with customers and with older people.

He was about to spend the weekend with his girlfriend in Plymouth and unfortunately managed to leave his bag on the train. I didn't notice it but the guard did and when Robin returned I apologised to his girlfriend for not looking after him.

PLYMOUTH

Lynn Fletcher came and collected me from the station and duly had a puncture. She took a picture of me mending it and for the first time I realised that I had a bald patch.

I had my first cigarette for a month and then off to the Hoe from where Francis Drake departed in the Golden Hind on December 13th, 1577.

Lynn took me to see her new flat and although it still had a lot of work needing to be done it had huge potential.

Afterwards we visited some friends of hers who lived in a converted barn, where all the threshing pulleys had been left in the roof space. He was an ex-submarine nuclear engineer. I couldn't believe how big some of the submarines were; carrying up to one hundred and fifty people.

On the way to more of Lynn's friends, we crossed a few cattle grids indicating our nearness to the moors. At one point she showed me the place where a schoolgirl had been murdered on a bus by the driver. It was an eerie night as we drove through a dark, foggy and lonely Dartmoor.

PLYMOUTH TO POLPERRO

After another awful breakfast at the hotel I went to Plymouth bus station and I couldn't believe what a smelly, sticky-with-chewing-gum place it was; it even had the local alcoholics and druggies to go with it. The only clean thing about it was the seagulls.

I bought a ticket to Looe. Plymouth harbour had some of the biggest ship maintenance buildings I have ever seen.

On the bus there was a Chinese woman with a mixed Chinese/West Country accent, which was rather interesting.

Later, we passed a field of daffodils and another with new-born lambs before going through the Cornish villages of Portwrinkle, Downderry and Seaton.

I decided to walk the coastal path to Polperro. Why do people let their dogs shit all over the place? I think dogs should be banned from seaside towns. Even when the owners pick up the shit they are just as likely to bung the bag into the nearest hedge! *'I think all dogs should be fed to the lions in the local zoo.'*

There were nice, easy stiles or kissing gates and little dog hatches. There was even plain wire where the footpath was close to the fence and barbed wire when further away.

An elderly Yorkshire couple pointed out a large seal in the bay and a couple of rather displeased lesbians with a collie dog disapproved of me throwing a yellow ring for it. Ramblers who don't make eye contact with me don't get away with it, as I always say hello to them.

At Talland Bay I passed a guest house saying: 'En-suite available, but no smokers and no pets'! I should have taken the number, phoned them up and said there were two of us: married, gay and HIV positive!

I had an uphill walk to the A387 past some interesting farm buildings which were ripe for conversion. It was blowing, misty and dull and all the hillsides were scattered with caravans.

POLPERRO

It's not very often that you're happy to be on a busy road with roaring traffic, but I was. I needed a bus or a lift but neither came, so I kept walking and made a half-hearted attempt to hitch. I couldn't believe it when two ladies stopped and gave me a lift. They hadn't even seen my face, which was probably why they stopped! They were on holiday from Exeter for a long weekend. The journey was short but welcome.

My 'walkabout' was full of surprises and Polperro was one of them. It's a small fishing village but still holds on to its working atmosphere.

I popped into The Blue Peter pub which was jammed full and two chaps were playing and singing: 'What shall we do with the drunken sailor?' on guitars. It felt appropriate. Dogs were welcome as long as the owners spent plenty of money, and well-behaved children were well behaved. It had been voted one of the best pubs in Cornwall.

I was amazed when the two women who'd given me a lift walked in. I bought them a drink and asked what they did for a living. Mary was a bit embarrassed as she said she drove a lorry and emptied recycling bins. Jo said she had her church and that kept her busy. We roared with laughter when I said, 'What a mixture; a dustman, a farmer and a born-again Christian!' It was nearly impossible to have a conversation here.

Polperro was full of hotels and B&Bs but most said: 'No Vacancies'. *'Why can't they just say that they have f--ked off for the winter?! Only JA would come down here out of season!'*

One place was open, but a little girl very nicely declined to accept me. I knocked on another door and the owner shouted out of the bedroom window in his vest, 'Don't open till April.' *'Thank Christ for that!'*

Milly's B&B seemed to be the only place trading. I even got proper bed sheets, a shower and a bathroom three fists wide. I also had a storage heater, which would probably have been better heating a mouse hole. Then as I was thinking I was about to freeze I found another electric heater.

I went out to eat and thought I had picked the right place but it was a bit rough and only had three things on the menu: 6, 12, or 18 ounce steaks, with chips, peas and tomatoes. Prices ranged from £5 to £8.50, plus £1 extra for a sauce! The food was about as plain as the customers.

As I left I got the impression they were saying, 'What the hell's he doing here?'

At midnight the B&B was like an oven – I thought I'd pulled the fire plug out, but realised that I'd pulled out the one for the kettle instead.

Next morning I was given a first class breakfast. There were no buses to Fowey at this time of year, so I started hitching.

After about twenty minutes I got a lift from a sixty-year-old man who helped my little legs recover. He had only been to Kent once in his life to go to his daughter-in-law's father's funeral in Rochester. I was dropped off in the middle of nowhere, but I just enjoyed the Cornish countryside: the sunken roads; the wind on my back, the leaves overtaking me, and the birds disappearing into the hedges, never to be seen again. A merlin flew past me going against the wind about four feet off the ground and going like a rocket. Unbelievable!

I passed some old grain stores, rather beautiful but unused for years. It was good to see that they had not been converted.

There were newborn lambs and they and their mums were sheltering from the wind. I saw kale being folded off – not a sight you get in Kent. The fields had stone wall boundaries backed up by electric fencing – a good stone wall is an ancient beauty.

I saw twelve cars in an hour and all went past me. *'Good job I have some legs.'*

At Polruan, for a very reasonable fare, I took the little diesel ferry boat operated by a captain with nicotine-stained fingers.

'How many times do you make this crossing?' I asked.

'Several,' was the not very informative reply.

FOWEY TO ST AUSTELL

It's hard work writing up *Walkabout* in a restaurant when slightly pissed and eating an oily salad – particularly when my pen became covered in oil!

I caught the bus to St Austell.

I think PVC (Personally Vandalised Countryside) windows have done more to muck up architecture than anything. Lovely old houses have had them put in and now look like a lady who's had a face-lift that has gone very wrong.

At St Austell most buses seemed to have 'Eden Project' written on them so I flashed my 'all-day' ticket at the driver only to be told it was with the wrong company. He asked if I was 'a senior'. I couldn't believe it! *'Moi, 'a senior'?'* I was too shocked to reply... *'To hell with it, I am a senior.'*

It didn't take long to get to The Eden Project.

'OK, as I look so old I am going to ask for a senior ticket.' 'One 'senior', please.' I expected her to call me a liar, but she didn't say a word. I even checked my change. *'I'm a senior, I'm a senior, I'm a fucking senior!'*

The message from this place is: 'Reduce, Re-use, Recycle and Reinvent'.

For a Monday in February it was fairly busy with school children and young families and a few dedicated gardeners. The whole set up was better than I had imagined. Outside it looked so green it was almost black, having had a lot of compost and seaweed put on it. The whole place is heated by water and that is heated by gas. Plants come from all over the world and signs tell you what their uses are and how they can help the environment.

Rice is the oldest domesticated crop, traceable back fifteen thousand years.

I never knew there was such a thing as a horseradish tree, but there it was, and then I saw a papaya tree heading for the roof. The avocado is also called 'testicles' by some local tribesmen.

Cola nuts were once used for the drink but have been replaced. Cashew nuts are difficult to pick and apparently roasting them removes the poison.

In the middle of my visit Valerie phoned to say that Lenham had had a lot of rain and the roof was leaking. I told her about the 'senior' experience, which she really enjoyed.

There was a stand showing the difference between natural and synthetic dyes. I never knew that coal tar is the main source of the synthetic ones.

The next dome was 140m long and 60m high with nine hundred species of plants.

The fig tree is the oldest cultivated tree and provided essential shade for the Ancient Egyptians.

There was a sign saying that we piss 16kg per year. Thought it was much more than that, but the moral here is never eat yellow snow!

The Greeks consume twenty-two litres of olive oil per person each year, whereas we only use half a litre.

On the appraisal form I gave them ten out of ten, as it's well worth a visit.

I then caught the bus back to St Austell.

'I am a senior, hee-hee-hee. A dirty old man, that's what I be, hee, hee, hee!'

At the bus station I inquired about times, but the booking office bloke was writing a report and never even looked up. He appeared to have been in the job about fifty years too long. I commented that the station was much better than the one in Plymouth. He said nothing for about a minute, then still with his head down, he said in a lovely Cornish accent, 'Bit of a shit-hole!'

On the bus the driver whizzed along the country lanes – to make up time I suppose. On the journey I saw bored teenagers playing on the swings at the high-rise blocks, making me realise how lucky I am to have a big garden; an old tramp eating fish and chips with his hood up, as if trying to hide from the world; rooks carrying twigs to build their nests; and a farmer spreading nitrogen.

TRURO

Wow! What a cathedral! I couldn't find a hotel so I ended up at the yellow house. I'd been turned away by the place next door because they only did doubles. I stayed with Mrs Lowe and it was probably the first proper B&B I'd been to – a bit tatty but clean and when you opened the drawer in your room there was no Bible. Instead there was a salt and pepper pot, a knife and fork and a plate – all there to eat takeaways in your room. There was a shared bathroom and separate loo. *'What do you expect for £25?'*

I popped into the nearby pub. It looked nice enough on the outside, but was a disappointment inside. I had a pint of beer and planned to eat but the waitress, a fat sloppy girl with her tattoos and bare midriff, put me off. I never thought *'a senior'* would be put off his food by a bare midriff! She also smoked in between times.

The Ristorante Pizzeria was a much better bet – a seafood salad and pizza and two glasses of wine left me feeling somewhat merry. At the next table was a family of young and old but they did not intermix. Strange how people can sit next to each other and not talk.

And so to bed.

Mrs Lowe my landlady had problems: her first husband died; then her second husband died as well; and her daughter and the rest of the family lived miles away. She'd had a window cleaner who'd offered to paint the front of her house, but he never turned up when he said he would. 'All he had to do was ring,' she cried. Then when he turned up the next day his ladder slipped and knocked her front light off and when he started to paint the house it was the wrong shade of yellow. *'Want any more?'*

Later, I visited the cathedral – what an amazing place this is.

TO FALMOUTH

The girl at the bus station said, 'You can take the quick one or the slow one, but if I was you I would take the fast one which is leaving later than the slow one.' So I took the slow one and enjoyed the ride.

Cornish houses are nearly all painted white with slate roofs and seem to stick out like little shoe boxes. They all look the same. *'How would you know how to find your house if you came back drunk?'* There were, however, some new houses near the boatyard painted in natural colours.

The driver dropped me off near a sign to the castle. Falmouth has the usual smart seaside hotels and seemed to be full of old people taking their 'shitters' for a walk.

PENDENNIS CASTLE

The sign said: 'Closed', but it was open. I told the ticket girl and she replied that she would look into it. She then proceeded to try to sell me English Heritage membership, which I declined, and likewise the brochure.

I managed to get by on a concessionary entry, saving a pound, but I don't think she believed me. *'My imagination is now playing tricks with me.'*

What a stubby fighting little castle this is, with several levels. On one level there was a cannon with smoke and sound effects which was done rather well. There was a large fireplace in the entrance with a bread-making oven to its left, and the tower right on top had a little fireplace for the guard. I enjoyed the castle and the long walk was worthwhile.

Falmouth harbour is the third deepest in the world, formed by a hidden underground valley. A lot of coal was taken down here to feed our fighting and colonial shipping crews. There seemed to be no taxis in this part of the world, and I was not used to all this exercise, so I flagged down a bus.

'Are you going to the bus station?'

'There is no bus station.'

'Well the centre then?'

'It's called The Moor.'

I thought, *'Well, take us to the fucking Moor then, you miserable little shit!'*

A sign on the bus read: 'Fare increase – insurance has risen by 89% and fuel costs have increased dramatically over the past twelve months.'

FALMOUTH TO HELSTON

I seemed to be stuck here as the next bus was not for two hours, so I decided to have a cup of tea in the café opposite. I joined the smokers and the unemployable. *'I think I am unemployable in the real world.'*

At last a bus came. We went through loads of small hamlets and passed daffodil farms and freshly planted potatoes. The mobile phones kept ringing and the fatty behind was cramming yet another Cornish pasty into her face with a big cheery smile.

This part of the world is pretty hilly with some interesting intensive farming and poor farming mixed in together.

We passed Culdrose air base and the driver told me that sometimes he wondered if the jets would take the top off his bus. This is a huge military base with helicopters and planes buzzing about, but it's certainly not a tourist area and most of the folk seem to be living one day at a time. There's no need to come down this route twice.

I finished up in Tesco car park, a wind-swept, dirty, fag-littered stop. I bought a sandwich and watched the local yobs converging, spitting and smoking.

Another dirty double-decker bus turned up. I went upstairs and could hardly see out of the windows. I thought this would be a good place to become a peeping Tom as you could sit up here and look into people's bedrooms, especially going round corners in the built-up areas.

Branches smashed into the bus as we wound our way to the Lizard. I walked down to the Lizard and dipped my toe into the Atlantic. Suddenly, a hail storm came from nowhere and we all ran for shelter. On the way back I thanked volunteers for repairing the path and I got a big smile in return.

At the bus stop there was a group of young boys standing around, which was a good indication that there was a bus due. I asked them when it might come and what they thought of tourism. One said it didn't worry him, whilst another in camouflage clothing was half-heartedly trying to thumb a lift and sending swear words at drivers who passed. A polite young lad on a motor bike asked what I was doing.

'A 'walkabout' with no itinerary.'

'Cool, man!' came the reply.

A single-decker bus picked us up. I wasn't looking forward to doing the same route but the homeward journey seemed quicker. We got stuck behind a tractor and trailer and the fat bus driver was growing more and more agitated.

I was going to give Helston a miss and go to Penzance, but I was so tired and I got dropped off in the town centre. I went to a pub that advertised accommodation for £30 but when I asked they said £60, so I gave it a miss. I went past a rather smart restaurant saying 'Bed and Breakfast', but couldn't open the door. Inside, the lady was setting the table so I indicated 'bed' to her and she said through the window that there wasn't one, but that the restaurant would be open at 6.30pm. *'If she can't be bothered to come to the door, then I can't be bothered to come to her 'up-your-jumper' restaurant.'*

I met Mike who offered me a single room for £35 and I knocked him down to £32. It was a nice room and after a wash and brush up I went out.

After looking in several places I settled for Figs – a rather fancy bistro; colour code red. I didn't get off to a very good start when I asked the owner the price of a glass of wine. 'It depends what you want,' he snapped. Then I asked him if I could change tables and he wasn't very happy about that. Then he wanted my order and I wasn't ready – I was on the point of walking out but was too hungry to do so. In the end we were the best of friends and he asked me what had brought me to this part of the world. He asked if I drank red wine and brought me a sample. The way he kept placing things in order made me wonder if he was gay.

The food was delicious: a lovely salmon salad in a crusty pancake thing with red cabbage and red pepper-type things on it – I love good food – and for the main course there were slices of chicken in an orange sauce. With a glass of wine it came to just under £20, so I gave him £23 and he was grateful for the tip.

It was the end of another interesting day, to say the least, and Helston wasn't as bad as I'd thought.

HELSTON TO PENDEEN

After an excellent breakfast of scrambled eggs and salmon – in the company of the other guests, who were only interested in today's weather – I told the owner he had an excellent business and off I went.

It was a cold and windy morning in February. At the bus stop I chatted to a lady from the Philippines, who having met her husband whilst travelling in Hong Kong, had married him in 1980. However, her eighty-year-old parents were still cattle farmers in the Philippines and she hadn't managed to visit them very often as, with children, it was too expensive. She'd brought up her children to be respectful, but she felt that in our society yobs were breeding yobs. I asked her what had been her biggest shock whilst living here and she said it was the lack of snow – with only three snowfalls in twenty-six years.

Some elderly folk boarded the bus, flashing their yellow cards like football referees, and outside young hoodies hung around.

I decided not to get off at St Michael's Mount and suddenly we were in Penzance. I went straight on to St Just.

A stuck-up couple got on the bus, giving the impression that they were too good to travel in this way. I felt like taking the mickey but behaved myself!

ST JUST

Christ, it was cold as I made my way to the same pub I'd stayed in two and a half years ago. I was going to have a cup of tea as it was only 10.30am, but seeing all the old boys having a drink I thought 'forget that' and had a pint of Tinners, the local brew, instead.

I had an interesting chat with three ex-tin miners, one of whom – Sid – had been on the bus with me. They all meet up once a week, to have a drink and play pool. They told me that they'd been miners for thirty-six, seventeen, and twenty-four years – it sounded more akin to giving me their life sentences – but just like the textile industry it had all come to an end now.

'Christ, George, I wish I had kept all the rocks. Some of them came out looking like miniature light houses. Would be worth a fortune now.'

'Aye'.

They told me that the deposits of tin are like a black seam, but not very wide.

'Aye, £2.50 a week.'

Gases weren't a problem. Arsenic could be extracted and when the dust was shipped to Holland they extracted sulphur for match heads.

'Aye, the finest tin in the world, Cornish.'

'Aye all finished now and won't come back.'

I asked if they smoked, but none of them did. Harold, who'd just two front teeth left, had packed up five years ago and felt much better for it.

I asked them if Geevor Tin Mine Museum was open. They told me to ask for Fred, tell him that I'd met the Three Musketeers and he would let me in.

It was very interesting talking to these chaps. I asked about John, the taxi driver who'd given me a lift when I'd had the plane. Apparently, he'd retired, had had a leg off and been in hospital for six weeks without smoking. I remembered John – from two and a half years before – giving me a lift from the airport, and when I went to pay him and was fumbling about with small change he'd said, 'Give me what you've got,' and happily drove off.

The publican was also the same one as last time but seemed friendlier.

ST JUST TO LAND'S END

It wasn't an easy place to get to on public transport, so I tried hitching and the first car that came along stopped. Mary, who had so much mess in the front of her car, put me in the back. *'I've never known a girl talk so much in my life.'*

She had been a care worker and now did it privately. She said that she couldn't stand the way some nurses just didn't care about their patients and were only in it for the money. 'My patients loved me and always wanted me because I treated them right. I would talk to them looking into their eyes and not at the ground. I always pick up women – not usually men – but you looked all right!' She was puffing away at her roll-ups. *'I've never seen so many roll-up smokers as down here.'*

'I'm just going to cook lunch for a ninety-seven-year-old gentleman. It'll take me half an hour and then I'll take you the rest of the way.'

I thought, 'Why not?' and that's what my 'walkabout' is all about.

I sat down on a rickety bench and tried writing but it was too windy.

When Mary reappeared she told me that her children lived in Plymouth and came down every weekend. 'They love me and I love their dad. Everybody loves me except their dad who was too busy with his work to love me. He left home and I cried myself to sleep every night. Now, I've accepted it and know he won't be back, but it's still hard. I went out the other night for the first time in ages. All the girls told me that I looked good. Yes, I am fifty-three but everyone says I look younger. Everyone loves me and now I just put my time into my old folk. The man I've just been to, Pat, spilled tea all down his front the other day and he said it wasn't what it looked like. When he messes himself I don't get uptight. I just tell him that there's a fresh set of clothes on the chair. I love old Pat.'

Mary went out of her way to drop me off at Land's End and I told her that if she ever happened to be in Kent, to look us up.

LAND'S END

It was just what I expected really – a dump. I asked Mary what she thought of Peter de Savoury (a property developer) and she said, ' Oh, we had to get rid of him as no one came here.'

And it's not much better now – just a brightly coloured theme park. How could a fairly important tourist attraction be so tatty? Maybe it's OK for the average tourist, but I hated it and will never return. They even plastered the place with large yellow no parking lines and they couldn't even get those straight.

On the way back to St Just I chatted to some horses, grazing on the grass that was growing on top of the walls, which was much more interesting than the tourists ignoring my hitching thumb. Nobody seemed to give a damn about a backpacker on these roads.

I asked some boys if I was on the right road for St Just. Cheerfully, they pointed me in the wrong direction, but then thought better of it! I passed some little churches, the smallest I'd ever seen, and then fields of cauliflower. *'Do the locals ever nick them?'* In the distance I could see vegetable farmers hard at it, and by now I didn't mind if I didn't get a lift. I wanted some of this and I waved at a forklift driver who looked like a manager.

This was the first farm walk on an intensive vegetable farm; with sprayers, forklifts, four vegetable planters, a plastic-laying machine, a fertiliser spreader and tractors carrying the plants. This was real farming with a huge gang of East European workers – Poles, Latvians, Lithuanians and Russians.

The man on the sprayer was a very reserved Englishman who wouldn't let on much. He was busy with his herbicide and slug pellets but was a bit of a fuck-head compared with all the others.

Another good-looking young man on a tractor was from Lithuania and was having his lunch. He told me that he'd been over here for a couple of years and taught Russian as well as doing farm work. I shook his hand and congratulated him on his good English, which he denied. I said it was better than my Lithuanian.

Across the road was the planting gang. I took a load of photographs as I hadn't seen this type of farming before. After the fertiliser and slug pellets had been put on, the planting gang came through with several people gapping up the plants and picking up the dropped ones. They were such a cheerful bunch and it restored my faith in humanity. One girl, with a huge smile and something special about her, gave me the biggest welcoming smile you've ever seen and then carried on laying the plastic. The foreman pointed her out later as being the best plastic-layer in southern England. I kept asking one lady where she came from. She tried to take her glove off to shake my hand, but I told her not to worry and grasped her hard-working hand as if to say, 'Good for you.'

The man I'd waved to earlier was going the other way on the forklift and I thought he was the manager. I think his name was John Boat or Badd or Barr, or suchlike – definitely John. The company, Southern England Farmers Ltd, rented land all over the south. He had enormous respect for his work force; they were planting cabbages and the plastic would be taken off in April. He said that pigeons were a big problem, particularly with the cabbages. John was a very busy man and had to get on. I told him he was a special guy to run this operation, but he would have none of that. *'Laying twelve-metre wide strips of plastic in a strong wind is a skill. If I'd been doing it, it would've been half way to America by now.'*

This was all so much better and more interesting than Land's End.

The more you walk the more you appreciate a lift and Mr Hen was a very welcome one – I'd seen him earlier doing deliveries in his big red van. Mr Hen had twenty thousand chickens, as well as beef cattle and a taxi. Even though there were two trays of eggs on the front seat and the rest of his office seemed to be on the other seats, he still picked up little old JA.

'Where are you going to, lad?'

'Geevor Tin Mine,' I said.

'Going right past it, lad, but...' – always be careful of the word 'but' – 'got three or four drops first, lad.'

'OK.'

'Well, it's up to you lad, you either stop with me, or take pot luck and see how far you get. If I see you I'll pick you up.'

'Oh, what the hell, I'll help you deliver.'

Ninety minutes later I was still helping Mr Hen to lug the big boxes of eggs around every store in St Just.

'You must be known as Mr Egg round here?'

'Nay, lad.'

'Are they free-range or battery?'

'Aye, lad, all battery since the wife left.'

I asked, 'Why's that? More work involved with free-range?'

'Nay, lad, the wife left and I had to pay her out big time, but we're all right and slowly getting back again. What do you do for a living, like?'

'Wheat farmer in Kent.'

'How many acres, lad?'

'Two and a half thousand.'

'Bloody hell, lad, they say you never see a poor corn farmer. Aye, wait till I tell the boys, lad, they'll never believe it.'

'Have you got any other family?' I asked.

'My lad, a boy of twenty-three.'

'How do you get on with all this farm assurance?'

'Y'know lad, if more of us told 'em to fuck off they wouldn't keep putting this on us.'

As we continued to deliver to the local shops I asked if they took any cracked eggs.

'Nay, lad, they all go down the septic tank since that salmonella outbreak.'

Next, we did a delivery to the pub; one across the road; and one to the butcher, who had two really old collie dogs.

'Bring this box in, would you, lad, and put it next to the other one?' Then, 'Sorry, lad, we brought the wrong one. Can you bring it back, lad?'

'Do you ever get a holiday, Mr Hen?'

'Aye, lad, only just come back from the Costa del Sol and going to Minorca next month.'

'What do you do when you're out there?'

'Aye, bit like you, lad, go and discover the different farming land.'

'What about chicken housing when the new laws come into force?'

'Aye, lad, I'm fifty-four and I don't know if I want much more of this, all the worry and that. But the lad is dead keen. I wanted him to do a course in Scotland but he didn't want to go. And the new building would be £350,000 – a lot of fucking money, lad. I don't know if I want it.'

'How do you get such brown shells? Is it the breed of chicken or the food?'

Mr Hen thought for a while and then replied, 'Aye, lad, funny you should say that. We've come to the conclusion it's the vaccination before twelve weeks. Sure of it – bloody strange, lad.'

I said, 'I've just been in the field with people planting cabbages. They're from all over Europe.'

'Bloody immigrants are all over the place down here. Locals don't get a look in, you know.'

'They just know how to work. The English are too lazy.'

'Aye, lad, I got two of them coming over next week. Czechs, I think.'

He didn't seem to have too much time for them and I don't think they were going to have much fun working for him. He had built the business up over many years: he had over twenty people working for him and said that he used £2000 of feed per month. He enjoyed his holidays, as life at home was not much fun with just him and the boy.

He ended up taking me to the entrance of the tin mine and we said farewell.

GEEVOR TIN MINE

The mine had closed long ago and was now only open for tourism. It was too late to go down the mine but there was plenty to see on top. I met Jim, who showed me round and I told him about the Three Musketeers. He just smiled.

The winder house was a feat of engineering in itself, enabling them to get the men up and down the shaft.

I'd never really understood what a hard, tough job mining was and it wouldn't have helped with the cold wind blowing up your jumper from the Atlantic.

In the old days they used to drill and wedge the ore out, or burn up against the face to get it out one way or another. When dynamite was introduced it made life easier. Jim used to be a 'detonator' and I asked how far he used to stand back – about four hundred feet. I told him he must've got it right because he's still here. He said he got pushed and bruised a bit, laughed and walked off.

Apparently one small lorry would only yield enough tin for a box of chocolates.

I walked on to Pendeen and popped into the North Inn, to find a room for the night. They had one, at £25 per night, and I didn't even bother to look at it first. Fortunately, it was clean and cosy, warm and brand new – in fact, it was paradise!

Pendeen, like so many Cornish villages, was perfect. It had a couple of pubs, shops, a school and a doctors' surgery, and that was what I could see from the pub. The only thing that spoiled this gentle architecture was the replacement PVC windows.

By now the pub had a steady trickle of customers. 'Hippy', with his charm and good looks and long fuzzy plaited hair, was entertaining all the guests with his jokes. I told him about the vegetable farm I'd visited and the Eastern Europeans and got the impression that he didn't like them. He muttered something about not being prepared to work for that small amount of money. I thought to myself that they wouldn't want him and his dozy mates either! He said that you can't blame the farmers but who would want to work for that money? He didn't like big business and the arrogance that goes with it and admitted being 'anti-capitalist'.

An old boy came into the pub with either a young wife, or a granddaughter. He was left on his own as she and Hippy went off to play pool together in the back.

The 'Lifeboat' girls came in to empty the ship of coins and had all sorts of problems opening up the boat. They struggled for over half an hour with a huge bunch of keys.

I said, 'Good job you're not the captain of the ship, or I'd be drowned by now!' I gave them some money for their collection.

I love the way the locals gather and wiggle their arses on the bar stools as if this is their life and it's great; not needing anything else, just pub, fags and mates.

PENDEEN TO ST IVES

It was a lovely sunny morning when I started walking along the B3306 and it turned out to be a fantastic walk. What amazed me was that in this touristic part of the world there still remained so many quaint old stone farm buildings and houses that hadn't been converted. If Fred Flintstone had poked his head out of one of these buildings it would not have surprised me!

Friesian cows looked scraggy and stood knee-high in mud, looking at me as if to say, 'What the heck are you doing down here at this time of the year?' The farmers were spreading slurry and the poor old cows were trying to find some fresh grass.

Gorse fires along the roadside had left exposed the rubbish that people had thrown out of their car windows. A sign at the National Trust site at Trevean Cliff said that because of the gorse fires the mine shafts had been exposed.

An ATS tyre van stopped.

'Any chance of a lift?' I asked.

'Only going to the corner, mate.'

As I watched his van disappear into the distance I wondered why he'd stopped in the first place.

The old tin mines with their tall chimneys and outbuildings have been restored for future generations. *Well done, those folk.*

After a sign saying: 'St Ives 9 miles', I walked for two miles and there was another sign still saying: 'St Ives 9 miles'. Very funny, Mr Sign Man!

It's not very often you see a farmer in a ditch with a spade: he was completely engrossed and had his collie dog tied up beside him – only his head was showing. From about fifty yards I shouted out, 'Good morning,' and he shouted out, 'Morning.' He seemed quite shocked to be spoken to.

Porthmear Farm is something out of this world – it would be a developer's dream.

A big brown and white cow was looking proudly over the wall with her new-born calf – all the same colour – and looking at me as if to say, 'Haven't you got anything better to do?'

The farmyard collie was barking away but was no threat to my ankles.

I passed a dead-end looking pub and was quite pleased it was closed. I said hello to a delivering coalman but got no reply.

Hitchers take note. Always smile at the driver if he doesn't pick you up and always put your hand up to the driver coming from the opposite direction on lonely roads, as well as smiling. If at some time later in the day he comes back, he might just pick you up. This happened today and has done so in the past. *'The art is to keep smiling.'*

After a long walk it's always good to see brake lights come on. Mike, in a Volvo, stopped: his front seat covered in everything but the kitchen sink and loads of twenty pound notes. He was an interesting, hard-working, well-spoken man, a bit grey through smoking and with a great love for Cornwall. He had been a farm worker on a dairy farm, a deep-sea trawler man for ten years, and was going to go mining but the pit closed. He grew daffodils to sell and cut and sold logs.

'You don't do anything the easy way.' I said.

He told me that he'd passed me going the other way and the only reason he had stopped now was because I had smiled and waved. He dropped me off opposite John Leach, the world-famous potter. I'd never heard of him but didn't want to admit it.

St Ives is a nice smug little tourist seaside town with a large curving bay. It also has its share of the bullies of the gull world – the herring gull. I love feeding these brutes and watching them fight it out.

I went into a small 'stuffy' coffee shop and was told where to have coffee, so as not to take up the viewing table where people might come to eat. Anyway, the gulls enjoyed her biscuits.

St Ives = 7/10. Coffee shop = 2/10.

'One ticket to St Erth, please.'

'Hang on, I'm on the phone'. After five minutes, 'Sorry about that, can I help? The ticket costs £4 and you can get off where you like. We are only a branch line.'

Something about this woman pissed me off with her little 'I-am-doing-you-a-service' attitude.

I laughed when the train turned up – it only had one carriage and there were only three people on board when we arrived at St Erth.

I caught the train to Redruth, where I had a cup of tea in a fish and chip shop whilst watching a group of highly made-up fourteen and fifteen–year-olds with their fat midriffs sticking out.

'Cup or mug?'

'I think I'll spoil myself today and have a cup.'

'Yes, my mum likes bone china,' said the cheery type serving.

I said goodbye to Truro as we made our way to Newquay. I had a bird's-eye view on the bus until it rained and then I couldn't see a thing. A branch smashed into the front and made a young girl jump. I saw a buzzard in a tree at eye level. *'Hi, Buzz!'*

I hadn't seen a pheasant in Cornwall, or a rabbit – nothing – no woods and no pheasant cover. I was told by John Mac that it was because Cornwall is so narrow and the salt air doesn't help the natural environment.

It was a walking and hitching day. There was a huge block of purple rape and a farmer spreading nitrogen.

I arrived at Newquay and to get out of the rain I walked into a takeaway where I met Raja. He'd been born in London and his parents came from Bangladesh. He had five brothers and had met a Polish girl whom he was to marry next September in Bangladesh. She'd gone back to university to finish her degree in physics. Raja seemed to have relatives all over the world. I asked how many guests he was having to the wedding.

'Not many,' he replied, 'just eight hundred to a thousand.'

I thought that if I stood there much longer he would have a thousand and one! I asked him about the Victoria Hotel opposite.

'Very expensive!'

It's large and dead-looking. The receptionist was too busy to attend to a common little backpacker having the cheek to ask if he could look at their £50 single room.

Eric, the porter, was summoned to show JA to his room. I was expecting something quite grand and when the door opened it looked like a broom cupboard.

'Goodbye and thank you, Eric.'

Eric was an upright man and had worked in this privately owned hotel for six years. I imagined he could well have been a butler in his prime.

Next door was a modern Travelodge type of place and once more I was given the key for a room inspection. I booked a room and the best part of this place was Mike, behind the bar.

'£40, sir.'

'Is that the cheapest room on offer?'

'Yes, sir, £10 off if you don't have breakfast.'

With that, the only other two customers in the place jumped up and said that they were leaving early so could they have a discount?

I went down early for breakfast, but all the doors were locked and apart from the goldfish it looked dead, so I went back and packed up. I came down again and there were signs of life.

'Beans with egg on top, please.'

'No trouble,' said the beaming girl.

NEWQUAY TO TIVERTON

A young girl got on the bus with a baby – very much playing the young mother – aged twelve to sixteen with heavy red lipstick, a big floppy red hat and a pink handbag. She was a bit of a madam.

It was a freezing cold day and yet she opened the window and sat up the front, leaving the rest of us to freeze. I know why she opened it. The fumes were coming from her baby.

The field boundaries changed and the stone walls changed into earth banks – something I hadn't seen before.

John, the bus driver, told me about an American he'd picked up and that every year he would come back and walk a bit more of the English coastline. In fact he told me three times.

Wadebridge has a funny little bus stop, but whilst waiting I popped into the lobster museum. Why has the lobster population gone down? Answer: new technology; three times as many pots put out as three years ago; and pollution. And why is the lobster different from us? Because, like the crab, its skeleton is on the outside.

Back at the bus stop I met Sergeant Smith who was ex-army, and when I remarked about the state of the bus shelter he said, 'They should bring back National Service and give them a bloody good hiding.'

Then I was told about when he was shouted at by his Sergeant Major – two of the cadets had fits and had to be taken out of the army!

'*Well, if you thought I had got rid of mum and baby on the last bus you were wrong. She is now changing the baby on the back seat and that's why the driver has the door shut. 'Walkabout' is never dull.*'

Everyone was giving the baby great big smiles as they got on and off the bus. '*Why am I the only one who hates the bloody thing?*' You should've seen it in its new change of clothing – looked like a baby panda! The baby was, by now, howling. I would rather have a dog on the bus – they don't cry; they don't shit on the bus; they don't smell; and they don't need pushchairs!'

'How long have you been driving buses, Mark?'

'Only about two years and before that I was in banking for twenty years.'

Mark was a bit of a nervous driver and a smoker so we made a good pair as we both had a quiet fag on the bus when everyone else got off.

'What sort of banking?' I asked.

'Clerking and that sort of stuff.'

'All they want is young people now.'

'Yes, blinking mini-skirts selling a pension and all that. It's not for me. They offered me a package so I took it.'

He said that the worst holidaymakers were the ones with Volvos who hog the road and take everything with them, bar the kitchen sink, and they contribute nothing to the local economy and live in expensive holiday homes.

An old lady said, 'Cor, that John Betjeman Centre café is a blessing. Cup of tea for thirty pence with a biscuit. Never have coffee, expensive wherever you go, but people pay so they keep charging.'

Our new driver should've been in a Grand Prix. John was about fifty-six and he wasn't hanging around. I was telling him about Mark, the last driver.

'Oh, Mark, yes, he's a Wadebridge man,' as if every driver has his own village or town. Apparently a lot of these buses don't go back to the depots at night but instead go to farmyards or drives.

BOSCASTLE

John talked about the disastrous flood and said, 'The water was coming down here like a river and I tell you what – if I hadn't had four-wheel drive I would've been washed away. See that bridge? It was swept away.'

I told him about our hurricane in 1987.

'Aye, I was down in Kent just after it. I used to drive for a national haulage company, and I knew Ashford pretty well, as I used to deliver to the REME. I had a drop at Chatham that had to be craned off and I had to be there before 9.00am as the crane was to be commandeered by the council to clear up.' He repeated this about three or four times.

Poor Boscastle reached fame through flooding: the worst being on August 16th, 2004 when seven inches of rain fell in one hour over the surrounding area. Strangely enough, hardly any rain actually fell over Boscastle, but the river rose seven feet in an hour and Boscastle, being the sump of the steep-sided valley, was nearly destroyed.

Seven helicopters rescued one hundred and fifty people from roof tops and seventy-five cars, five caravans and six buildings were washed out to sea. Amazingly enough no one was killed. The villagers couldn't praise the pilots highly enough. Now that the village had been rebuilt most people seemed happy with the insurance payouts and all seemed nearly normal.

I went to sit in the middle of the bus. I was hanging on for dear life with this guy.

BUDE

This is a funny little seaside town and the first job was to find a connection. Then I was told there was no public transport and I was stuck here. The only way out would be to go back to Exeter.

The coach was waiting and I gave the driver a twenty pound note.

'I've only just come on duty,' he snarled, 'haven't you got anything smaller?'

I found a fiver and asked, 'Where are you going next? Tiverton?'

'Not worth it,' was the reply. *'Christ, I have a misery guts here! The coach is a forty seater and there are only three of us on it.'*

48

Mr Misery and I hadn't hit it off and every now and then we made uneasy eye contact in his mirror. But I have to say that he was a very careful driver and we were going up some extremely narrow lanes. I just thought he was rather tired. Bus driving is not easy with bendy twisting roads and hardly any passengers.

The countryside was becoming more wooded and I saw my first rabbit for ages.

By now I was the only passenger on the coach and I told Mr Misery that I felt very privileged.

'Well, I should charge you more.'

'I reckon I should get a discount when the coach is full.' There was no reply.

'Where do you want to be dropped off, bus or train station?'

'Train, please, and thank you very much.'

Exeter station was cosy and warm. I had a hot chocolate while a group of probable young farmers with hard-working greasy hands sat next to me.

The train soon pulled into Tiverton. I found out from an apologetic woman at the bus company that there were no more buses that day. I rang a taxi service, which I only do if it's unavoidable – I don't like arriving late at hotels but a 'walkabout' is never simple. A cheerful Scottish lady driver came and took me to a local hotel.

I thought I would have a bit of luxury after my busy day. I went upstairs to a large landing and an average-sized bedroom. With the restaurant closing in fifteen minutes I had to get a move on. There were loads of morons at the bar afterwards, so I went to bed.

The next morning breakfast nearly slid off the plate with grease and the tomatoes were nearly green. There was an air of excitement at the hotel because of an impending wedding. The sister of the bride came shyly into the restaurant and said that she had a problem with some arrangement and asked if she could display the balloons. The waiter, instead of jumping to it, just made her feel more awkward.

I felt like kicking him up the rear end. However, when I got back home I wrote a letter suggesting that they should keep the lady manager, but sack the chef – for his shit food – as well as the rest of the moronic staff.

TO BRUSHFORD

Later in the morning I looked up some farmer friends, who'd moved to Somerset after winning the agricultural jackpot when they sold some of their land for development. They had bought a dream estate with a huge mansion and four hundred acres to go with it.

I failed to thumb a lift so I caught a bus. The countryside on the A396 to Brushford was amazingly beautiful. No wonder John and Julie had moved down here.

Dawn was looking after me on the bus and would tell me where to get off. Half way across a bridge she told me that we were in Somerset and that I should go past the church, turn left and then I'd be there.

The church was very beautiful and I reached the end of a sweeping drive and checked the letter box to see that I had the right address.

As I wandered into the garden it wasn't long before I heard John shout, ' Why didn't you phone? I would've given you a lift.'

John and Julie had bought this place about two years previously – a 14th or 15th century building which had had major work done in the 1920s and 1960s. John said the main things still to do were the roof and windows. They had just finished renewing the central heating – with its seventy-six radiators and two boilers making it look like the engine room of the Titanic. The attic had a lead sump for water and this was all piped outside the house. Every room had its own character and there was a bell rope, a priest's hole, different moulding and panelling and old and new parts of the house.

I hadn't realised what a hands-on-man John Mac was – he could turn his hand to anything. 'We have about ten or twelve bathrooms.'

The house is surrounded by some of the most beautiful countryside in the world.

We drove off to Simonsbath and hit a load of snow. It was unbelievable as we'd not seen any until then and in one place we had to turn round as the road was blocked. I don't think Julie ever believed our story when we got back.

We had some of John and Julie's homemade sausages and I then retired to my magnificent bedroom. I couldn't resist pulling the bell rope for room service and heard a muffled, 'Fuck off,' from below!

With seventy-six radiators I lay in bed with all my clothes on, freezing cold.

Next morning Julie said I was very honoured because John had got up at seven o'clock to take me to the station. Patrick, the station master, opened up for me and I told him that the station was a credit to him and his team. It was clean and warm with nice tables and chairs, and was ideal for *Walkabout* writing. The waiting room didn't take long to fill with fairly 'stuffy' clientele. Bang on time the train arrived.

It was party time on the train and I thought the football boys were going home, but they were on their way to the Carling Cup Final in Cardiff. There were beer cans and bottles all over the place. *'I've never seen such a mess in my life.'* The Taunton Reds were in full swing – I enjoyed it because it gave me more material for my *Walkabout* – although I thought most of them were fuckheads!

'Go get some ice and a bottle opener!'

'I got the fucking family coming!'

'I bought a car for £1500 and sold it for £2000.'

'The fucking oil's worth more than the car!'

When I came back from the loo the football boys were in my seat, so I said, 'You're in my seat.'

Surprisingly, they didn't mind and moved out.

At Westbury station the fans changed for Cardiff. The guards came along and upgraded us all to first class because of the broken glass. *'Good riddance!'*

A young girl was chatting on her mobile to a friend for an hour, in which time I got to know about her hair-do, nail varnish and her latest boyfriend. She was still chatting when we drew into Paddington and I said to the young guy sitting opposite me that I was glad I didn't have her telephone bill.

Home Sweet Home!

CHAPTER FOUR

Taunton to Liverpool

It was May and it was time to get back down to Tiverton. A £71 ticket got me on the Friday morning train with a mixture of business people and holidaymakers going west. Laptops were out, some for work and some for amusement. I nodded off and soon we were at Reading; a modern busy city with some very smart offices. It was very windy and a cloudy day with drizzle.

Next it was on to Swindon, Bath, Taunton and Tiverton Parkway. I had arranged to meet our friend, Fiona Doyle, but phoned her to say that I wouldn't be doing so. She said she'd just driven past the entrance to Tiverton Parkway and wanted to know if I would like a lift to John and Julie's. I declined as I didn't want to push their hospitality.

This walking job isn't much fun when it's peeing down. I crossed the road and, with no plan in mind, just walked up a very rural lane. In no time I was in the middle of nowhere – no houses and just isolated farms. The verges and hedgerows were oozing with every wild flower you could think of and they were all competing with each other. *'God is one great gardener!'*

After a while I tried to thumb a lift but had no luck. *'Who wants to pick up some nutter in the rain?'* As luck would have it I went round the corner and there, like a mirage, was the Staplecross Inn and it had just opened at 4.00pm. I had a beer and met the driver of the car who had just passed me. He said he didn't pick me up because I had 'something or other'!

I asked if there was a bus to Brampton and the pretty barmaid said, 'Yes, on Thursday.' *'Today is Friday. I'm going to be here a while then! Ho, ho, ho!! Well, I thought it was funny."*

I started walking and finally a friendly farmer gave me a lift in his Land Rover.

'Going to Brampton?'

'Yes, jump in.'

John was a local farmer, divorced when he was thirty and had five children. He had only just done a deal with either selling or buying the Staplecross pub. He seemed to have land all over the place and also owned a pub in Exeter.

He knew John Mac and Ian Kemsley. He liked his shooting and preferred picking up with his dogs.

When I asked him, 'Who shall I say picked me up?' he said to say John from the Exeter pub and they would know who I meant.

The phone rang and it was John Mac.

'Where are you? You're staying with me and I'm coming to get you!'

As it was peeing down with rain and getting dark, and I had no idea where I would be staying, it didn't seem a bad idea at all.

I popped into the pub at Brampton whilst waiting for John. Some of the old boys looked as though they'd been sitting there for a hundred years, but they were quite welcoming.

What a taxi driver John Mac was, and soon we were going down his driveway with all the rhododendrons out. He proudly pointed out a pink one in full flower.

We all went to Dunster for a meal and then I hit the bed in my amazing room.

I was woken by a loud thumping noise outside my bedroom. I was expecting Fiona to break in but was disappointed to find it was the cat that wanted some company.

Later on, I looked out of the window and saw

the cat playing with a mouse – then the puppy joined in. This would've made a perfect photograph, but by the time I got there the mouse had run into the house, leaving the puppy very mystified.

I said my 'goodbyes' to them and John dropped me off on the road to Minehead, where I walked and walked.

It was a quiet road and I walked with the river below me. I found that if I cupped my ears I could hear three times as much. *'The human race should be like elephants and have big ears.'*

My poor old legs were about to say enough is enough when another Land Rover stopped and gave me a short lift to Bridgetown, or some damp little hamlet in the valley with a pub called the Badgers Holt. Earlier, I'd passed the priory estate owned by the League against Cruel Sports, who seemed to have imprisoned themselves with barbed and electric wire. They only bought the land to stop the fox hunters, stag hunters and shooters from having some fun, and I suppose that every now and then a local throws a brick through the window.

Mr Reynolds gave me a short lift – he was a shooting agent and he knew John Mackelden and Ian Kemsley.

I was now back walking and hitching and taking in the nature around me. I saw some different wild flowers but nothing like yesterday's.

People down here don't like hitchhikers and I don't blame them. Plenty of shooting and gamekeeper types drove past.

I couldn't believe it – at last there was a bus and it stopped. A well-spoken young driver gave me an 'all-day' ticket and we were away.

There was more stunning scenery and after Dunster we were soon back at Minehead. *'I didn't really want to come here but on this job you go where the bus takes you. What is it about seaside towns that make them seem like the sump of humanity? What a sloppy breed of holidaymakers there are in these places, including me.'*

I asked some old boys about the steam train, but the silly buggers only knew about the Butlins' little white one that drives around Minehead.

I walked down to the bottom end of Minehead and found the old steam train from Minehead to Bishops Lydeard. A one-way ticket cost £8.50.

The line was originally opened in 1862 between Taunton and Watchet (twenty-three miles long); it was closed by British Rail in 1972 and re-opened by volunteers in 1976. All the staff on the railway were volunteers.

En route, the countryside unfolded with the hedgerows bursting with wild flowers.

The first stop was Dunster, then Blue Anchor, Washford, Watchet, Doniford Holt, Williton, Crowcombe, Heathfield and finally Bishops Lydeard.

I didn't realise what a team you need to run this railway: there were guards, drivers, conductors, signal men, mechanics as well as those who ran the restaurants and souvenir shops. I was told that this particular train used sixteen tons of coal a day.

I caught the bus at Lydeard. It was full of rowdy children, who, after asking about my camera, all left the bus in good humour. One young lad was wearing eye-liner. An older boy apologised for their behaviour, and I told him that I didn't mind and that they were harmless enough.

TAUNTON TO BURNHAM-ON-SEA

I didn't have to wait long at this rather smelly bus station before getting on board the number 14 to Burnham. *'Why do bus stations seem to have their own smell?'*

I talked to Auntie Mabel in the queue behind me and she said she used to be married to a policeman. She said that when they'd retired they were going to go walking on Exmoor but by that time they were too clapped out. I asked her who the MP for Bridgewater was but she said she wasn't that interested in politics. *'There seemed to be a bit of a sad streak in Mabel.'*

This is another British seaside town. I went and asked the owner of a B&B if he had a bed for the night. The man, with a fat gut and dressed in his slippers and slacks, said that he only had a double room and the price was £50. I felt like telling him to stuff it up his jumper, but I didn't.

I found a fairly rough old pub with stacks of unwashed glasses on the bar. I had a beer and asked about a bed: £70 en-suite and £50 without. I burst out laughing and said it was Burnham-on-Sea and not the London Hilton! She went to see the manager and the price then became £50 or £35. I looked at the room and it was a lot smarter than the pub and the landlady, so I took it.

I met Graham in the bar, who was a retired aviation engineer. He did hydraulics and propellers. I said I owned a huge jet and we chatted like old friends. Nowadays, he does DIY and drives cars for a hire company.

I went and had a shower before walking my feet off around the place looking for somewhere to eat, trying to avoid Indian or Chinese. I couldn't find any English food and ended up having an ordinary Indian meal. I didn't tip them and got out quickly.

I woke up quite early and wrote a few pages of *Walkabout*. I was glad I had paid up the night before and it was OK to leave quietly. I don't think I could have stood a breakfast in this smelly place. Just before escaping down the fire escape I put on my wet-weather gear which turned out to be just as well.

The street cleaners were hard at work. I said to them that it took a good man to get up on a rainy Sunday morning and do this job.

There were no buses at this time of day so I had a long walk out of this boring little seaside town in the rain. Having left at 7.40am I walked for over an hour and a half but the exercise was good for me. One hundred and three 'hitched' cars passed me and then dear old Angus stopped for me in his twenty-five-year-old Volvo and gave me a lift to Weston-Super-Mare. He was very proud of his car, as it had had only one owner from new and had a full service history. He said that you don't get many hitchhikers these days and most people don't pick them up anyway, because a few idiots had given them such a bad name. Apparently, he had worked on Guernsey for three years running an underground car park for Barclays Bank.

He went out of his way to drop me off.

THE ATLANTIC HOTEL

I reckoned I deserved my breakfast and passed all the usual rat-holes and went into the only building that looked grand. This must have been the hotel for the oldest people in the Western Hemisphere. When I walked in and asked for breakfast this really baffled the skinhead head waiter.

'Are you a resident?'

'Not yet, but I'm booking in for tonight.' *'Kidding him!'*

He then escorted me to the reception desk where I asked the stuck-up little lady if she had a room for the night.

'No, we're fully booked. We have two coaches.'

'Well, what about breakfast?'

'That's only for residents, but we can give you a coffee.'

'But outside it says you are open to non-residents.'

In the end I told them to stuff their coffee up their jumper.

She muttered, 'If that's the way you want it.'

What a strange lot. I went down the road and had a very nice breakfast with a Cypriot family.

'Now, how do I get rid of this delightful little seaside town?'

I went up the high street and found a double-decker bus with 'Bristol' written on it and asked the driver if he was going there. He muttered some remark about 'Bristol' being written on the front of the bus. *'I'm just checking, Mr Lasthole.'*

Bristol bus station was brand new and spotless. Looking at places of departure on the screen and wondering where to go I really couldn't stand another seaside town. I tried to find a tour bus to show me around Bristol, but gave up and went back to the station and caught a bus to Bath.

Bath on a wet Sunday was full of sloppy looking tourists, including me. Chewing gum was stuck to the pavements and cheap stall traders seemed to take the beauty from this lovely city. It was jam-packed with coaches. Bath deserves better than this.

I took an open-top bus and we all stayed downstairs in the dry. The guide reminded me of Ronnie Corbett and really did know his job. He explained everything about Bath – the place where Londoners would come for some fun – gambling, whoring and hot baths. Some of the locals were jealous of their lifestyle and used to pee in the baths! One could see evidence of the window tax, and where the expression 'daylight robbery' came from.

The Victorians put the shops into Bath and in Georgian times they liked high pavements.

We went over a Venice look-alike bridge, then around a circular building built on the same principle as Stonehenge. In those days the river was much more polluted: Avon is the Celtic name for 'river'.

Queen Victoria hated Bath because one day someone there said that she had fat ankles and she never forgave them for that. On one occasion, whilst travelling by train through Bath, on her way to Bristol, everyone wanted to wave, but she asked for the blinds to be drawn down. The story goes that she had a memory like an elephant and legs to match!

Vanity Fair was filmed here and apparently Jane Austen lived in Bath for a while. It was also in Bath that some old coffins with scratch marks on them were dug up and so after that bells were placed on the corpses' fingers.

I went into the station and the train was there, so I rushed past the ticket sales and jumped on. I felt like a naughty school child. As luck would have it, when we arrived at Bristol they were checking tickets. So I handed him my Tiverton to Lenham ticket and he just glanced at it and waved me through.

BATH TO GLOUCESTER

I thought I'd better not push my luck any further so I bought a ticket. It was just as well, too, because there was a conductor and only two carriages. I bought a sandwich at the station and soon we were whizzing through beautiful countryside.

Well, this was another wet, dirty old fag-end bus station. A film crew called 'Vertigo' were out at the back making a film called *Outlaw* and some streets were sealed off because of it. They seemed a pretty basic load of young film makers, but when they packed up they shared all the food with the homeless-type losers; some of the youngsters were playing silly buggers with the equipment when they weren't looking.

I had a look at the timetable and it seemed that the Ross-on-Wye service didn't run on Sundays, but the bus driver said that it did and that there would be a lot of young people with loads of baggage.

There was a beggar with two dogs making a nuisance of himself, and I was approached by another air-head who said he was homeless and hungry and wanted money. Instead of telling him to clear off, I took the easy way out and gave him a pound, but then regretted it as I watched him walk from the bus station and, outside the local pub, I heard him say something like: 'This place is full of foreigners.' *'Yes, and they're better than you, my friend.'*

When the bus driver turned up he said, 'If you want a cup of coffee you might as well have it now as I won't be leaving for three quarters of an hour.'

So I went to the local pub – a typical football pub – with large screens showing football, plenty of cheap beer and large bellies to go with it, and a sloppy waiter cleaning the tables by flicking the bits onto the floor.

GLOUCESTER TO ROSS-ON-WYE

Well, I'd travelled around the south coast on empty buses, but now I was standing, after helping some youngsters on with very heavy luggage. I tried to find out what they were doing but their English wasn't good. After a while I discovered that they were Ukrainian workers: this was intensive fruit country.

When I asked one of the locals how far he was going he replied, 'As far as my council tax allows.'

Ross-on-Wye sounds a poncy name and when walking around it I noticed that several hotels were closed. There was a notice on one door thanking all his wonderful customers, but that he was off for a well-earned retirement and hoping to improve his golf handicap.

I found a pub-type hotel that was fairly expensive, but it was late at night and I was not prepared to bargain too hard. The single supplement was 10% more than the double, so I offered them the double as I couldn't understand why I should have to pay more. They didn't argue and said that they had a job to bring it up on the computer. Anyway, for £62 I got dinner and breakfast so it was a good deal.

After climbing twenty-seven steps to my room in this rabbit warren type of place, I then went to the restaurant and couldn't believe how smart it was. They were even wearing ties.

I went to bed thinking that the highlight of the day was getting out of Burnham-on-Sea. *'Don't be cruel!'*

ROSS-ON-WYE TO CARDIFF

I caught the bus to Hereford. I reckon this area should be called the Garden of England. The only things which didn't look good were the arable crops. Some of the barley and rape was flat and the potatoes looked as though they had only just been planted. Everywhere was waterlogged. Much of the sugar beet had temporary rabbit netting around it. I could tell, agriculturally, that this was a progressive area because new packing houses were being built and there were acres of polythene.

'Well, here I am and it's peeing down with rain.' I had no will to traipse around this city so I caught the coach to Abergavenny. It was another steamed up bus. An old artful farmer got on board, and I asked what he had done with the weather. There was no answer! Was he deaf, or did he only speak Welsh, or was he just plain rude? The latter I suspected. Seeing an old man put his feet on the seats confirmed to me that he was a bit of a pig. The only window steamed up was the one next to me.

There were plenty of these grand old barns sitting around in farmyards waiting for someone to do them up and put some money and love into them.

The bus followed the railway line and we passed into Wales.

I arrived at Abergavenny where there is certainly some history. I went into St Mary's Priory Church and asked if this was a city.

'We are most certainly not! We are a town!' They proceeded to tell me the history of the church and how it cost £400 per day to run. It didn't go down too well when my mobile phone went off.

A large medieval sculpture of a recumbent Jesus had just been returned from the Tate Gallery.

The two ladies gave me a leaflet to take round with me, but not to take home! The old girl was so proud of her church and I gave a little donation.

The tithe barn stood outside the church and dated back to the 12th century. It was built to store the produce of the local community who in turn paid tithes to the monks of St Mary's Priory. In 1590 the barn was raised to make it into a two-storey building and in the 1700s the roundels, stone shelving and pigeon holes were added. Over the years it had been used for many purposes, from a base for a travelling theatre in the 17th century to a carpet warehouse and discotheque in the 20th century. It also housed a food hall, a shop and an education and exhibition centre. It had been painstakingly restored in 2002.

I had lunch in the Lazy Days café, a thriving little place, and I congratulated them on their politeness.

Abergavenny Castle was open but the museum was closed. The approach to the castle was through the gatehouse, which is the youngest part and was added in about 1400 in response to the threat from Owen Glynder. It had a long narrow passageway which was originally vaulted and with rooms above which must have been comfortable, judging by the large fireplace on the south side.

ABERGAVENNY TO BRYMAUR

We were getting into industrial Wales now and some elderly people on the bus pointed out where the disaster at Aberfan had happened. You can see where whole hillsides of the coal mining valleys have been grassed over.

Fred told me that his father had asked him whether he wanted to go down the mines or join the army. Fred went into the army and went to the Sudan and Palestine – and survived.

I said to the couple on the bus that I thought Maggie Thatcher wasn't very popular round here and the man said, 'No.' As I got off the bus he continued by saying, 'I wouldn't mention Maggie Thatcher round here.' *'He obviously thinks I'm stupid.'*

You can go down a coal mine called 'The Big Pit' so I jumped off at Brymaur bus station. Now this was a great place to be at 3.00pm with alcoholics drinking cider, and what was frightening was that they were very young. And everyone was smoking for Wales – I think they beat Cornwall.

As luck would have it, the last party was at 3.30pm. I joined a school party and teachers, and went down in a cage after being fitted up with lamps and a gas mask. We had to leave behind our cameras, watches, mobile phones, cigarettes and lighters and anything else that could cause an explosion.

The pit had opened in 1860 when the shaft was eight feet wide. By 1880 it was extended to eighteen feet. At that time children as young as six worked there.

Compressed air took over from steam in 1953. We were given strict instructions to close the ventilation doors.

When the coal was dug by hand it came out a lot cleaner and when mechanisation came loads of rock came out with the coal.

'How do you separate the rock from the coal?'

'By floating it in water, as the coal is lighter than the rock.'

We were told of the man-made disaster at Aberfan in 1966, when a landslide covered a whole school and one hundred and fifteen children died along with twenty-nine adults. Since then they have mixed cement with the slurry to stabilise it.

Smokeless coal was used in the war which was invaluable; smoke could be seen for miles and the Germans used to easily pick off the smoking ships.

Down the mines canaries were used to check for carbon monoxide as they were more reliable than machinery and did not break down.

The stables that housed the pit-ponies are still there. In 1938, when the coal industry was nationalised the miners got two weeks' holiday instead of one.

The Davy lamp, invented by Humphry Davy, was one of the best inventions of modern times.

I managed to find my way into the wrong shed and all the workmen in there asked where I was from.

I said 'Kent.'

'Betteshanger?' they asked.

There were two American women waiting for the bus, but I decided to start walking; it was a fair way through the industrial estate. After about ten cars I managed to hitch a lift.

Bob was a tough, greasy, hard-working and tattooed lorry driver who drove a heavy low-loader and travelled and worked all over the place. He was born in Colchester and met his wife in Wales.

He had two identical twenty-three-year-old twin daughters and when I asked if they were very close he told me that they fought like cat and dog and if he tried to separate them they would tell him that it was their fight.

One was expecting an unplanned baby which had come as a shock; she was on the pill but had been given antibiotics. *'That's what she told her dad, anyway!'*

I thanked Bob for the lift and made my way to the bus station. An alcoholic was just being loaded into a police van. The usual mouthing went with him.

BRYMAUR TO PONTYPRIDD

'This is not exactly Daily Telegraph country down here!' This is a poor old part of the country and everybody goes around looking pissed off. Local elections had ended with plenty of Labour posters around. *'Haven't seen any Tory ones. I wonder why?! I know I live a sheltered life but you wonder what Labour has ever done for all these people. They keep voting Labour and get more pissed off by the year.'*

Pontypridd is a real rat-hole. (As someone said later, 'Where men were men and women were glad they were women.') As I couldn't stand the idea of staying in Cardiff I thought that as it was getting late I would stay here. *'Not a good idea.'* It was only 6.30pm and all the shops were 'grilled' up, and even the loos had roll shutters on them. I couldn't even find a hotel and it gave me a really creepy feeling. In fact I'd felt safer in Mexico City, where at least one in six people was an armed policeman.

I found the station which matched this rat-hole and smelled of urine. The only pleasant part of it was the jackdaws.

I met an Asian lady at the train station and asked if she lived here. She told me that she didn't and that she found it the same as me – a creepy hole.

I was pleased to take the fifteen minute ride to Cardiff.

Not many metres from the Great Western Railway Station I saw a Travelodge so I made a beeline for it and booked in.

CARDIFF TO PEMBROKE

I didn't have a good night and decided to ring Linda, a lady I'd met in Thailand and again, purely by accident, in Guatemala. She lived in Barry so I took the bus out to there.

A sign in the bus said: 'WE CANNOT THINK OF A WORD FOR PEOPLE WHO ABUSE OUR STAFF.' These were the punishments: 'THREE MONTHS FOR AFFRAY; SIX MONTHS FOR ACTUAL BODILY HARM; SIX MONTHS FOR SUSPECTED THREATENING BEHAVIOUR.'

Linda's house was what I expected. It was a pretty muddled higgledy-piggledy place with nothing really finished, because she was always flying off travelling around the world. I stopped for about an hour and then carried on my way. She offered to drive me back to Cardiff but I took the bus.

In Cardiff they have a different bus system and they don't give change. My 'all-day' fare cost £3 but I only had a fiver. I asked all the people if they had any change but got no response. *'Surprise, surprise!'* But the driver found some out of his own pocket.

Studs! Every young person here seems to have one stuck somewhere on the body. *'Perhaps they hold them together!'*

I felt quite young on this bus as we wound our way through every housing estate in Wales, with the old people proudly showing their free passes.

It was now nearly midday and I needed breakfast. The only place I could see was the Prince of Wales so I had a chicken salad and chips. *'I left a note on the table saying: 'Dear Chef, these chips are nearly as old as me and I am 56! Love, Table 50.'*

I bought my ticket to Pembroke and sat and wrote some *Walkabout* while I waited.

CARDIFF TO PEMBROKE

My lunch was now sitting on my stomach and it felt like a hedgehog. I would write a proper letter to them when I returned home. Neil, from the farm, rang with various technical questions and said that they had sprayed thousands of acres. *'To tell the truth, when you're away like this, you just let them get on with it.'*

In Cardiff station they had a 'break the glass for cardiac arrest equipment' thing. I had never seen that before, but they probably needed it for all the smokers here.

The train rolled out and we all changed for Swansea. Steel manufacturing is still king of this part of the world, with its huge factories. Thank God they are still making money, in spite of huge competition from China.

We arrived at Swansea after an interesting journey with the sea on the left. The train rolled out of Swansea after they had put a ramp down to let a lady in a mobile wheelchair get on board. She certainly knew how to drive it and parked it in the carriage like an expert in a car park. Her companion looked just like Albert Steptoe when he took his cap off. He started reading *Computers for Seniors* and had a new colour printer in a package.

This is a pretty part of the country. It's always good to get back out into the countryside.

We stopped at Carmarthen, passing a milk depot with huge tankers all lined up, and got to Pembroke late afternoon..

I don't know why, but I didn't get off at Pembroke but went on to the docks. I thought this was a quaint little holiday town, only to find two huge oil refineries and a massive dockyard. I hadn't yet seen any accommodation and I looked like a lost sheep wandering around.

This is a working part of Wales and I was well away from tourism. I went to Asda to see if I could get a taxi to a hotel. No taxis – then two arrived. The driver of one was fat and toothless and took me to The Cheddar Bridge Hotel.

'Nice view up there, mate, right across the estuary.'

'What's it like in Pembroke and how's it treating you?'

'Good, mate, good.'

The hotel looked fairly tatty, but they seemed to think they were rather up-market. The receptionist said, 'The only room left is the suite at £80.'

I replied, 'Too expensive and wasted on me!'

'We could do it for £70.'

'I hope you sell it!' I couldn't be bothered to haggle with them in this dead-end hole on top of the hill l, so walked back down into town.

I went and found the Welshmans Arms which I had been told a few days ago was a building site, and a friendly place it turned out to be. I got drinking with three guys from Grimsby – a father, his son and a mate – who were shotcrete blasters working at the oil refinery. The following day was to be their last; they'd been all over the world but had only seen the building sites! They used to be fishermen until the Icelanders put in place a 250-mile exclusion zone which killed the industry overnight; all we have now is a 12-mile exclusion zone. I asked if it was Ted Heath who'd sold the fishing industry down the pan but they said it was Harold Wilson.

These men didn't eat coley. They said it's a dirty eating-fish that spends its life on the sea bottom and that people should see the filth that sticks to them. They ate haddock which was much cleaner and lives in the middle part of the sea.

I got talking about fat girls and got shushed as the landlady's daughter nearby was no midget and was actually there eating chocolate biscuits. I got shushed again when I started talking about the Chinese as one of their mates had married one!

The pub did B&B for £25. The two new chandlers in the pub reminded me of Del Boy and they laughed when I told them.

'By the way, have you got a room for the night?'

The landlady asked the maid, 'Have you finished room three yet?'

There was a lot of banging and hoovering going on upstairs, and I spent the next hour getting drunk and talking to the concrete boys.

'I suppose you old boys make a fortune?'

'Just a bit.'

They knew Sheppey and had been concreting at Sheerness Steel.

They suggested that the best place to eat was at The Swan, a fair walk to the other end of town. So when the room was ready, I had a bath and a little laugh at the new paint over the carpet and the en-suite department. *'I am a stuffy little snob. What do you expect for £25? The Ritz?'*

On the way to the Swan a car pulled up and the girl driving asked me the way. She was young and local and before I could explain she just took off. It didn't sink in until the next day that she was 'on the game'. She had taken one look at me and driven off. *'It's sad that I'm so ugly that even they don't want me, even if I pay.'*

I walked a long way but it was worth it. I stood in the street looking for The Swan and there it was right behind me – a proper local pub and restaurant. It was nice not to have a tourist place. The landlord looked a little like a grown-up Hell's Angel and had a twitching neck. He must have had a good wife, or mother, whom he said did the cooking. I had a lasagne and it was excellent. When I asked him who had cooked it I said, 'You want to look after her because she's good.'

I asked an old boy at the bar if he lived in Pembroke and he replied, 'No, in Pembroke Dock. Two generations and proud of it.'

There was a local family who had just finished eating and the father and eight-year-old son were at the bar. The boy was talking about the ozone layer and the publican was taking time to explain. I thought he was a bright lad and as I left I said to the father, 'You're going to have trouble with him, but you'll also have fun.'

I went back to the Welshmans Arms and to bed. The concrete boys were well away now in front of the open fire.

ONWARDS FROM PEMBROKE DOCK

Well, what a day. I didn't get the earliest of starts and left at 9.10am. There was no one around and I left the keys in the door. I'd been told that they couldn't do breakfast but I could get it next door in a sort of transport café. However, it smelled of stale oil and was empty so I gave it a miss.

I walked for a while and flagged down a bus in a rather dangerous spot under a bridge, but luckily it stopped just beyond. It took me to Pembroke and I asked the driver to drop me near the castle, where I got rid of my horrible Cardiff bread on the swans; not that they complained.

I really felt I had to see Pembroke Castle, where Henry VII, Henry VIII's father, was born in 1457. The castle was built in 1200 and has many towers that were copied from the French castles. I could've been more knowledgeable, but was too mean to buy the guide book. The entrance fee was only £3.50 so I didn't have the nerve to ask for OAP rates, as the lady on the desk was grumpy enough as it was.

I met a young chap going round who was doing a risk assessment for the partially-sighted, as he was going to be visiting on Thursday with a party of eight mainly elderly people. He told me that he'd been here once before for a firework display and that it had been so windy that when the rockets reached the height of the wall they went horizontal.

It seemed funny looking out to sea from the turrets over the modern oil refinery.

I went into the paper shop and there was a very severely disabled man in a wheelchair. The lady carer was flicking through the pages of a pornographic magazine for him.

It was a funny old-fashioned town with shops that in Kent would be past their sell-by date. I went for a coffee and was served by a very attractive waitress wearing a T-shirt with 'Little Miss Naughty!' emblazoned on it.

Kids have kids here – not only are they fat and ugly, but they actually manage to find someone to make love to them! They usually waddle onto the bus with a pink pram and great fat legs.

We passed little fields of grass with some cows but not much else in the way of livestock – certainly not sheep.

Little uninteresting men came and went with their fat uninteresting wives. Couples were in town on holiday and trying to make out that they were happy. Two youngsters got on the bus with snog marks on their necks; I couldn't believe how such a young girl could have such a wrinkly face. As soon as the bus stopped, they all got off and lit up! *I'm not really a grumpy old man, but these youngsters are a useless generation of fat, smoking, lazy no-hopers.'*

The bus wound its way round Pembroke Dock again on the way to Fishguard. I was pleased to get away from here.

A man got on with a teddy bear on his rucksack and looked a bit frightened; he possibly had learning difficulties.

For the first time we saw some woods and a 'new' Iron Age fort. Most passengers didn't sit, they slumped. The bus didn't hang about. In spite of my rudeness about everyone, most thanked the driver when they got off.

HAVERFORD WEST

I couldn't bring myself to have lunch in a Wimpy bar so I went and had a baked potato in Cardigan. Every one of the staff was smoking in their tea breaks.

I decided I needed some exercise and saw a little rural route which I took. This was the first time I had really copped out with the weather and I got soaked. I saw some very old farm buildings and walked past some dairy farms, but saw no one to talk to. A man on a tractor and baler passed me by; I made a sign about the weather, and he laughed. There seemed to be quite a lot of new house-building going on. I passed two churches right next to each other, both with their own graveyards.

I spotted a small unconcerned bird with a white head, sitting on the electric cables, but I couldn't identify it.

I was now getting seriously wet. I thought someone might take pity on me. A red van stopped and it was Ray from Essex. He worked as a maintenance man at the caravan site.

I didn't realise there was a big RAF base around these quiet lanes.

Ray Short's lift was just right. He dropped me off and went shopping. He'd offered to leave me at the main road but I said I'd be fine.

I passed the entrance to a large hotel and rang them on my mobile for a quote. 'Are you with the air-force and have you been here before?' I was going to get the corporate rate of £70 per night. 'We have several vacancies.' *'In other words, we are empty!'*

I said I really didn't want to spend that much so walked on in the rain. It seemed a pretty dead place.

The roads were narrow and bendy with high sides and were perfect for getting knocked over, especially in the rain. The art is to keep crossing the road to be in the safest place. This game is not such fun when you're soaked through.

I couldn't believe my luck when a bus came out of the junction in front of me. I flagged it down, once more in a dangerous spot, but he drove on and then stopped for me, only for me to find out that he was going south, not north. I apologised to all and he drove off.

I was back on the A487, soaking wet and trying to hitch. Ten cars passed in a very short time and then a smart BMW Estate car stopped. *'The happiest sight for a hitcher is that of brake lights.'*

JIM PRYOR

Meet Mr Pryor: twenty-nine years old, smart looking and well dressed. He was a tree surgeon, but when I said to him that he didn't look like one he told me that he mainly did administration nowadays and the HSE. He had a team of seven in the busy months and four at this time of the year, as the birds were nesting. We talked about the teenage generation and he said how quickly they had gone off. Apparently, when his nephew came out to work with him he was puffed out in minutes.

I asked Jim how he coped with all this Health and Safety. He replied that he'd had a nightmare job last October. He'd had several big oaks that needed felling and everything was against him – they were at a crossroads, there were lots of wires and they were on a bank. The day before he had cut off all the branches, then the next day he'd hired a crane to take the trunks down. Everything was going fine until he put the chain round one of the trunks and then as he cut off the last section 5.5 tons of oak trunk swung out and the crane went over. At that point all hell was let loose. The crane driver panicked and tried to jump, instead of staying inside. He broke his leg, and chains and shackles went in all directions.

Everything was in complete chaos. The air ambulance and fire brigade came and two more 80-ton cranes lifted up the one that had toppled over; after they'd cut off the jib which was extended.

The worst thing was that Jim had more work to do the next morning. He was all for packing the whole job in, and suffered a total loss of confidence. However, he did finish the job. 'Thanks for the story and the lift, Jim.'

I asked a shopkeeper if he knew of anywhere to stay and he muttered away as if I was asking him to direct me to the moon. I went to a pub and asked what their bottom rate was. She said they didn't do bottom rates – just £45. I said I would think about it. It's always a good idea to take your time with these places, for just around the corner I found the ideal place.

Lima House had dried my clothes out nicely, and with breakfast in the conservatory I was given a show by jackdaws eating off the bird table, together with blue tits. The colours were amazing – I'd never realised before what a beautiful bird the jackdaw is.

I noticed that Mrs Donewell had a certificate on the wall saying that she'd just graduated and asked her what in.

'IT, but it was a bit of a late start and I had a struggle towards the end, but I did it.'

Everywhere I went I just seemed to miss the bus. Some of the girls waiting for the bus looked like gypsies, with their hard looks, gold earrings and cigarettes. I met Gordon at the bus station, complete with his backpack and like me, a map in his hand. He was getting off just before Aberystwyth and was staying in hostels for £13 per night. He did voluntary work in IT and now had his new agenda after being pushed around for forty years by different people. He'd been retired for sometime and he said to me, 'Obviously, you're retired.'

I met a lot of people today with terrible disfigurements. One man on the train had had half his face removed; a lady on the bus had moles all over her face; and behind me a man only had one finger on one of his hands. It must be terrible to have a facial disfigurement. At least with me when you have five toes missing on one foot you can cover it up.

An old boy called George got on the bus with an old raincoat, and his flies undone. His eyes were full of sleep but he was quite well-spoken and read the *Daily Telegraph*.

Things were going fairly well until we went into North Wales. Our 'all-day' tickets had to be renewed and the old boy went mad and really gave the poor driver what for. He just wouldn't let it go and was going to phone up headquarters.

'Why don't you?' said the driver, knowing what the answer would be.

I thought he was going to chuck George off the bus, but when I renewed my ticket the old boy just said, 'I'd better have the same as him!' *'Never a dull moment and I was enjoying it all, but the rest of the bus was very serious.'*

I'll probably never know if George was a tramp or a millionaire.

ABERYSTWYTH TO CAERNARFON

Gee, this driver didn't hang around and must've been running late.

We passed several wind farms which were being serviced by a huge crane; a farmer was patch-spraying a grass field of thistles; and then we passed woods which seemed well-managed and attractive with the different shades of green.

We were in Powys country and the children were all speaking Welsh, which was fascinating.

I saw a tree harvester way up on a hill and wondered about the men who work it. Now we were driving through very narrow lanes with stone walls climbing up the steep hills.

We arrived in Dolgellau early afternoon having been through some real Fred Flintstone country. Hidden in the hillside was Bristol Nuclear Group, generating electricity for us mortals.

'CYMRU IS NOT FOR SALE' was written in large white letters across some farm buildings. *'Who would want to buy it anyway?'*

I went into a café that was split into two, upper class and lower class, and you know where I was! I asked for a salad and was told I needed to go 'upper class', not in so many words – but I felt more comfortable 'lower-class'.

PORTHMADOG

'How can anyone take this place seriously with a name like that?'

I had a long walk, but I knew a bus would come so I wasn't too worried. All I had to do was to be in a safe place when it came.

Well, the cars didn't stop and the bus didn't come and I was lying down among the wild flowers writing *Walkabout*. I decided to walk on towards some bendy roads ahead. As soon as I did that the bus turned up and fortunately stopped. I love buses when you have walked miles.

I needed a good laugh and got it from the children on the bus. One particular lad, about thirteen, with black hair and big brown eyes, answered my question about which language was taught in the schools.

'Welsh, a lot of crap really!'

'Do you think I would get a lift if I was hitching around here?'

'No chance, unless you dress up as a sheep. They don't like the English, but show them your money and that's a different matter.'

'Do you live here?' I asked.

'Yeah. Used to live in England but came back. Have you travelled to many parts of the world?'

'A few, and if you get the chance you should do so as well.'

'I will, I love travelling,' he said.

I hopped off the bus way out in the countryside. I saw some buzzards in a field feeding off a dead sheep – they looked like vultures. Pretty yellow poppies were growing in the hedgerow as we passed Caernarfon Creameries, a huge set-up in the countryside. No way was I going to get a lift and even the sheep farmer passed me as if I was dog muck. *'Next time I'll have a sign on me saying: 'Kent Farmer, or Ex-Kent Farmer, or Agricultural Waster!'*

'Stop!' Even waving a five pound note didn't do the trick.

Y FFOR

'I thought I was a funny bugger, but I'm obviously not on my own round here.' When I walked through this place I saw a big fat lazy bugger getting out of a taxi with three packets of twenty cigarettes in his hand. He waddled back to his council house and I wondered if he'd ever worked. I thought what a huge waste of taxpayers' money it was supporting him.

Once more, I found that I'd just missed the bus. So I walked on past empty cigarette packets printed with: *'Smokers die younger.'* Just when you're feeling a little sorry for yourself, a bus comes along. People jump on and off and the driver is a friend to all. A couple of boys sat at the back of the bus sharing iPod earpieces.

There was an interesting girl on the bus sporting a pair of green wellingtons. It looked as though she had come off a dairy farm. She was writing notes and I would've loved to have known more about her. Would I get the chance?

Another couple got on – a big fat girl with an honest face and a mouthy beer-drinking husband; the man I described earlier with only one finger on his hand.

I said goodbye to 'one-finger' and stepped onto the next little bus to Caernarfon. The smart girl jumped on as well but I still hadn't had a chat. I was getting good value out of my dear old Rover ticket today, and again the smart girl jumped onto the next connecting bus. I said to her that it looked as though she'd had a hard day on the farm. She told me that she'd been working on a compost farm as she was doing a PhD on composting and was going back to her university in Bangor. She looked a little embarrassed when she told me what she was studying, but I said it was the thing of the future and when she got her PhD would she be a Doctor of Compost?! Her interest was compost in flower production and we talked about the farm at Lenham and satellite navigation.

We said goodbye, and I went to find a hotel in Bangor. I looked at a B&B run by a spotty Polish man but decided to give it a miss. The one next door was full. It was a funny place and I couldn't find the hotel area. Being a university city it was full of young people. I nearly walked my feet off. I went to a pub and asked the young girl behind the bar if she had a room. She said they were full and carried on reading as if I wasn't there.

I booked in at the Garden Hotel. It was run by a smart Chinese family. When I asked if they had a room, Sandra screamed with delight as they had just checked out the last guest. She was a little breath of fresh air and told me her life history in three minutes. She'd done a degree in languages, Chinese and Spanish, and had even been to China for a couple of years. She was now helping her father run the business. He'd become very stressed and she was shocked at how much he had aged when she came back.

I had a wash and came down for a meal. Sandra's sister was taking her mock GCSE exams and she was having revision lessons from her mum.

Frank was my Hong Kong waiter and was a cheerful Charlie. When I went to bed at 10.30pm Min was still doing her revision.

BANGOR TO CHESTER

Once more it was raining. After going out of the hotel I found that the railway station was immediately opposite. There was a train to Holyhead. Bangor is the only station in the country with a tunnel at either end, apparently. I asked Mr Bilks if this was the right train for Holyhead.

He was a big man with a goatee beard and was eating a pasty. He used to work for British Rail and had done so for twenty-five years, so he now got free rail travel. He lived in Holyhead and also drove the school bus – and 'trained it' to save diesel. 'You have to keep mind and body active.' He also liked digital photography.

Apparently, this station used to be really smart some years ago. It had separate ladies, gentlemen and family waiting areas and was heated by coal. Recently, Mr Bilks had offered to clear the station's rubbish but he'd been refused.

I took a photograph of the ornate bridge and tried to get him to stand on it but he wouldn't. He also told me about a steel bridge that had burned down and I asked him how a metal bridge could burn. He said that it had been coated in tar to stop it rotting.

He told me he used to work on steam trains for many years and I asked him what the greatest difference between steam and diesel was. He said it was the fact that you didn't have to start so early with diesel as there was no stoking up to do. With steam they had to arrive three hours early. You worked your way up from cleaner to fire-lighter to stoker and then finally you could take control and become a driver. He said that most trains nowadays have air suspension which gets rid of most of the noise.

He'd also been a special constable and had served in the RAF all over the world. He'd served in Malaya in the war and had had the job of sorting out shot down aircraft, which usually meant flying in a helicopter and parachuting down. Then he would take out the armaments and blow them up. They were wrapped in plastic so they would implode rather than explode. When parachuting, if you got caught in a tree you had a winch system that would get you down. Most times you got there before the enemy, but not always.

One time he was on sortie duty in the jungle working with two Ghurkhas when suddenly a shot rang out and down he went with a bloody ankle. The Ghurkhas just put one finger to their lips and two minutes later came back holding two heads. He spent the next eleven weeks in hospital. Luckily enough the shot scraped the bone without breaking it, but he said that it had felt red hot when it went through his leg.

Mr Bilks was such a modest man that I had to drag all this out of him, but fortunately he told me that he had written down his memoirs for his grandchildren. He'd also had three books of poetry published, but used a pen name to avoid any hassle.

I asked him if anyone spoke only in Welsh and he told me that his mother-in-law hadn't spoken any English and had lived to be 103 years old.

When I asked him what he thought of the young today he replied, 'Load of crap.'

HOLYHEAD

The train journey was through a wet, rocky part of the world, and was covered in windmills. Mr Bilks had said it was a very windy area and I wouldn't want to be a farmer here.

Spot the feet

There were funny little shops, really old-fashioned. Even the garages doing the cars up looked like something from a past era, with old engines scattered all over the place and a greasy character under the car. All you could see were his boots sticking out. The 'clean' sheet he'd put over the car looked as though it had been up a chimney.

St Cybi is a 14th century church surrounded by slate gravestones.

I gave a donation to the Salvation Army man and had a chat with Eddy the street-cleaner. He had moved from Surrey four or five years earlier. He said he'd never been happier and lived in a caravan. He used to go to a farm when he was young and later in life wanted to return to a more rural type of life. He said that some parents tell their children not to worry about dumping rubbish as he was paid to clear it up. He'd had one lady whose dog had crapped right in front of him and he offered her a plastic bag to clear it up but she just walked away. He'd learned to be patient over the years.

Anglesey is full of scruffy flowering hawthorn hedges.

MABEL

I met this ninety-one-year-old at the bus station. She'd lived all her life on Anglesey. She suffered with degenerative eye disease. 'Damn nuisance,' she said, 'the trouble is that my body has lived longer than my eyes.' She lived on her own and when I asked if she had any help she told me that she could have some, but then she wouldn't be able to find what she wanted – at least she knew where things were and every day she went to the café for her lunch.

I was trying to go to the north of the island, so when a bus with 'Bangor' turned up, I jumped on. When I asked the driver if he was going straight to Bangor he said, 'In a roundabout way!' In other words, we wiggled across Anglesey passing RAF Mona with a sign saying: 'NO TO BIOGAS.' I asked the boys and girls on the bus what it was all about but they just looked at me as though I was stupid.

Someone had spilled milk and cream in the back of the bus. I noticed that the lady in front had strawberries in her basket so I said to her that I'd got the cream, but I didn't get much response. I don't think I've ever seen so many unhappy looking people as there are in Wales and miserable looking parents with miserable looking children. I was surrounded by kebab houses, Pizza Huts, Chinese takeaways and the usual rubbish shops.

I had a sandwich at Bangor railway station then got on the train to Chester, having had to rush to get my ticket first.

When I got off the train I didn't really know how to go about seeing the place, but as luck would have it I saw an open-top bus, so I jumped on board. I sat right up the front, just opposite the Irish lady guide – I took an instant dislike to her. She must have thought me a miserable bugger, because I didn't make eye contact or laugh at any of her stupid jokes.

She told us that Chester had the oldest racecourse in the UK and used to be the main entry point to Wales. The then wooden bridges had been burned down; the ones that connected to Wales.

I saw loads of narrowboats and the guide told us about a clock face on a square tower. There were clock faces on every side, except the one facing Wales! At one time the city was enclosed by a huge wall. I didn't realise that the Duke of Westminster owns most of the place and earns £40 per minute in rent.

On the back of the bus was a sign saying: 'COME AND JOIN US. £18,000 PER YEAR AS A DRIVER.'

CHESTER TO LIVERPOOL

When I first started my 'walkabout' the railway stations had no litter bins. Now they have see-through plastic bags for security reasons.

The journey to Liverpool was through some pretty industrialised land and this was my first time ever in Liverpool.

St James' station is at the end of the line and I had to get into a huge lift to reach the main street. Who should be standing next to me but the old boy I'd met backpacking in Aberaeron. He said he'd come back a day early because of the weather. I asked him for the name of a cheap hotel and he said to try the Mount Pleasant area.

Half the centre of Liverpool seems to be a new shopping centre with a mass of white tower cranes above the skyline.

I went and had a beer in the Hotel Liverpool in the city centre. It had a huge clock with some fine joinery and I had a chat to an Irishman about places to stay. He also suggested Mount Pleasant but said to watch my back as there are some dodgy characters there. Prices here were £170 per night, so I left.

I found Mount Pleasant and booked into a small but fairly smart hotel. I had no option as the others were full.

I had a shower and a rest before going off to Friday night in Liverpool. *'I think I was the oldest old git in the city with all the youngsters out for a good smoking Friday night.'*

After a fairly long walk I found a good restaurant and enjoyed my pasta in a kind of garlic oil, with cut up baked potatoes. The restaurateur came and asked me if all was well and where did I come from? I told him I was from Kent and he asked if it was anywhere near Bluewater. *'He didn't connect the county with The Garden of England but Bluewater, for Christ's sake!'*

It's always good to get out and move on, especially from these greasy 'fry-up', smelly hotels. It was time to have a look round Liverpool and get back home.

LIVERPOOL CATHEDRAL

Wow, this is some building. It stands on St James' Mount in the city centre and is the seat of the Bishop of Liverpool. Its official name is The Church of Christ in Liverpool. It is the largest cathedral in Britain and the fifth largest in the world, although this title is disputed by the Cathedral of St John the Divine in New York.

King Edward VII laid the foundation stone in 1904. On completion of the altar the cathedral was consecrated in 1924, but regular services were not held until 1940.

With the interruption of the Second World War and inflation, the completion of the building only happened in 1978, which was too late for the architect, Giles Gilbert Scott, who died in 1960.

I couldn't believe that at 9.00am there were so few people around – just a young man from Colombia and me.

In the cathedral there was an article from the *Medical Foundation*: 'For the Victims of Torture', and a story written by John McCarthy, the British journalist who was kidnapped by Islamic Jihad terrorists in Lebanon in 1986 and held hostage for more than five years. It said: "I was at this conference and someone said to me, 'What is it like to be living in the free world?' and just walked on, smiling." Later in the day, John found out that this man had been held hostage in Argentina for several years. John had been so wrapped up in his own experiences that he had not realised that others had experienced much worse times than he. Some had been tortured and been left in a foreign country with nobody and when they finally returned home their families were dead. John realised how lucky he was.

I am not a religious person but I felt overwhelmed by this place.

Again I chatted to another well-spoken voluntary gentleman picking up litter outside the cathedral. He proudly told me how they'd cleared the area down below which was used by the druggies and that now when people visit they clear their own rubbish and take pride in the place.

Walking to the bus station, which is nearly in the centre of Liverpool, I couldn't get over how dilapidated the Victorian buildings and warehouses were with their backs pulled down. Some only had their fronts left and these were supported by scaffolding. It was as if the planners had only just realised that they had some important architecture and the history that went with it.

TOXTETH RIOTS

On Friday 3rd July, 1981 the arrest of twenty-year-old Leroy Cooper on Selbourne Street, watched by an angry crowd, led to a fracas in which three police officers were injured. Over the weekend that followed full-blown riots broke out on the streets of Toxteth with pitched battles between the police and youths throwing missiles, including petrol bombs. This also extended to other cities in the UK.

I jumped on a bus and went through this parish. I couldn't believe that I would see rows and rows of boarded up houses. It was nearly thirty years ago since the riots and I thought it would've been rebuilt and regenerated. I jumped off and walked into Granby Street where some of the fighting had taken place. It was difficult to realise that I was walking down a street in the UK: with boarded up houses, rubbish piled up in the front gardens, wrecked cars, and houses with the roofs burnt off. But there was also some fantastic Victorian brickwork. Even the police community centre was closed with the roller shutters down.

In addition there were the odd druggie-looking chaps floating around, but also some very tall, smart Somali women in their traditional costumes. They were such a contrast to the poor housing.

Across the road was the Somali Welfare Development Trust Centre. A man shouted from across the street, 'Can I help you?'

'I'm just having a look round,' I said.

'Come over here and I'll show you round.'

I was lucky to meet Ismail Hersi who ran the centre. It was like a corner shop in *Coronation Street* with a few computers in it. He was no doubt well respected in the area and had a dignified air about him. I called him the Mayor of Toxteth.

The centre was a place where young Somalis who'd just arrived in the country could learn English, and those who got behind at school could come here after hours and get some help from volunteer teachers.

He showed me some pictures of Somalia, both before and after the war. They mainly showed buildings that had been damaged. He asked me, as a farmer, how I could help. We had a chat about corrupt politicians. He showed me a newspaper cutting about Toxteth, saying that after thirty years it was still bottom of the pile. It had a picture of him in it. He said there were no shops or post office and the residents had to walk miles to get to a shop. 'They promised us the world but gave us nothing.'

Children are bullied at school because some of them have had no education. One Somali boy had said that he might as well get a gun and go back to Somalia and have some fun.

Apparently, the politicians would come round here when they wanted your vote, and you never saw them again. Ismail showed me some of the files on how the schoolchildren were getting on. He showed me some of the spelling mistakes. I had a laugh when he showed me that one of the words they were asked to spell was 'university'. It was the same word I'd had trouble spelling and I showed him my notebook where I had been trying.

He then showed me round some of the streets. There were buildings with lovely brick frontages which were mainly Victorian and the pity was that most of the buildings were roofless.

We exchanged addresses and I made my way back to the high street to catch the bus. A man was trying to manoeuvre his wheelchair onto the bus and I gave him a hand. With a full bus and standing room only we went back to the main bus station.

Unfortunately, the rail ticket I had was a 'return' from Tiverton and I was in Liverpool. I explained to the ticket collector, but not very well, and he said I was OK. I don't think he really understood what I was talking about.

This was to be my first ride on a Virgin train, leaving Liverpool at 1.15pm. The idea was to go to Bristol and pick up on my proper ticket. We went through Runcorn and had to change at Crewe and Derby. Then there was an announcement saying that those who wanted to go to London should change at Derby. The conductor stamped my ticket and I took pot luck and went straight to London with no problems.

My company for the rest of the journey was a Welsh actor going to London for lessons, and a Chinese Liverpudlian – a smart-arse with a gadget with which he could read everyone's text messages on the train. I didn't like him!

We also passed a sad looking Stoke-on-Trent, with old brick kilns towering over the railway line, and then the JCB factory with its shiny new JCB 360's waiting to be dispatched. At last we arrived at Euston station and I was soon back at Lenham again, after another interesting fourteen days.

LETTER TO THE PRIME MINISTER

Dear Prime Minister,

During a recent visit to Toxteth in Liverpool, I met a Mr Ismail Hersi who very kindly showed me round the area and discussed some of the problems there.

I was shocked at the state of the houses and the conditions in which some of these people were living. I wondered if I was even in the UK.

As quoted in the *Liverpool Echo*: 'Why is Toxteth still bottom of the pile after all these years?'

Would you please inform me what has been done and what is to be done in this area?

Yours sincerely,

JA Boyd

1O DOWNING STREET
LONDON SW1A 2AA

From the Direct Communications Unit

Mr J A Boyd

Dear Mr Boyd

The Prime Minister has asked me to thank you for your recent letter.

Mr Blair would like to reply personally, but as you will appreciate he receives many thousands of letters each week and this is not possible.

The matter you raise is the responsibility of Department for Communities and Local Government, therefore he has asked that your letter be forwarded to that Department so that they are also aware of your views.

Yours sincerely

S CAINE

Please quote reference
in all correspondence: **CO/RC**

HOUSE OF COMMONS
LONDON SW1A 0AA

JA Boyd

Dear JA Boyd

Thank you for your recent letter.

Parts of the Princes Park ward (Toxteth) which you recently visited are deprived and are amongst the poorest wards in the country. Change has been slow, I accept, but regeneration taking place.

I have passed your comments on to the Chief Executive of Liverpool City Council, Colin Hilton, about your recent experiences.

The city of Liverpool has embarked on its renaissance and I am hopeful that areas like Toxteth will benefit.

Yours sincerely

Louise Ellman MP

SERVING THE CONSTITUENTS OF LIVERPOOL RIVERSIDE
Telephone: 0207 219 5210 (Westminster office) 0151 236 2969 (Liverpool office)
Fax: 0207 219 2592 (Westminster office) 0151 236 4301 (Liverpool office)
www.epolitix.com/webminster/louise-ellman

JA's Observations Tiverton to Liverpool

1   Fat horrible lazy youngsters.

2   Amazed at the amount of heavy smokers.

3   Welsh language still being used.

4   High price of property.

5   Poorness of the people.

6   The effects of closing down the coal mines on the people of Wales.

7   Toxteth shock. (Am I in the UK?).

8   How run down Liverpool was. (Since I have been it is now improved).

9   How de-populated some parts of Somerset are.

10   What a poor old place Pontypridd was.

11   What a spoiled little brat ja is.

CHAPTER FIVE

Liverpool to Glasgow

It always takes me far too long to get myself organised for 'walkabout'. Valerie was my taxi to Headcorn for the 7.28am train to Charing Cross.

My first good deed of the day; I gave a chap 20p for a pee when he couldn't find his money!

I only had ten minutes to spare for the Virgin train to Liverpool.

I couldn't believe how many first class carriages there were, and when I eventually found a second class one I was lucky to find my own table.

'This is travelling in style, as we whizz through the beautiful countryside. It's a funny feeling when the train goes round the bends at high speed.'

The only stops were at Rugby, Coventry and Crewe, which is the graveyard for old trains; Virgin and British Rail amongst them.

The train seemed to be full of fairly gloomy people, except for our smiley restaurant manager, Charles, who told me that he'd never actually met Richard Branson. 'Very big company and he's a very busy man,' he said, with another huge laugh.

The train went slowly through Manchester Piccadilly and I could see the famous football stadium.

Bang on 2.40pm we arrived at Liverpool Lime Street Station. Now I felt I was really in Liverpool, passing Cunard House, the Royal Liver Building and the Albert Dock. I popped into the museum, but I didn't really have time to study the slave trade and hoped to go back there the next day. With no records they reckon that millions of slaves were taken from the West Coast of Africa. I also saw pictures of a bombed part of

Liverpool, with people getting into Anderson shelters. People hated going into them, especially when their houses were nearby.

I saw a couple of ladies shopping in the high street; probably mother and daughter, with the longest and saddest faces I've ever seen. I wanted to take a photograph of them but couldn't.

On the side of a bus was written:

'IF YOU SPIT AT OUR DRIVERS YOU WILL BE PROSECUTED. OUR DRIVERS CARRY DNA TESTING EQUIPMENT.'

This city was about to become the City of Culture in a few months' time!

Later in the day I took a ferryride down the Mersey; it was interesting looking back at Liverpool from the river.

The Anglican Cathedral, which took seventy-five years to build, dominates the skyline – it's such an imposing building; and apparently the Metropolitan Cathedral was built on the site of the largest workhouse in the UK.

Huge oil tankers were pumping oil into the storage depot and I was hoping this lot wouldn't blow up while we were here.

I now needed all my clothes as the cold wind ripped up the river. The cannon that went off at 1pm every day, except Sundays and Bank Holidays, was for ships to set their chronometers by.

We saw a huge brick vent that had been built to let out the traffic fumes from the tunnel under the Mersey.

When we got to the pier the sunset over Birkenhead was beautiful.

I thought my homing instincts would get me back to the hotel in Mount Pleasant, but I found myself going right round in a circle and then over a flyover. I flagged down a taxi and Jim, the driver, told me I was going completely in the wrong direction. He'd worked in London on the building sites in the eighties because there was no work in Liverpool: 'I was one who got on my bike!' He had a bit of a moan about all the blacks and said he didn't mind the ones that worked, but not the hangers-on.

I've never been so organised. I'd pre-booked the hotel and they'd even put me back in the same room as before.

November 5th sounded as though the war had started and the walk to the restaurant had its fair share of piss-heads on the way, with even a drunken singing prostitute. This place seemed to be full of beer drinking, smoking footballers. *I'm so glad I'm not the one who has to employ them.'*

I went to find the restaurant that I'd been to the last time, only to find it was full of p--- h---s , so walked up the road and found a Chinese buffet/takeaway.

If you sat down you could get all you could eat for £7.00, but if you took it away you could get all you could eat for £3.70. With dirty seats and food not that tasty or that hot, I thought: *'What do you expect for that money?'* At least the staff were much smarter than the Liverpudlians.

So, back to the small but smart hotel room for an early night.

METROPOLITAN CATHEDRAL

I didn't realise how close I was to this cathedral. It was completed in 1967 and straightaway it had leaked. The aluminium roof had failed due to thermal metal fatigue. In wet weather the water poured through, and the asphalt blistered and broke. 2,800 acoustic baffles and 257 benches had to be repaired and six million pounds was needed for the refurbishment, of which two million was provided by English Heritage. I think the cathedral raised six million and borrowed one and a half million, which they still have to pay off. The archdiocese sought damages from the architect, the engineers and the builders. This was settled out of court and the sum they got was considerably less than they'd wanted.

I was the only person walking round the cathedral and I said to the security officer, 'Some place.'

He replied, 'It's a great place.'

I lit a candle.

MERSEY MUSEUM LIVERPOOL

I went back to the museum because of the excellent portrayal of the slave trade. The demand for sugar in Europe put pressure on the growers to grab some Africans for the plantations. In the early days of the slave trade, in 1700, more than one in five died coming over. By 1800 the British suggested that a surgeon travelled on board, but this was for the convenience of the crew and not the poor old Africans.

The main trade was in sugar, cotton and tobacco, with the slaves in the bottom of the boat. Some might have marched for a month before reaching the coast. They were then placed in a compound to await the ship. Some of the women were raped by the sailors on the way to Europe and America; other slaves were branded by their 'owners'; and different tribes were separated so that they couldn't rebel. The process of breaking their will and separating them from home and family was called 'seasoning'.

I thought there were some miserable people in Eastern Europe and always blamed years of Communism, but I have never seen such unhappy people as in Liverpool and Southport. I got the feeling that their lives had been shafted.

An alcoholic, a harmless but horrible little man, was trying to take on two polite police officers and inviting them for a punch-up should they want one.

As I walked back from Albert Docks I passed some beautifully built Victorian warehouses, with curved steel and lovely bricks. The pump-house was being re-pointed, which was no small task as it had a tall chimney. In the distance the 'Paradise Shopping Centre' was being built and had some eleven cranes dominating the skyline.

It was so different this time in Liverpool. Last time it had been a quiet weekend, but this time everyone was out buying their goods. Last time I'd never realised the influence of the Anglican Cathedral as it looks over the city.

TOXTETH

'Never go back to the same place twice,' but I did, as I wanted to get some photographs. I had also thought it might be better not to push my luck in a deprived area.

I didn't want to get bogged down with Ismail so I didn't ring him.

I couldn't get my bearings and had to catch another bus as I had gone too far. Then I realised I was on the wrong road. I asked some motorbike mechanics where Granby Street was.

They said, 'What do you want to go to that shit-hole for?!'

I replied, 'That's the place.'

Even before getting to the right area the new flats looked as though they had been burned down or smashed up. I tried to take some discrete photographs and also took off my pocket waistcoat, so that I wouldn't look too conspicuous.

I crossed the road and found the worst of the housing, and quite by chance I stumbled on Ismail's office. The shutter was half up and I got no reply when I knocked on the door.

A policeman stopped me in a large white van and asked what I was up to in this area, and why I was taking photographs. He told me to be careful about flashing a camera but I would probably be OK at this time of day.

I tried to explain to him that I wasn't a complete idiot and thanked him for looking after me.

I went to catch the bus back to Liverpool and there was the same wheelchair man I'd helped last time – so I did it again.

LIVERPOOL TO BLACKPOOL

In other words from one shit-hole to another. *I've seen enough of Liverpool and its happy contents.'*

I went to Lime Street Station and caught the underground to Central, after a very polite ticket information officer had told me the way.

I changed at Hillside for Royal Birkdale and before long we were in dear old Southport, with some more miserable-looking folk. I had some soup and a roll and caught the next bus to Preston. I thought it seemed such a shame to have people living in houses on top of this beautiful topsoil.

Preston is the home of the cotton manufacturing industry. Eventually I got on a crowded train and was sitting backwards on my way to Blackpool. I didn't want to arrive after dark.

I took a £4 taxi to a hotel. I'd said to the driver that I wanted neither a shit-hole nor a palace and got dropped off at a street full of B&B places.

I got a room in the Westholme Hotel, where I had a wash and brush up and was looking forward to some good food: *'In Blackpool, if ever you did.'*

I know I was out of season but I couldn't believe how dark it was down on the front and it looked dreary and shuttered up.

I was tempted by a fish and chip shop, but went further into town and asked the taxi driver for a recommendation. He sent me to an Italian restaurant which wasn't that good, but it was adequate. I had two large glasses of wine which made the smelly loos in the restaurant, and Blackpool, seem that much better.

BLACKPOOL TO CARNFORTH

I had a better fry-up than yesterday and then went out on the dear old Blackpool streets. I hadn't realised I was quite near the Tower, which was closed at the end of the season.

I asked the taxi driver what was worth looking at in Blackpool. He said the Tower and the Winter Gardens building. Both were shut. Whilst waiting for the bus I went to the first Roman Catholic Church to be built in Blackpool. It had been designed by a twenty-year-old architect and had a steady stream of punters coming in and out. The average age was about seventy-five.

There was a vagrant hugging the radiator for warmth and a kindly lady who gave him some money.

'Now a service has started and I'm right in the middle of it. Time to get out.'

In Liverpool everyone calls you 'love' and in Lancaster they say 'like' all the time.

Hooray for Lancaster, a working town and a change from the cities I've just been to.

ST PETER'S CATHEDRAL

I got caught by a ninety-year-old ex-church warden type of lady, who told me she took her holidays in Lourdes. She said there was a big do about to start in half an hour and TV cameras were coming. I slipped away quietly.

All the old mills have been turned into offices, flats and coffee houses. Some have interesting staircases and some warehouses still have the original wooden hoists.

I went to Lancaster Castle only to find out that it's a prison! After all these seaside resorts I was ready for a castle, but instead I found barbed wire round the top and prison vans outside, telling me that it was a fully working prison. It has been going for nine hundred years, has working courts inside and about three hundred inmates. The man in the tourist office told me that there was a rumour that they wanted to turn it back into a castle and open it to the public, but the cost would be huge. I saw a man come out of the prison doors, saying: 'I'm free, I'm free!' I think he was joking (or was he?). I believe it's now not a prison.

LANCASTER TO CARNFORTH

On the way back to town I went past the Lancaster Boys' Grammar School. The pupils looked really smart in their dark suits.

Going back over the canal I put my head over the bridge to see if the alcoholics were still there, and yes, instead of three there were seven or eight. Unfortunately, I couldn't get a photograph. *Two things I must do. Have a chat to the alcoholics and talk to the person selling the Big Issue.*

I couldn't quite make sense of the bus station so walked up to the train station, after asking a young man the way. He didn't know, so that gave him the excuse to ask a pretty young lady. I said to him that that was a bit cheeky. 'Absolutely!' he replied.

When she'd given me the information to get to Settle, I clambered into a busy, two-carriage train to Carnforth, mainly full of cheerful schoolchildren.

I asked the very tired looking hotel manager what Carnforth is famous for and apparently it's the railway station.

I walked through the town to see if I could find a better hotel. If I see a banner up advertising 'Live Football' outside I avoid them.

Another hotel looked tidy and OK, but I thought there would be more life in a mortuary, so walked back and booked in at the Royal Station Hotel – a funny place right on the street junction. There seemed to be no staff around and I felt a real shit when I asked the busy lady if I could see my room and she had to walk up forty-three steps to show me a rather shabby but clean room. The price was £29.50 and it seemed that the further north I was going the cheaper they became. I asked if there was any heat in the room and was told it was on a timer, but as it never did come on I found some extra blankets.

Dinner was a nice surprise. I went to the bar and caught up with a big chunk of *Walkabout*, and ordered Yorkshire pudding pie, bread and two pints of beer. The pie was delicious and amazingly the whole lot came to £7.93. I was beginning to like this place.

I'd gone to bed early but didn't sleep well so by the morning I was uptight with doing the *WA* during the night. I was feeling a bit guilty about calling it *Walkabout* and with the small amount of walking I was doing maybe it should have been called 'Busabout'.

Breakfast was not included, so I checked out and went to the railway station to try to organise a trip to the Yorkshire Dales, but the friendly station master said I could get to Settle but would have a long wait. I went back to the hotel and asked the girl there. She was the one who had cooked that lovely Yorkshire pudding and I told her how good it was. After that she couldn't help me enough. She said that all the food at the hotel was home-cooked and I told her about all the shitty fast food I'd had elsewhere. The staff here in a rather dull hotel made it shine.

She said I would have a struggle to get to the Yorkshire Dales, so instead I decided to carry on up the west coast to include the Lake District.

I had breakfast in a café called The Pit Stop. A taxi passed the window with a sign on it saying: 'Soiling charge – £75'. A vagrant was chewing a lollipop stick and waiting outside the post office in football boots with yellow studs.

It was nice to get back amongst smiling people. The lady in the pub had told me that Morecombe Bay was the main holiday resort for the deprived people of Leeds and there were also children's homes there.

CARNFORTH TO BARROW-IN-FURNESS

This really is a large smart station for a little village and I reckoned it must have been a shunting yard for trains going to Scotland. A Virgin train went roaring past shaking the baskets of plastic flowers. It was so good to see a station with no rubbish. Only three of us were waiting and soon we were on our way.

The rain had stopped and now I could see some beautiful countryside unfolding. I'd never seen rushes growing tall in the middle of hedges before. It's a bird watcher's paradise and I saw just about every type of wading bird in the Saltings. It's also serious sheep country and I saw a sheep that looked like an old English sheepdog. It's called a Herdwick, or so I was told. Most times when I asked a question the answer was: 'Don't know.'

I saw a wildfowler walking along the river bank and two herring gulls pecking the eyes out of a dead bullock.

A field of kale flashed by and the huge industrial complex – maybe it's an oil refinery, but I never found out.

The train made a lovely 'bangdebang, bangdebang, bangdebang' sound. No continuous rails here.

BARROW-IN-FURNESS

I didn't know quite what to expect here. I suppose I thought it would be another shit-hole seaside holiday camp, but it seemed that in its day it was a busy shipbuilding town.

BAE systems was printed on a huge building and when I asked a lady who had lived there all her life what went on here, you can guess the answer – 'Don't know'.

I thought to myself: *'You stupid lady! You've lived here all your life and still don't know.'* But she did know that all the lovely brick buildings had been built for the shipbuilders.

In just forty years it had grown from a tiny 19th century hamlet into a large industrial town. at one time it was the biggest iron and steel centre in the world with a major shipbuilding force and now it's building nuclear submaries.

The railway was built to carry iron ore and slate and limestone to the new deep water port. Its prosperity grew with the development of the steel and shipbuilding industries.

There's a forty-five acre public park and there are 247 Grade II listed buildings. The population grew from 300 to 8000 in 1864 and by 1881 it had jumped to 47,000. It peaked in 1939 and has now dropped.

I don't know why, but I was drawn to the dock complex, with its huge building and housing for the workers. I stopped someone and asked him what was being built now.

'You won't see much, like.'

As I walked through the town I was struck by the number of pubs. I went to catch the bus back to the town and was told by the driver that I was on the wrong bus. I had held him up buying my 'all-day Rider' ticket.

I asked a lady for directions and found that she'd married an army man and had lived in Germany for four years. She'd had five moves in her life and was happy to stay at home. She looked as though she had smoked a few cigarettes in her life. We passed Furness General Hospital and Maternity Ward which was quite a new building. I saw a fairly young woman struggling to push herself uphill in a wheelchair.

ILVESTON TO BROUGHTON-IN-FURNESS

Well, on 'Buzzaround' you have some luck and I got my own minibus waiting for me. I reckon the smaller the bus the better the view. Albert, the driver, said that sometimes he only has four or five passengers all day. Once more the countryside was stunning. The bus turns round at Broughton.

Let me introduce you to Mr Charisma – I'm the only customer. I ask him several questions. 'Don't know.' I ask him when the holiday season started.

'Don't know.'

'Can I get to Ilveston by public transport?'

'No.'

'Get me out of here!'

A prickly pub with a Mr Prick, the landlord's son, in charge for the day.

BROUGHTON TO CONISTON

Well, it was early afternoon and I wasn't going back the way I'd come, so the walk would do me good, and it was nice to be walking in the countryside. I took quite a lot of photographs of gateways. *'How sad!'*

I went past a row of young conker trees, but they all had conker canker.

'I wish I had a cardboard sign saying: 'Kent Farmer' on it. I might get a Land Rover to stop then.'

As in Cornwall there are lots of Fred Flintsone buildings. I walked on, thumbing for a lift. I was enjoying the walk but a lift would be a bonus. Thirty cars later, I got one. A four-wheel drive went past and indicated that he was about to turn left, but in fact it was to pick me up.

A funny bugger, this one was. I'm going to call him Mr Stern. He was listening to the news and when I started making polite conversation I was told to shush! So I never said a word. When the news stopped he started talking and when the news started again I had to keep quiet once more. I felt like telling him to stuff his lift.

Mr Stern had a voice to match, and a sense of humour to fit. This old bugger really was a funny combination.

He gave me a detailed breakdown of his knowledge of the Herdwick sheep: what colour it is when born; how it goes a lighter shade of grey every year; and how it always retains its white face. Then we had a chat about where I live and he said, 'Where they're building houses on all the low lying areas?' and then he rattled on about where they have built houses near him and put them high on brick rubble. Then I got to hear about how a high tide is made up with the wind behind it, and: 'Have you heard of Beatrix Potter? She lived round here and she kept Herdwicks.'

I said, 'You really live in a beautiful part of the country. Have you lived here all your life?'

'Forty years. Came from the Midlands.'

This guy really had no sense of humour at all and I was left wondering why he'd picked me up, especially when he was in the middle of the news!

He dropped me off at Coniston.

Suddenly I felt that I had been cloned. There were hundreds of John Arthurs about; late middle-aged people all stumbling around with backpacks and instead of feeling different I was one of thousands. I suppose I was in prime walking country and every other shop seemed to be selling outdoor gear. *'Help!'*

I went into another pub and on the door was a sign saying: 'No packs inside.' I muttered something unmentionable to myself and found another pub, with yet another Mr Charisma. Again, I was the only one in it. *'I'm beginning to wonder if it's me.'* Another pretty ordinary tomato soup. Why don't these guys warm the bread up?

The Tesco bus comes to a place as remote as this, bringing shoppers back, but it won't take some local piss-heads back with it. They're too smart to do that.

DONALD CAMPBELL CBE

Well, I never realised he died up here. Always thought it was on a salt flat in America, until I saw a sign saying: 'Donald Campbell's grave' – in fact it was a memorial stone to him and also to his mechanic.

The promised bus seemed not to be, and with two bus stops in different places I wondered if I'd missed it. So I decided to hitch and the second vehicle to come along, a Land Rover, stopped. This man was a joiner and a local man. He had already driven past me and when he stopped I said that not all backpackers are idiots.

'Wanna bet?' he replied.

He was a nice enough fellow but again he had no sense of humour. All his friends were farmers, as was his father. He loved fell-hunting and went to Devon to watch stag hunting. He said all his friends moaned about farming, but they were always changing their Land Rovers every three years and having new tractors. He dropped me off in Ambleside.

Now in amongst the tourists, mainly walkers, a chat to a bus driver told me what bus to catch and that it wouldn't be long. He told me not to get caught out by the winter timetable. He couldn't believe it when I told him about the sign in the bus concerning spitting at drivers in Liverpool.

A street trader was just packing up for the day. He was selling some beautiful coloured clothes from India. Apparently, a relation of his lived out there and sent them over. He worked a four-day week touring all over the place and said he'd been in this job long enough.

AMBLESIDE TO KESWICK

I was told how to pronounce Keswick on the top of the bus by a couple of teachers who lived in Snowdonia.

What a way to see the countryside.

They told me that many of the stone walls in Wales had been built by the soldiers after the Napoleonic War.

The teachers had their motorised home parked in Keswick, but found it much more fun travelling locally by bus. Their home was being decorated whilst they were away. In the process of slagging off Liverpool the husband told me to be careful as his wife came from Birkenhead. He used to do outdoor pursuits. Currently, he was doing Nuffield scholarships but didn't like the way it was going so he was going to get out of it.

Arrived at Keswick. There is no shortage of places to stay here and I'd never seen so many places selling outdoor pursuit gear. *'How do they all make a living?'*

I went into a shop selling clothes and maps and asked about a map showing Scotland as well. Judging by the looks I got I may as well have been asking for a map showing somewhere on the moon.

'You won't find a map of Scotland here. You'd do better to go to a garage and get a road map.'

'For Christ's sake, I'm in Cumbria, next bloody door!'

It was now dark and the place was full of B&B houses. Some looked a bit fancy and there was an old lady in her garden, with a sign outside. She told me she had a room, so for £25, which included breakfast, I had the choice of several rooms. I took an en-suite one. How I hate that phrase! The lady checked the grout to see if it was dry after her tiling in the shower. She was well into her seventies and had a great sense of humour. The towels she brought up were mouldy in one corner and the rest were frayed but OK. The sheets weren't ironed but were clean, I think!

The shower was an old plastic type and I had to wrap Sellotape round the hose to stop the water pissing out. The hot water couldn't decide whether to come or not, but just about managed to.

I asked for another blanket for the big double bed. I was given a lesson on the keys and she told me a few eating places but I was so wrapped up in my own importance that I forgot what she told me. She did say that if I was late I was to come in by the side door.

The Oddfellows Arms is owned by Mr Maloney who also owned race horses; all over the pub there were pictures of his triumphs, as well as other photographs of racecourses elsewhere in the country. His racing colours and badges were also there and pictures of him covered in badges. I never actually met him because he was away.

There was a couple eating next to me who had come down for a few days in a caravan. The husband looked as though he'd had a bit of a stroke, but she was a chirpy old bird. It cost £11 per night to park the caravan, but more in the summer.

KESWICK TO CARLISLE

The landlady, Mrs Sexton, gave me a receipt for £50 rather than the £25 I'd paid. I had breakfast facing out of the window. It was a strange room in which nothing matched, but it was quite fun in a way – especially the prints of nudes! Her husband cooked the breakfast, but only one other person came down for it.

Funny names: a shop selling outdoor gear called Trespass; another called Been There Done That, Fat Face, and Tithe Barn Trading. Every time I go away I buy a friend a stupid present and I had just found it. It was a china watering can that said: 'If friends were flowers I would pick you!' I thought it was funny, anyway.

I found out the time of the bus and it gave me a chance to visit the Pencil Museum.

I had forty minutes to kill, so an adventurous chap like me needs a fix. So here we go.

Until I came out of the building I didn't realise that the museum was inside the pencil factory. Derwent Coloured Pencils are the main product, but they can't compete with the ordinary mass-produced pencils.

I was the first person to go in when the doors opened at 9.30am. Crowndale graphite was the main component, but in the 19th century they discovered that it was better when mixed with French clay. Graphite was also used to make cannon balls. It was discovered in 1500 by shepherds, and the factory opened in 1832. Each pencil is 184mm long and they are dusted in French chalk to stop them sticking together. The factory can produce six hundred a minute, and sixty million a year. I also saw a fly press which was used for slitting pen nibs.

David Tee was the technical manager from1939 to 2001 and he was responsible for taking the company forward. During the war, pencils were unpainted because of a lack of resources. *I'll never look at a pencil in the same light again.'*

Another bus trip with an 'all-day' ticket. The ticket would eventually get me to Carlisle.

Two happy young girls got on the bus. Their accents were so strong I could hardly understand them.

We were driving out of the Lake District where we had been spoiled with the views, but the autumn colours were something else and the leaves were golden. We were on the A66 and the rams, judging by their harness marks were doing a great job! The schoolchildren were doing a great job as well, judging by the chewing gum all over the seats. Cockermouth School went by and it has the ugliest buildings I've ever seen.

'Where do you live, mate?'

'Cockermouth.' *'What a name!'*

A gentleman on the bus said that Cockermouth was famous for Jennings Brewery. There's also a steel factory that makes railway lines, but it's going to close. All the coal mines, even the open-cast ones have been shut since the eighties.

WORKINGTON

Workington, a good name for a working town. This is where real people live and struggle each day to survive. There's no fancy tourism, and no easy touches; just get on with life. It's funny to think it's less than an hour from where I'd been surrounded by hoards of backpackers as I was the only tourist here.

I noticed loads of hairdressers and nail shops and that the house prices, at last, were falling: detached houses for £150,000; and an end-terraced house for £75,000.

I could see a bus with 'Silloth' on the front and then couldn't find my 'all-day' ticket. The driver said, 'You need a ticket before you get on.'

Luckily I found it.

Opposite me, sitting in the back of the bus was the hardest, toughest looking man I had ever seen. He was built like a tank and covered in tattoos. I could feel him eyeing me up and down, and I wondered what the hell I was doing on his bus. I thought that if I made eye contact with him he wouldn't need much excuse to kill me! As I turned round to get something from my rucksack on the seat behind he said, 'Aye.'

I asked him, 'How are you getting on?' With that we chatted like a house on fire. 'Lived here all your life?'

'Aye.'

'Lots of industry here?'

'Aye, a lot of people work in t' fish factory.'

'The paper factory makes paper board and building material or cardboard?'

'Cardboard, aye.' And pointing, he said, 'That's the street where I lived all me life.'

We said our goodbyes and Ian, the hard man whom I thought had wanted to kill me, had only wanted to talk.

I've never seen a CD hanging from a telephone wire before. I reckon it's to stop the racing pigeons colliding with them. A wind farm mingles in with the industrial heartland and a football stadium with rusty towers sits on the outskirts of town. This is a tough old working town with no frills.

Maryport is a smaller version of Workington with row upon row of workers housing. There are no trees. I'm not even sure if there's a town centre, but maybe I was there when I got off the bus. I asked if there was a café nearby and the old boy smiled and pointed across the street. In amongst the terraced houses was a small sign saying 'café' and when I opened the door it was full of people eating their lunch. I didn't realise it was that late.

I shared a table with Mary. 'All right if I sit here?'

'Aye.' She had two sticks behind her chair. She was tucking into a huge pile of shepherd's pie and chips. She said, 'See those walking sticks? That's what happened to me. I was a school cleaning lady and caretaker. I was buffing the floor one day and someone rang on the bell and the buffer took off. I went down and broke three vertebrae. The doctors said I would be in a wheelchair in three years' time, but now here I am.'

Breakfast cost £2.75.

'Busy place this,' I said.

'Good value for money, that's why.'

'Lived here long?'

'Last five years and it was the best thing I ever did. The pace of life is slower here. Where do you come from?'

'Kent, between Ashford and Maidstone. Do you know it?'

'Yes, I lived in Ashford for five years and I have a relative at Ramsgate, and family halfway. My children say, "Why don't you go abroad for a holiday?" I say that I haven't visited all the places here yet, but they don't understand.'

'Where do you want to go next?'

'To the Outer Hebrides. My grandfather was stationed there in the war. He was in the navy on HMS Midlands. He was on it all his life and I want to find out what all his medals were for because my grandchildren keep asking. Where are you walking to?'

'Just going north.'

'Go to Silloth. It's a beautiful walk.'

'How far is it?'

Anne, the waitress, said it's about ten minutes by car, about five miles, but in fact it's nearer eight.'

'What! Are you trying to kill me off?'

'Well, the stroke club walks it.'

'Now you're trying to make me feel guilty! So if you read about a backpacker being found dead by the side of the road it'll be your responsibility! If I try to flag a bus down to pick me up, will it stop?'

'Depends how hard you flag.'

'What about if I threw my rucksack in front of it?!'

Mary and I roared with laughter.

I shook her hand and said goodbye. It was an interesting half hour in a café with local people, and it was the centre of the community. I left with a warm feeling, unlike many places in the south where you leave feeling that you have been shafted.

Mary was right. It was a beautiful walk and the exercise would do me good. Bussing around is a good way to do it and you can pick where you go, but walking in the middle of the day gives you the chance to get a lift if you want one. With the days getting shorter you really don't want to be out much after 4pm.

I walked past some builders with a trailer on the back of their van loaded with large bricks. They were coming very carefully off the kerb. I caught up with them again and they were tightening up the wheel nuts. There were only two left. As I walked past I said that it was just as well they were not in the Grand Prix. The race would've been over. They smiled.

A lone golfer was going round the course walking up the fairway next to me. *'God, he's worse than I am.'* Once more I felt very pleased with myself that I no longer played.

A beautifully kept cemetery came into sight, behind wrought iron fencing. An old man was cutting the grass between the headstones with a push mower, and an old lady was getting back to her car after visiting a loved one.

I reached the Solway Firth, where they've used large lumps of concrete as breakwaters. It didn't actually look that bad.

To my left some farmers were growing rape. A local had just filled his car boot with driftwood, and some very careful motorist had put plastic mats under the wheels of his car which was parked on soft sand.

I thought I'd done enough walking and after only five cars an old boy stopped.

'Where are you heading for?' he asked.

'Silloth.'

'Jump in. I'm only going to Allonby.'

'Nice part of the world you have here.'

'Aye – been up here for ten years now. I worked in Hemel Hempstead for thirty-eight years.'

'Kodak?'

'No, I was in teaching and glad to get out of it. I took early retirement at fifty-eight. I'm on my way to the leisure pool. I used to drive coaches, but I have Parkinson's and they took my PVL away. I don't often give people lifts these days.'

His hands were shaking, and I was beginning to wonder what I had let myself in for.

The thing about walking is that you see all sorts of things. I saw a very old building tucked up behind some houses and asked two old boys if I could look round. It was an old Quaker coach house; rather tatty but with lovely windows. They had these places all round the coast.

Another bus came along and it was the first I'd seen for an hour and a half. The driver accepted my Stagecoach ticket. I was the only one on the bus and he told me all about his daughter who had just had a serious operation. It made him realise he wanted to retire and see more of his grandchildren.

Silloth in the sixties was a swinging seaside resort, with some of the widest cobbled streets I've ever seen in this country. It has a really nice old-fashioned feel to it.

A market trader was selling vegetables and huge swedes.

'They're bigger than supermarket ones,' I said.

'No supermarket rubbish here and all things here are locally grown and don't sit in warehouses for months covered in chemicals.'

It was 2.20pm and all the cafés were closed so I went to a very old-fashioned golf club for tea and cake, served by a young Italian waiter.

I caught the 3.00pm bus and chatted to a lady with a glass eye. I asked her which political party was in power here and she hadn't a clue. She got off the bus in the countryside and her house was the saddest looking place I've ever seen, but she was a happy soul.

We arrived at Carlisle just as the light was fading.

As I remember it, it was a pretty grey, dull old town. I then went to look for accommodation. I asked the postman. He said not to stay at the pub but to look at the Ibis Hotel. I was booked in by a Polish man. Once more my Mastercard failed to work.

You get what you pay for in life and this was a nice little room with everything the traveller might need. The bathroom had the best shower I've ever had.

Went for another 'all you can eat Chinese'; the food was tasteless and if I'd eaten my lawnmower cuttings it would've been more flavoursome! And don't you just meet the pigs of society in these places? I saw one lady go up three times, with the table manners of a pig. In fact I think I prefer the company of pigs.

A good-looking, well-to-do mum with three very young boys came in. They were playing havoc and it was fun to watch. When checking out I said to her that it looked as though she had her hands full. She nodded. She was a bit 'up-her-own-jumper'.

CARLISLE TO NEWTON STEWART

I didn't like the idea of breakfast in the Ibis so I left a little note for the cleaners, thanking them, and left. I went to the station but the train to

Castle Douglas was not for another two hours, so I walked to the bus station where a bus left every half hour.

It's quite an art finding the right bus stop for the right destination, but fortunately the inspector was really helpful. Two ladies from Carlisle were about to make their first visit to Dumfries. An American joined us who was over here on holiday for two weeks. He was on his way to Hadrian's Wall and I was tempted to join him, but I'll see it on my way down the other side next year.

Anyway, back to my American friend. He worked as a laboratory technician in a nut factory that specialised in peanuts and cashews. Apparently, they had an ultraviolet machine that could blow out any unwanted ingredients. He was loving his holiday and commented on how friendly the British are; back home no one would speak to anyone else at a bus stop.

Carlisle was bigger than I expected and took some time to leave behind. We passed one or two dead looking farm buildings.

The bus stopped at a superstore which stood out like a sore thumb out in the countryside, and so they'd tried to blend it in but had failed miserably. I think it was called 'Suits You'.

We really were having some fun today. After several splutters the bus ground to a halt just inside Scotland. We were just outside a cemetery and the driver rang for a replacement bus. I asked him if he had his hazard lights on and he told me he had pulled over enough. I didn't like the idea of sitting in the back of the bus so I moved to the middle and started writing. I walked to the driver's cabin. He did have his hazard lights on. *'There are some dead-heads on this bus. I think even if it catches fire they'll still sit here! Oh well, at least with writing Walkabout I never get bored.'*

About forty minutes later a mechanic arrived with a spare bus and loads of tools and a battery starter.

We were now in Scotland and you could see the changes in the countryside already. The farmers really love their white paint.

The bus was now filled with pretty angry rough old working or unemployed people. They were all nodding their heads, and had got frozen to death waiting. At least we were sitting on the bus with the heater on. One of the rough lot behind me had hair down to his shoulders and smelled of fish. I tried to squeeze some conversation out of him, but it was quite noisy in the back and I had a job to understand the accent; funny really as one of the reasons for doing 'walkabout' is to chat to people which I couldn't do when abroad. And now here in Scotland I couldn't understand what they're saying anyway.

We now had eleven on the bus. There was a shop steward type reading the *Daily Record* and a young mum with very badly behaved children, who kept throwing their sweets down, and shit-head little mummy kept giving them back. The children were sticking their tongues out at people they didn't know and I felt like giving them a smack round the ear, or telling the mother what morons they were.

DUMFRIES

Arrived at Dumfries; back again with really unhappy people. The rain just added to the misery. There were some really dopey looking men around. I went and had coffee in a fancy coffee house – in a huge cup with two handles and a fancy price tag to go with it!

I found a house where Robert Burns (1759-1796) had lived, but it was out of season and closed. As luck would have it the door suddenly opened and the curate showed us round. In the corner of the amazing graveyard at St Michael's Church is a huge tomb to the friends of Robert Burns, and in the corner there's one to his daughter who'd died aged fourteen and his son who'd died aged two.

I jumped on the bus to Castle Douglas and only then did I realise the beautiful bridges on the way out of Dumfries. I arrived at a gloomy, wet and grey Castle Douglas.

I couldn't believe the number of butcher shops there were in such a small town. One had five people working in it. *'Oh dear, at the end of the town is a brand new TESCO.'* It's only a matter of time before the supermarkets squeeze the lifeblood out of all these shops.

The number 500 bus turned up and I was expecting a pokey little thing but it was a luxury, brand new, forty-seater Stagecoach, and it was full. My seat was at the back and I was squashed between a young couple and their luggage.

It was now dark and I couldn't see the road signs, and I was missing some great countryside. I couldn't hear the driver when he called out the stops, so I ended up in Newton Stewart. I was sheltering in the bus stop as it was pouring with rain and I was joined by two scatty teenage girls. I asked where the hotels were and they told me there were three up the road. They couldn't make out why I was here, but it was nice that they didn't mind chatting.

It was Friday night and they were going to get some money off a friend and get pissed. They all came from big families. They asked if I had children or was married and thought I was mad. I asked one of the girls about her brothers and sisters. She said she had one half-brother and a step-sister. I asked the other girl if her parents were still together. She looked rather sad and said she didn't know her father.

I found a hotel and the young man who booked me in was doing his best and gave me a double room and a radiator to dry my clothes.

One side had a working bar but the other was like a night club. Upstairs was all under construction and was a bit cheapy-cheapy.

The restaurant was unwelcoming and empty and being refurbished, so I went instead to the Bruce Hotel. It was the best and warmest welcome I'd had on 'walkabout'.

As soon as I walked in they made me feel welcome by shaking my hand, both husband and wife; and the staff were all smart and polite, too. The man whom I assumed was the owner, reminded me of Mr MacKay in *Porridge*. He really knew how to work his customers; asking how the meal was and saying, 'I haven't seen you in a long time!' I really felt I was in Scotland now. There were some lovely tartan carpets and a man, dressed in a kilt, came in with his wife and mother. His mother had a bib round her neck. She was very old and had a coughing fit, but Mr Mackay soon got her a glass of water.

Mr MacKay was nearly as interested in me as I was in him, and as he asked me if my meal was all right he noticed me writing *Walkabout*.

'Observation, I see' he said.

These are the reasons why it was a mistake to book into this hotel:

1. I think on Friday nights they fancy themselves as a night club with dreadful music playing until 1.30am.

2. The traffic.

3. Saniflo loo sounding as though it was trying to drown someone all night.

4. Fuck-head youngsters talking all night outside my window.

5. They'd spent a lot of money on this place and hadn't got it right.

6. The fan that goes on in the loo when you turn the light on sounds like a power station starting up.

7. And somewhere in this hotel there was a door that banged all night.

Next morning I felt like telling them to stuff their breakfast and going to the Bruce Hotel, but as I'd already paid for it, I didn't.

I was the only person here and no other place was laid up.

The lady asked me, 'Where would you like it?' I thought she had a twinkle in her eye but perhaps I was imagining it!

The waitress asked me if everything was OK and I said it was a very noisy hotel, especially with the night club. She called to the manager and I heard her telling him what I'd said. The egg-head never even came out to apologise. So in the book for comments I wrote my name and address and the comment: 'NOISY HOTEL – TRY THE BRUCE HOTEL NEAR BY.'

I walked up to the roundabout and the only people working were the market cleaner, who was tipping rubbish into a skip, and the post lady. I asked if the Christmas card rush had started and she said, 'No, but the parcel rush has.'

A friendly good-looking horse across the road looked at me with ears pricked. I went over to her muddy field and she buggered off! I then looked back across the road, saw a bus and flagged it down. I bought my £5 'all-day' ticket and was on my way to Wigmore. *'I don't know if I want to go there, but that's where the bus is going, so I'll go with the flow.'*

George, the bus driver, was happy today because his shift would end at 5pm. Apparently Wigmore is the biggest book centre in the country.

When we arrived there we saw a small minibus that was going to Port William and the surrounding areas, so I jumped on. I was the only passenger, which was fun and I really enjoyed this countryside.

We passed a pub that had a sign on it saying: 'If you misbehave in this pub you will be banned from all pubs in a 'Pubwatch' premises.'

The driver pointed out all the places of interest including the old RAF aerodrome from which the Lancaster bombers flew.

We passed a bronze processing factory and a huge distillery at Bladnoch, and I said to the driver that it was a bit early to visit at 9.30am. He seemed to know everyone we passed and nodded or waved to them all.

There was no rubbish around which was very refreshing. There were a few lambs grazing in the fields, and derelict houses all over the place. In the south of England they would be worth a fortune.

Well, the bus filled up with four children of whom three were triplets: James, Bryan, Ryan and big brother Cameron. The mother's partner was a lobster fisherman. She let me take a photograph of them and the hardest bit was to get them all together.

The countryside must be difficult to farm with its dunes and rocks. It made me feel seasick looking at it.

We passed the Isle of Whithorn and the driver continued to nod and wave at everyone. A farmer had made a right cock-up of some drilling, and all the youngsters were on their mobiles.

Some houses had red roof tiles which looked out of place in these parts.

We finished our round trip and were back in Wigtown where the bus was waiting to take us to Newton Stewart.

NEWTON STEWART TO GLENLUCE

It was a busy bus and nearly full. I was sitting next to Molly, who was a cheerful, happy lady and enjoying the chat. She'd just done her shopping and was going back to put her feet up and let her niece cook lunch.

One lady was debating with another about where to get off and I suggested she should get her morning exercise.

'I get enough exercise with me Hoover.'

We both roared with laughter.

Another lovely old girl with a real 'grandmother' face was someone I would've loved to have photographed but I couldn't bring myself to ask.

One of the 'debating' ladies, Mary, had lived in Carlisle for thirty years and had never regretted moving north. I asked if she would go any further north. 'No, I'm staying put.'

As I was feeling fat and lazy I got off the bus at Glencoe and started walking towards the New Inn. I walked along the fast flowing brown river that has an extraordinary arched bridge.

GLENCOE ABBEY

It started to rain so on went the wet-weather gear. I tried the museum door and although the light was on I couldn't open it. Suddenly a man appeared and showed me around.

The Abbey was built in 1190 and has been a ruin for five hundred years. I was really fascinated by the eight hundred-year-old land drains which were handmade and had interlocking collars. They are the only ones known about, and each had an individual marking so that if they were ever taken up for maintenance they would know exactly where each one came from.

The monks who came here didn't live long. They ate little and most died after twelve years. They wore no underwear which must have been a bit draughty.

Colin, the curator, who'd come from Somerset many years ago, was excellent at telling me about the museum.

He told me that three monarchs had, in the past, visited the place. The little tower was the gatehouse, a place for the mad monk to look after the arrivals and departures.

I asked Colin the way north and he gave me a wary look when I said I was walking and perhaps hitching. He said it was a quiet road with very little traffic.

Whilst walking round the Abbey I'd heard a banging. It was John Porter, who was dry stone walling; He had his sheepdog with him for company. I said what a marvellous job he was doing.

'Aye, aye,' came the response. 'Youngsters won't do it these days. I can do four metres a day and I charge £20 per metre. Someone told me that if I came south I would earn much more, but I'd rather be here. Aye, aye.'

He was bashful about having his photograph taken but I got him in the end.

I went past a field of happy donkeys and they all came towards me, but the annoying thing was that my camera had misted up.

I only saw one car in thirty minutes and the wind and rain was hard into my face.

Luckily for me the vicar and his wife picked me up. He was on his way to conduct a wedding service. I had to be a bit careful as I scrambled wetly into his car. I did not want to ruin his Bible or papers. He was going to marry a farmer's daughter. He said that they only seemed to get married after the sheep sales when a bit of money came in.

When we arrived at the church the heavens opened so I rushed for the porch for shelter. The photographer looked down his nose at me and the guests were arriving so I put my wet-weather gear on and got back to the road.

I walked past a pub thinking to myself, *'No, keep walking, you fat little man, you'll never get to Barr Hill.'*

The bride, all dressed in white, was driven past me and I gave her a big cheery wave.

I passed a farmhouse, a fairly small single-storey place with huge trees surrounding it. It reminded me of Argentina. All the wheelie bins had been blown over. Well, if I gave the impression of remoteness earlier on, I apologise. *'John Arthur wanted 'remote' and he has it now.'*

It was raining and windy and the wind made my leggings fill like sails and pushed me sideways. My hood, with my big fat head in it, didn't want to stay up.

The cattle looked at me as if to say: 'What is this idiot doing out in this awful weather?'

I came across some very nice sheep with the most amazing curly horns, and I thought that if I stopped here much longer I would start fancying them!

'Good afternoon, Mr Sheep, if ever you're in Kent, come and look us up. Good afternoon, Mrs Cow, and how's all your family? I am possibly going to eat you one day!'

I was feeling like a white man in a black country and the animals all looked at me with pity at my being here.

I was starting to think that this was not a fun walk, more a question of survival. There was no grass now bar a few stumpy bits. All the animals had disappeared. I kept thinking I could hear a vehicle but it was the water playing tricks on my hearing. I had one cigarette left and it was too wet to light. I was seriously worried about my health and my ability to get out of here.

At last a red van came from nowhere, so I took my hood down and gave a big smile, but he drove past as though I was a piece of dirt. I could still see the look on his face some forty-eight hours later. *'I hope you feel guilty when I'm found dead.'*

My zip had broken and on my jacket, the label read: 'Regatta – Great Outdoors'.

'Well, I don't think it's great. Normally when you break a zip you just repair it or chuck it away, but I'm relying on this anorak to keep me alive. At least if I'm dry my body temperature won't drop.' I botched it up by sticking the Velcro together. *'I'll always give a zip a bit more respect in future.'*

I pictured the headline in the *Kent Messenger*:

'KENT FARMER DIES WHILST WALKING THE MOORS. THE LAST PERSON TO SEE HIM ALIVE WAS THE MINISTER FOR NEW GLENLUCE CHURCH, WHO GAVE HIM A LIFT EARLIER IN THE DAY.'

I was thinking that I really should've gone into the pub and they would've warned me. I should've let someone know where I was going. I wished I'd studied self-survival. I thought about the film where a man killed a buffalo and cut it open so that he could shelter.

'But how am I going to catch my cow, let alone cut it open without a knife? Don't panic, just take big breaths. This will be a big tale by tonight.'

I tried to shelter by a wall but it made no difference as the wind was everywhere. I finished the last of my water and started regretting I hadn't had any lunch.

I wondered if the building and maintenance of these tiny roads was paid for by British taxes. There were no passing places which I think put people off using it. I kept thinking I could hear cars coming but again it was the water playing tricks with my ears.

In the distance was a big old farmhouse with a blue sheet covering it and I could seek shelter there. I had an empty plastic bottle that I would've loved to get rid of, but I wouldn't dump it in this beautiful wild countryside.

I could've crawled into a farm building and stayed the night, snuggled up in some warm straw. *'Some hope of that, as the nearest straw is hundreds of miles away.'*

I'd given up hoping that someone would come along. For an unfit person I was pleased with my legs which were going rather well. My knees and hips were OK and as I'd found out before on 'walkabout' you very quickly become fitter.

In the distance I could see green grass rather than the brown stuff and that meant more life, more animals and more farms, and maybe more people.

I was now getting excited. I saw a Land Rover and someone standing next to it. What a great feeling to see another human being! *'I'm not ready for the Good Lord yet.'*

As I approached the Land Rover the man was still there. 'What are you doing out there?' he asked.

'I'm a Kent farmer getting some exercise. What's your name?'

'Alex McCrow. I have twelve hundred acres. Just me and the wife. Aye.'

'Is that your farmhouse with the blue sheet on it?'

'Nay, owned by an Englishman; not there at the moment. What are you doing out in this?'

'All right, I know when I've been an idiot, but I thought I might get a lift.'

'Well, there are two young lassies over there with two punctures, aye, and two men have just changed a tyre and the spare is flat. If they get a tyre man out, they'll be charged double as it's the weekend. They got the puncture where the farmer was cutting the hedges. A thorn went through and they're waiting for the two men to come back. Where are you heading?'

I said, 'To Barrhill. How far is it?'

'Aye, it's a good eight or nine miles.'

I thought, *'Wow!'* and just then a rail worker drove around us. Alex said he'd take me, but I thought that advice was a little late as the man disappeared into the distance.

The girl in the punctured car came across and said, 'Got a light?' She was a bit of a fat, stupid girl dressed in pink.

I said, 'If you get going and pass me will you give me a lift?'

Pinky replied, 'Going the other way.'

I shook Alex's hand and said that I'd better get on. As I went past I looked in the car and there were three young girls and two babies. Alex was keeping an eye on them.

Just as I thought I was back in civilisation I was thrown back into the lonely Falkland environment, and my short-lived excitement at the prospect of a lift vanished.

At least it had stopped raining but the wind was still up my behind. The road was flooded at one point so I had to be careful that my feet didn't get wet. I stuck my head over a wall and saw a pheasant feeding. A hen pheasant then flew off close to the ground in this strong wind.

I was alone, walking under a large moon and I had no idea how long it would take to get to Barrhill. I was getting tired and it was getting dark. At times like this you need a sense of humour. And it was looking like rain again. I dug my head torch out, put my pullover on and pulled myself together.

It was now pitch dark.

There are two things you do not want to do on a 'walkabout'; one is to run out of money and the other is to be stuck on the moors after dark.

The Lord was looking after me and I could see car lights coming. I flagged down the driver. He stopped and gave me a lift. It was the best lift of my life, and Mark would have nothing for it. He said it was still a fair way to Barrhill. He was English and used to work in Kent, in Paddock Wood. He'd also been in the army and all over the world; Belize and Guatemala to name just two places. We exchanged a few stories and he told me he loved walking himself. He was now a police officer.

He dropped me off outside the Trout Inn.

'I'm alive, I'm alive, I'm alive!'

All the locals turned around when I arrived and wondered who I was. I had the best John Smith's I've ever had. It wasn't long before we were like long lost friends. Paul came from Medway, and was now retired from working on the oil rigs. He did three weeks on and then had one week off – it was hard. He bought me a drink. He used to smoke eighty cigarettes a day but had now given up. Then there was Jim. He drove a concrete mixer and he bought me another drink.

I went up for a shower and a nice sensible woman took me to my room. She was about the only one not getting drunk.

My room was strange. The outside of the pub and the bars were somewhat drab; then you walked upstairs. They seemed to have made an attempt to smarten up for the tourists. There were no keys and the only way I could identify my room was to stick the hoover outside. Everything was new. My bed was like a steel cot; the furniture was of wood covered with cotton. How it bore the weight of a television was a miracle. Saturday night at the Trout Inn was in full swing.

I had a chat with some deer stalkers who were also staying. Then it was cod and chips and more beers.

In addition to being a pub this place was also a community centre. A lovely old lady came in with her husband and just had a cup of tea.

I said goodbye to everyone and one old boy shouted out, 'You won't forget Barrhill, that's for sure.'

He was right. I staggered up to bed.

Well, they must've all gone home last night because there was only Anne, the landlady, and the deer stalkers at breakfast. The deer shooter said that every year they brought forty oak trees up and planted them. They were from Yorkshire and would be back again before Christmas. He was an HGV fitter and worked with large quarrying machinery. He said that in some forests they find ribbon of different colours, hanging on trees and the rangers can tell how many deer they have and what sex they are.

I couldn't make it out because last night they were all rolling up cigarettes and disappearing outside to smoke. The Scottish ban was due to be introduced in England next year and I said that if a Conservative government introduced it there would be a riot. They were keen to tell me that the Tories had also voted for the ban in Scotland.

I must explain to you about Sue, the boss of this pub with her husband. He was serving in the bar last night. He was overweight and didn't look too good; had probably smoked a lot of cigarettes in his life. Sue said they had bought this bankrupt pub to be a holiday home. At the time there were two in the village. Then out of the blue the other pub shut and this was the only place the community had. Everyone came here so they had to carry on and start the pub again. The beer turned up at 11am and the customers came through the door at midday. They didn't even know how to operate the till, and had never dreamt of running a pub.

They managed to get a chef and the food was so popular that people were booking up every night. The place was full, but it was not what they had come up here for. The chef's mood became very variable, being either up or down. Doors were slammed and sometimes the chef seemed to go mad. Sue was just a happy quiet girl, so she found it difficult. Then one night they had thirty people booked in and there was a big argument in public with the chef. Sue told him that if that was his attitude he had better go, and he did.

Sue said, 'I made the announcement to the customers that in view of what they had heard, all those who had ordered would be served and the others, unfortunately, would not. Apparently, there was a loud cheer and they'd pulled it off.

Her mother and father came up and gave a hand. They were good cooks. Sue could cook as well but didn't enjoy it. When Sue and her husband are away the locals man the bar. They did have a barman but that didn't work out.

Sue, who lives in Yorkshire, also has another job. She commutes up here for a long weekend every week and covers four hundred miles.

As we were talking the deer stalkers left and she gave them a big hug.

The pub needed new windows, a new boiler, new roof and other things, but it couldn't all be done at once, so she was going to get a new boiler and the rest would have to wait.

She said, 'I can't believe I'm doing this job. I like to be a free spirit and when I was twenty-one I swore that my life would be plan-free.' She loved driving onto the moors as it gave her a sense of freedom.

She wore the most amazing short skirt with little pop socks. She really looked the business.

Her friends came up a few months ago and said how much the villagers had changed. They had become all jolly and completely different. Sue said that it had been difficult to get them going, but now, with the slightest excuse they were all up and dancing all night.

Sue offered me a lift to the rail station, but I walked and as I left she gave me a big hug. She was just that sort of girl.

After a short walk I was there. I had time and was enjoying the morning and wondering why, after yesterday's exertions, I wasn't stiffer, although I did have a headache.

Some railway workers were operating a petrol-driven cart that goes up the track. I asked if it would have enough petrol to get me to Troon but I got little response. They still have working signal boxes up here.

I noticed that some kind soul had managed to do a huge crap on the line! *'Please mind the gap and do not shit in the station!'*

There was some interesting antique rail equipment in the station. It was a very tidy place with a brand new shelter. An old miserable farmer, who had driven past me and had looked at me as if I was dirt, opened the gates of the crossing. It was a dangerous place and on a bend. Then he drove a flock of sheep over the line.

I asked the station master for a ticket, but he told me to pay on the train. I never did see the ticket collector, so I had a free ride to Ayr.

The train came, all two carriages of it. There was a jet of air blowing from under the seat so I took my damp boots off and put them in the way to dry. I've never had so much seat room on a train before.

Once again there's a very old-fashioned feel to Ayr and it has a very beautiful Victorian station and a newsagents that is closed on Sundays.

I had a chat to a happy Indian taxi driver, but just as we were getting a conversation going some ignorant locals jumped into his taxi and without even looking the driver in the face gave him orders.

AYR TO SALTCOATS

'Bloody cheek. I've just had to buy a ticket for £3.60.'

There was so much space between the seats and there was a fair amount of rubbish on the trains. The only time I saw the lovely bridges going out of the cities was when I was on the trains. This time there were two or three, one after the other. The train was starting to get busy and went right past Prestwick Airport. I was thinking how busy this must be when the Open Golf is here.

A smart young lad of about thirteen got on the train with his fatty mother. She had a whole packet of pastilles and stuffed the lot in one by one. Mother was now washing down her sweets with lemonade. She was sort of slumped in the seat like a polythene bag full of water. Then she shoved her big fat hand into her mouth and started picking her teeth. Her jeans that were trying to contain her thighs were bursting at the seams.

The boy was much better behaved than his mum. He wore a smart St John uniform.

Whilst I was writing this, a pretty girl came and sat next to me. I hoped she wasn't reading my notes.

The train stopped at a station and while we were waiting I watched two engineers who had their heads in a big metal box. Being a nosy-parker I asked them what they were doing. Apparently they were fitting a new driver's toy, a station mirror, which would enable him to see right up the platform to make sure all passengers were either on or off the train. JA asked if it might not be just as easy if he simply looked out of the window. The answer was, 'No, because the station has a bend in it.'

The train was very relaxing. 'Let the train take the strain' is right, and after a few minutes it arrived at Kilwinning. 'This is a non-smoking station – Please mind the gap.'

'Can you tell me the way to the ferry?'

'Wrong town, mate. You want Ardrossan and the train has just left.'

'I know that, because I just got off it.' *'Prat!'*

I walked up the street and asked an old man at the bus stop where the bus to Ardrossan left from. He thought for a long time and then said, 'Aye, I couldn't tell you.'

'Well,' I said, 'I'll keep walking and if it comes by would you tell it to stop?'

About two minutes later I flagged down the bus and he looked at me as if to say, 'You should've got on at the bus station. It cost me 85p and Ardrossan was within walking distance. In fact it was the shortest bus journey I've ever made.

My 'walkabout' is all about a little bit of luck and I found I only had about an hour to wait. The very helpful girl in the ferry terminal booked all my island-hopping ferry trips. The ferry terminal here was brand new and the lady I was talking to said that I should've seen the last one.

A large group of schoolchildren had arrived for an outward bound week on Arran, and the teacher offered me a brochure all about the islands.

I was quietly sitting writing *Walkabout* when an elderly mother and daughter sat next to me. She had a large cardboard box and I offered to carry it on board. As we went up the gangplank I said to her that I hoped

121

she was not carrying drugs! This lady was about eighty and she said, 'No such luck!'

I was expecting it to be like an old bathtub of a ferry, only to find it was like a luxury liner.

The lady with the box was Jenny. She oozed 'specialness'. I was just thinking that I was sure she'd been something to do with medicine, and having given her a hand with the box I was going to find out. I knew she had retired to Arran fifteen years ago and that her daughter would love to move there when her children left home as she had fond memories of the place.

Jenny told me to avoid certain hotels as they would rip me off.

When we came to disembarking I picked up the parcel and said to Jenny, 'Would you be from the medical world?'

She said, 'Yes, I worked in the inner cities and before that I spent ten years with the Samaritans.'

'Seen a bit of life then?'

'Just a bit.'

ARRAN

Well, it was just about getting dark and I was feeling knackered. I'd never slept so badly on 'walkabout' as on this leg. I saw a huge hotel decided to check it out.

Now this could have been Fawlty Towers. There was no one at reception until the drinkers in the bar informed the barman. The price of the rooms was £28 or £33, including breakfast.

'Can I see the room, please?'

He took me up there.

'That'll do fine. Is there anywhere I can dry my clothes?'

'Yeah, just hang them on the radiators.'

'Are you sure you want my dirty clothes hanging in the lobby?'

'No trouble.'

I liked the attitude. In the end we put them in the ballroom where I met the chef, Robert.

I told him that I'd been informed that he was only cooking for the staff tonight.

'No, it's no trouble. I'm just doing pasta, chips and peas.'

I shook his hand and after that nothing was too much trouble. It's amusing what a handshake does. I could see Robert rising about a foot with pride at the prospect of feeding me and the meal was great.

This place was run down and the man at reception had been embarrassed at asking me to pay in advance. Apparently, three people had done a runner the night before and they had lost £100.

The bar had about six locals in it. I sat on my own in the corner watching Mr Lard playing snooker. It amazes me how much fat you can wrap around a skeleton.

The boss man had a lovely cheerful grin and went out of his way to help. 'If there's anything you want, just ask.' He told me that there was a Country and Western evening in the pub next door and made me laugh when he apologised for the 'intellectual company'.

CARPET FITTERS

I said I was sorry to hear about the money owed by the 'runners'.

'Aye, but no worry, we'll get it. The trouble was that there was no one here when they left. They'd paid for the first night and spent £100 in the bar. They went mental and I was worried about the women – bloody mental!'

Although it was a funny hotel, my room must have had a 16ft ceiling and had some brand new tartan curtains and a bedspread to match, and the little electric fire on which we were told to hang nothing melted my inner soles.

Back in the bar Mr Lard's stomach hung over the table as he took another shot. It really is a macho game, drinking and tipping the last drop out of the bottle into the glass.

I couldn't get to sleep no matter how many sheep I counted. I just kept having stupid dreams and did *Walkabout* all night. The funny thing is that I thought I was being shipwrecked, what with the noise of the sea and wind. Even though it was very windy and the windows were open, the room felt stuffy.

ARRAN TO PORT TARBERT

I had to get my backside into gear this morning if I wanted to look around this island, as I had to catch the afternoon ferry to Tarbert, so I didn't have breakfast and left before 8am. Brodick was bustling with early morning ferry travellers and bus passengers.

As luck would have it, dear old Mr Stagecoach had a bus waiting and it was to go round the whole island anticlockwise. I jumped on. It took three hours, picking up schoolchildren en route and dropping them off at their schools. There were sheep on the road and cows and deer, and a lady tending to her horse and companion goat. A puppy collie dog thought the bus was a plaything and the driver had to try to avoid running it over before it ran back to the farmyard. Seals were basking on the rocks and relaxing in the early morning sun. The bus was warm and outside the grass was bent double by the wind. We passed Lochranza where I would catch the ferry later on. I thought the island would just have one good school but there were several. One thing I noticed was the intensity of the colours here. The moors were a really rich soft brown and the wild sea was a beautiful grey.

A mother stood with her daughter waiting for the bus, with an umbrella shielding her from the strong crosswind. A father opened the door of his people carrier as the bus came along, and another opened the door of his house and ran with a very small infant.

A few swans were tucked in behind the rocky shore, the odd heron was looking for his early morning breakfast, and a few pheasants were strutting about as if they owned the place.

There was a stubble field with geese foraging for grain, cormorants ganged up on the rocks, spreading their wings and ever searching for food, and the hooded crows looked so smart in their grey waistcoats.

At Kildonan we picked up Arran's only punk girl. She had a hair-do and outfit worth a photograph, but I hadn't the nerve to ask. When we got to the bus station I saw her again and told her she was the most modern girl I'd seen in Arran. She took the compliment.

I also saw Mr Lard, back in Brodick, from the pool table last night and gave him a cheerful wave, but got no response. *'Surprise!'*

I didn't have time for breakfast, so I just grabbed a couple of packets of crisps and off we went. The seals seemed to have disappeared. The poor old bus driver didn't look well at all. There was something wrong with his eyes and he looked as though he would really like to go to sleep. When I got off the bus I asked him if he was OK and he said, 'Aye,' and then rattled on in a Scottish accent that I couldn't understand.

LOCHRANZA

I had a couple of hours to kill and plenty of writing up to do. I just needed somewhere comfortable to get on with it. I went to the Lochranza Hotel and rang the bell, but there was no answer.

Not much life around here at this time of year, but just around the corner I found a little café or really just a sandwich bar. I met Mini in her tiny café making soups and teas and sandwiches. There was nowhere to sit. I had pea and meat soup and a cup of tea and a roll.

The ferry waiting room had loads of comfortable seats and tables, but it was locked. So I was left with a choice between a telephone box and a draughty bus shelter. The wind was so strong that it nearly blew the soup out of the bowl. I felt like a little old tramp. Wrappers went flying out of the shelter and I tried to catch them. This was the first time I had ever been lost for a place to shelter on 'walkabout'.

It was starting to rain and there was no shelter on the walk up to the Lochranza Castle, so I ran only to find it locked. The doorway had been blocked off in 1625. *'Thanks a lot, mate.'* The other door was padlocked. The seagulls didn't need to make the effort to fly here; they just glided on the turbulence.

Walking up the road I met the gang of schoolchildren and their teacher who had been at the terminal. Bernard came from Halifax and had been coming here for many years with the teenagers. They would stay for about a week; it was hard work, but good fun.

I saw a deer and rushed to put a film in my camera but the animal tried to take it out of my hand thinking it was food. I couldn't believe it!

I could see the ferry some way off battling through the waves so I had time for another cup of tea with Mini. She had two builders in there sharing stories about aeroplane flying and rude passengers. Mini said she had also had her fair share of rude people in her shop and if they didn't say thank you, she would say to them, 'What is the magic word?' Parents would look at her as if to say, 'Watch it!'

Mini told me a story about a ferry captain who knocked the pier down when doing a hand brake turn with the ferry. He used to sail in all weathers but in the end was sacked.

I asked Mini if I could have a photograph and she agreed, but only on the condition that it was not sold or put on the Internet. She had once let someone photograph her and the next thing she knew she was on an advertisement for Arran.

I met a nutty woman down at the docks with two small dogs with their hair tied in bows. I said that they looked well cared for and she replied that they were.

THE MULL OF KINTYRE

This was a much smaller ferry and the sea was choppy. There were two walking passengers including me, one Calor gas lorry and about four cars filling the ferry. I was not quite sure why I had to book, but maybe in the summer they get too many people. We passed a fish farm and steep cliffs to get to the Mull of Kintyre. I met Ashley Walker on board. He had lived in Germany for ten years, working in the car trade, but he'd now moved back to Yorkshire for a quieter life. His wife was in the car feeling ill.

I couldn't get over how long the journey took and wondered if I was on the right ferry. I kept hearing banging. It took some time to realise that it was the children running about over my head. I suddenly smelled a wonderful smell and looked up to see a blonde bombshell with an older boyfriend.

We passed a wind farm sticking out from the Mull, with the blades gracefully turning. Just before it got dark we arrived at Port Tarbert.

The little bus that had awaited the ferry left without passengers and I wondered if I should have got on it, but the walk to the town was enjoyable and short. A few B&B places peered out over the harbour but looked dead after the summer.

I had another chat with the fishermen sorting prawns and all sorts of different fish from their nets. And for the first time ever I got a friendly response.

'Would you mind if I took your photograph?'

'Aye.'

I popped in a hotel and enquired about a room. A tall, short-haired girl barked back that it would cost £35 per night, with no smile and straightaway carried on talking to the locals.

The next door hotel said that they were full. *'Little liars!'*

I found the Hotel Victoria much more accommodating, but the room cost £45. The only thing I could bargain for was breakfast, so we settled for £40.

When I signed the visitors' book she said, 'Lenham! I used to run the Harrow Inn for three years and this pub was run by the same company that went bust.'

Funny after being in the Fawlty Towers place to come to this. It was all neat and tidy but not nearly such fun. There was fruit in the room and even tissues.

I had my evening meal, then rang Valerie and got my ears burnt over this, that and the other. I had left the hoover in one of the rented houses and she couldn't find the keys to get into it; and a bit of my life history to go with it!

A young girl had taken over from Maggie and she organised my taxi for 6.30am. She made me feel very welcome.

I thought I'd turned the radiator off, only to find that I had switched the shower off, so I woke up roasting.

Duncan, my taxi driver to the ferry, turned up on time.

The ferry this time was huge, with all mod cons. I got stuck into a big fry-up minutes after the ferry pulled out. For a fiver I had black pudding and other bits and pieces and plenty of fat. We were warned that in the event of the ferry sinking we were to remain calm at all times!

It was still dark at 7.30am. The businessmen kept checking their watches. As day broke, the islands on both sides unfolded.

We got to Port Ellen, back on dear old Islay again, where a boat was unloading malting barley. I went for a bus.

'Going to Bridgend?'

'Aye. £2.25.'

'You're robbing me.'

'Aye, you won't get away with anything here, boy.'

'Have you got an 'all-day' ticket?'

He looked blank and didn't know what I was talking about. After a short wait we were off through the busy port. We passed Islay golf course, which brought back memories of when we'd played there years ago, and suddenly there was the airport. I stopped the bus and booked a return flight back to Glasgow for a few days' time.

It's seventeen years since I was last here and a quaint little airport was now a little 'up-your-jumper' one. *'What have they done with the shed that served us so well?'* I was amazed at this mini-Heathrow with all its mod cons, including pretty BA check-in girls.

I was really enjoying being here and having a smoke whilst hitching to see Fiona. She was an old family friend who had no idea I was on the island. I wondered if she would be in. *'By gum, it's wet here and Islay really hasn't changed from being a peat bog.'*

After about five vehicles had passed, Bobby Wright stopped for me in his white transit van. He worked for Duffies Delivery Transport. He knew

128

where Fiona's house was and pointed it out in the distance. He said he was going fairly near and after waiting for him to drop off some deliveries he put me down at Whin Park.

I saw the church where years ago we'd gone to a wedding. It's one of only two round churches in the world, built to make sure the devil couldn't hide in the corners.

My next lift was with David Lance, who worked for the RSPB. After a short distance I was dropped off. Every little helps.

The next lift was with Alex. He had a really strong Scottish accent and told me he used to work for the council, but it was not much of a job. However, it carried a good pension and was better than a kick up the backside. He used to be a jobbing builder and had a little nodding dog on the dashboard. I said to him that at least he didn't have to pay vet's fees!

'Aye, and he don't eat much food either.'

We both roared with laughter.

He dropped me off right outside Fiona's house. For the next few days I saw him quite a few times going up and down the road.

FIONA DOYLE

What a bit of luck. She's in!!' As she came to the door she was talking to John Mackelden. All hell was let loose within minutes and the whole world knew I'd arrived. Anyone would have thought I was some sort of celebrity.

Her new house was undergoing complete renovation and the place was in chaos. The front garden was dug up. Today we were in luck as the builders hadn't turned up.

She phoned Mark and Rohaise and invited them for supper with their daughter, so after a cup of tea we went shopping.

Fiona was sure that eyes were peering and just to give them something to chat about I put my arm round her, but she soon shrugged me off.

When we got back home after a conducted tour around the island seeing lots more wildlife, we prepared the evening meal, rubbing salt into the pork. I peeled the potatoes and it was difficult to find all the right tools in a strange house.

Mark and Rohaise, Fiona's sister, have farmed on the island for many years, and are well known for being entrepreneurial.

There are about thirty-two farmers on the island, which is about the size of the Isle of Wight.

Fiona has the reputation of being a great cook, and still is. We tucked in to good food, good wine, good company and it all made a great start to exploring Islay.

I went to bed.

The builders had arrived and the radio was on full blast. In fact it was plumbers, as the builders couldn't be found.

To get to the bathroom I had to go through Fiona's room, so I decided it was easier to visit the garden.

All the dogs and the cat slept in the same basket. Last night the whippet scratched a hole in the new red carpet. With renovations going on and Fiona going on it's a madhouse.

This place really does see some weather. Rain and showers come from every direction.

What a day and what a drive! Rockside Farm is where Mark and Rohaise live. They've been here for thirty years and Rohaise runs a horse trekking business and a farm shop that sells local produce, including their own meat. The meat is cut and vacuum-packed. They run a shoot and there are pheasants and partridges all over the place.

There are no foxes on Islay, but plenty of otters.

With Fiona rattling on it was nice to go for a walk. I was carrying my rucksack, field glasses and camera and Fiona gave me a look as if to say, 'Why do you need a rucksack and make yourself look like an idiot?'

The next few hours would live with me forever. Fiona's binoculars are brilliant and bring the smallest bird right up close.

Barnacle geese rule here. They were everywhere; eighty thousand had come down from Greenland and Iceland. They're normally here from October to April, but they seem to be arriving earlier and leaving later. There were a few brents and white fronts as well. I saw what I thought were buzzards but Mark said they were golden eagles.

'Hares, my beautiful hares, pop up all over the place and at night the deer come out.'

I walked across the barley stubble. Mark grows about two hundred tons a year for his distillery. I've never seen daisies as a cereal weed. Mark said that the geese brought it over in their shit and spread it all over the fields.

KILCHOMAN OLD CHURCH

The Church of Scotland, or whoever, wants shooting for letting this church become derelict. I found it on my walk and couldn't believe that they'd built some pretty plain holiday homes close by whilst letting this church fall down. I had to be careful walking round the outside to make sure I didn't tread on a nail. It made me feel quite sick that this landmark, sitting as it did on a hill, could end up in this state.

A barley stubble field had a small strip in it left for wild birds. A hare jumped up with its bluish bottom. Fiona says they are bigger than our hares, but I'm not so sure.

An old pumping station lay rotting on the ground, and a surprised sheep did not expect me to creep up on it. Fieldfares and skylarks flew about as well as some other smaller birds.

KILCHOMAN MILITARY CEMETERY

'IN MEMORY OF THOSE WHO DIED FOR OUR FREEDOM
IN THE 1914-1918 AND 1939-1945 WARS.'

'Why do they call it the Great War?'

These graves look out to the sea like so many on Islay and around Scotland. They're all very well looked after by the War Graves Association. We all have a lot to be thankful for.

There was a flock of feral pigeons flying about, and Rohaise's ponies were enjoying their winter break grazing in the fields. I walked back to Rockside along the road and saw loads of chaffinches feeding on the teasel; what a magical sight.

Rockside Farm drive gateway is famous for its whale vertebra and jawbone found in about 1850.

Mark told me that otters are as bad as foxes and take ducks and pheasant chicks. He also explained how Islay fields had been drained at four to five feet apart, mainly by soldiers after the First World War; the Irish had helped, too. Some drains were horseshoe shaped and placed on a board – the deepest were six feet down.

The last time I was up here, seventeen years ago, farmers had had enough. The geese had caused so much damage eating all the livestock grass and devastating cereal crops and they needed to control them but some species were protected. Now farmers and conservationists have come together. The farmers are compensated for giving the geese 'bed and breakfast' for the winter months and everybody seems happy, including the geese. Compensation of up to a million pounds is divided between the farmers.

The goose population has increased from twenty thousand to eighty thousand over the years, and the better the grass the fatter they go back to Greenland and the more chicks they have. Even some of the brent geese are nesting on the island. This has never happened before. Maybe global warming is coming to Islay.

They have about sixty inches of rain here each year but it depends on where you are on the island.

All the family work together and today they are all dressed in white, cutting up meat, and vacuum packing it ready to export to upmarket restaurants in London.

Farming up here is tough and you have to know how to add value. When I asked Chloe if she loved Islay or hated it she said, 'A bit of both.'

Mark and Rohaise have a share in the company that has rented some of the buildings to Kilchoman whisky. Mark said there were several shareholders, then showed me round and explained the manufacturing process, which was rather similar to making petrol.

The wish was to be self-sufficient and to use his malting barley, with the residue being fed to the cows and the surplus liquid sprayed on the fields as it has nutritional value.

The distillery has a shop and a café which at this time of year is sometimes closed. However, in summer the farm is swarming with people and Mark has to be ever vigilant about safety issues.

Back at Loch Gorm the plumbers were just about to go home. More plaster had fallen into the porch. Fiona sent me up to the village shop to buy some food for the night.

ISLAY TO GLASGOW

For the first time I had a fairly good night's sleep and managed to creep into Fiona's room twice to use the loo. She said she pretended to be asleep.

The builders were back with the radio full blast. Fiona was afraid that the Polish builders had done a bunk as their tools had gone. She tried to stop a couple of cheques but the big one had been cleared. In no time at all, the entire island knew about it. (However, they ended up finishing the work and everybody was happy.)

The whisky sample from Mark's distillery was only 68% alcohol.

After a lazy morning Fiona took me for a drive down to Port Charlotte and Loch Gorm villages. Every other builder's van we stopped and talked to. One gardener person asked Fiona if she had any work as he was a bit short. She gave him the job of replacing the wire in the boundary wall. She pointed out all the places which were either owned by her mother, or Gavin, or which used to belong to them. 'That was ours and it broke mum's heart when we sold it.'

We went past a farmyard with a curved outbuilding which used to belong to Fiona's family, too. A car stopped and it was Fiona's friend from the post office and we were invited in for tea.

Another van stopped and it was a carpet layer with a young lad. They were trying to pair Fiona up for the Christmas dance!

I had to stop at the distillery to buy some whisky to take back with me. I was the only customer all day and was served by a very pretty girl. It was now late afternoon and I tried to bargain.

She said, 'You won't get anything for nothing and we'll even have your shirt buttons if necessary.'

I told her she was now talking my sort of language.

The three bottles of whisky had seriously overfilled my rucksack.

During the drive back to the airport Fiona was on the phone the whole time and looking out of the window. With one hand on the steering wheel she was fluffing up her hair and wasn't wearing a seat belt. *'If I mention anything I'm told I'm an old woman or a wanker!'*

We checked in 'Heathrow style'. Fiona was giving me a daggers look because I asked if I could be upgraded to 'Club Class' for the twenty-five minute flight. She said she 'had to come here again'. *'Snotty little madam!'*

My boots were taken off as the security check was the same as at big airports.

We were called through to the departure lounge and I said goodbye to dear Miss Doyle and boarded the plane. We had a very pretty stewardess and our ten passengers were so quiet that I mentioned it to her. She told me to wait until the plane started up and how right she was, as it was certainly a noisy little bugger. With the wind up her jumper I was amazed how quickly we were over Glasgow. It was a clear bright night and you could see for miles.

Now several years on from my visit to Islay, Fiona's guest house is up and running and has the best reputation for food and hospitality on the island and is well worth a visit.

GLASGOW CENTRAL

I wandered about for a while and saw a middle-aged Asian chatting up a blonde Glaswegian prostitute. I found my station, checked that I'd got the time right and then went to find a place to eat as I had three or four hours to kill.

I saw another Bella Italiana restaurant and I gave it a miss. I wandered into the £100 per night Quality Hotel in the station. It was a huge old hotel that had a wide staircase with low steps – a real old Victorian place. A young, good-looking Greek girl showed me round and told me I could have a meal for £12.95 for one course or £14.95 for two.

A man behind me was sitting having his meal and asked if I would like to join him. As we were both alone I did.

Gordon had arrived on a steam train and been on it for five hours. I imagine he was going to stay in the hotel. He told me he used to run the South-East line and wanted to know what I was up to. We didn't talk for long as he was tired and went to bed. He left his jacket behind, but then came back for it. He had a quiet air about him and I got the impression that he was quite an important man.

I asked the Greek girl how long she had been over here and she said about three years. I asked her what she liked about the UK and she said the best and worst things were the people.

I had a chat with a man selling *The Big Issue*. He told me that he paid 50p for each copy and sold them for £1.50. He was pleased that someone had taken the trouble to talk to him and asked me where I came from and whether there were gangs in Kent. I told him that we probably did have them but I didn't know of any. He said it wasn't safe to walk in the Glasgow streets at night.

The station was another huge construction of rivets and RSJs and it was so spotless that you could've eaten off the floor.

I was allowed on the train early and the ticket collector told me that my ticket was first class.

The train was very clean and as I walked past one carriage it looked brand new. Later I found out it was the Royal Carriage.

It was a luxury not having to share and I could spread out, and do what I wanted when I wanted. I went straight to bed and catnapped for about an hour and then went to the restaurant. Here everyone called me 'sir' and I liked it! I felt I was quite an important little man!

I started writing up *Walkabout* at a small table. Some Scottish businessmen were doing some serious drinking and the man opposite looked like a slimy bit of work. He was on the phone even at 1.30am. I heard him say, 'Well, I don't want to walk away with nothing.' I went to bed.

By 1.45am we were in Carlisle and I slid my little blind aside to see what was happening. It seemed that soon afterwards there was a knock at the door to say that breakfast was being served.

As I got off the train at 6.30am, loaded down with my whisky, I staggered onto the Euston platform, half falling over. I shook my head and said, 'Good morning' to someone. It turned out to be Princess Anne with her bodyguard and apparently she'd been in the Royal Carriage.

The bodyguard said something but I don't remember what. Princess Anne smiled as if to say, 'Who is this idiot?'

I fell asleep on the train back to Lenham and dreamed about HRH.

All night long she kept knocking on my door.

I said, 'Go away, I am too poor,'

But she kept coming back for more.

Bang, Bang, Bang,

'Don't you realise I am Royalty?'

I said, 'Yes, but I got loyalty.'

Bang, Bang, Bang,

'I will offer you a salary.'

I said, 'Why don't you fuck off?

I am going back to Valerie.'

I said to Valerie, 'It's hard to sleep with you when I've slept with Royalty!'

CHAPTER SIX

Glasgow to Thurso

It was exactly a year ago since ending the 'walkabout' in Glasgow and it was time to get back up there. In the meantime I had been to Africa, and had had a trip from Moscow to Beijing mainly by train. It had been an interesting summer.

I caught the train to London and then took the sleeper to Glasgow. In the bar at the station I was asked to a wedding in Lahore, and I was also asked to pay the fare of a hard-looking young girl, to get her home. I declined both.

The old boy serving in the carriage was the same man as on the train when I came down last time. I told him about Princess Anne and he said that she often uses the train. I slept well with all my clothes on as I only found the heater control at the end of the journey. I found the sink as well.

I opened the curtains and it was just getting light and the station sign said: 'Welcome to Motherwell.'

There was a knock on the door and coffee and three sweet buns were served. The buns were fed to the pigeons in St George's Square later on.

On arriving at Glasgow I gave the conductor a tip and thought he might give me a nice compartment on the way back – but, alas, it didn't work out like that.

I asked about going to Mallaig the next day and was told that the train would leave at 8.21am from Queen's Station up the road, so I went there to familiarise myself with the area.

I asked at Buchanan bus station which was the best service for the west coast and got two different answers from two different people. The station has a great bronze of two young people embracing each other. I thought how right that seemed. I asked the conductor what was the most deprived part of Glasgow and he told me it was Possilpark.

'Take the 54/75 bus in Hope Road if you want a really dodgy area.'

When I got out there I didn't think it was that bad and thought he was being a bit hard on them.

I watched a mother and toddler walking along and she didn't interact with the child at all, which seemed rather sad.

RUCHILL HOSPITAL

I could not believe what I saw on a hill in amongst the modern developments. It was an old Victorian fever hospital with an amazing tower. So I got off the bus and made my way to see it.

'Excuse me, can you tell me what that building is?'

'Dunno.'

It was a strange place to get to with buildings all around, and trying to find access wasn't easy. I asked another lady about it and she was pleased to tell me.

'Aye, that tall tower is the water tower. The place was closed down about ten years ago. It suffered a lot of vandalism but has security on site now. It's an old fever hospital. You can walk round the fence.'

I walked to the entrance. High security gates prevented access, so I climbed through someone's garden and jumped over a wall. Hey presto! I was in the grounds.

Ruchill Hospital was opened in 1900 as a Glasgow Corporation Infectious Diseases Hospital. It initially had four hundred and forty beds and by 1915 two hundred and seventy-two beds had been added for tuberculosis patients. It had one hundred beds when it was absorbed into the NHS in 1948. After 1960 young chronically sick, geriatric and psychiatric patients were catered for as the numbers suffering with tuberculosis fell. The hospital closed in 1998.

The area around here has been characterised by a high degree of deprivation and social problems. However, from the 1990s much of the poor building stock was cleared to be replaced by newly-built housing association and owner-occupied homes, improving much of the area's character.

The two gatehouses had been stripped of their slates. *'Wow! I'm enjoying this. What a wonderful age the Victorian building era was.'*

The centrepiece was the 165ft water tower, which was required because of the height of the site.

I walked across the waste ground in front of the building, but I had to be careful of the holes that were appearing. I couldn't believe what I was seeing and I was clicking away with my camera. I saw a security guard outside a Portakabin and avoided him and his big fat gut.

On the way out I saw a man from the inside opening the gates and was tempted to go out with him, but I didn't want a confrontation so I decided to go out again through the garden.

A man nearly jumped out of his skin when I said, 'Good morning – lovely hospital!' He talked about it with pride and was so pleased that someone had actually stopped and spoken to him.

It was now 10.00am and time for breakfast. The place I went to was run by two keen, smoking girls, but it was very cheap and very clean.

'Fried breakfast with sausages and bacon well done, please.'

'Give us a couple of minutes. No problem.'

I had bacon, sausage, black pudding, potato, beans and fried tomato, and all for £2.

Kevin was waiting for his takeaway. He chatted to me with a strong Scottish accent, which was hard to understand. He told me how the money he was earning wasn't good. He was helping to put cheap kitchens into council houses and sneered at the tenants.

I told the girls what a great café they had and carried on my way. I caught the bus back into town and tried to find the tourist information office, which nearly walked me off my feet. Things don't seem to be that well sign-posted here and I couldn't find the bus station, or the tourist office, but did find the Remembrance Day ceremony in St George's Square. It annoyed me that young people walking through the square weren't buying poppies and avoided the soldiers who were selling them. *'You lazy little f--kers. You wouldn't be here if it wasn't for them."* I put £10 in the pot.

At last I found the tourist office. I booked in on the open-top bus and it was just leaving at the other end of the square, so I ran.

This really was a good way to get around and learn about the area. Now I know why all the hotels were booked – there was a big football match going on between Lisbon and Celtic. All the fans were out and they didn't like it when I told them I thought they were from Spain.

There was some really beautiful architecture in Glasgow and it was clean and free from beggars.

Glasgow has a population of six hundred thousand.

The man on the bus gave us a full history. 'Here was the last public execution in 1845.'

The cleaners were clearing up after the firework display in Green Park. There was a huge greenhouse and it seems that the architects really do like their glass up here. We passed Lord Nelson's Column and Trongate Tower. The tower was where they kept an eye on weights and measures. We also passed a Victorian bridge.

GLENLEE TALL SHIP

I jumped off the bus and could've spent half a day here.

The ship was built in 1896 and had five thousand working days before it finished in 1922. She transported coal from South Wales, lumber from the Pacific ports, nitrates and guano from South America and also grain from South Australia. She wasn't the fastest ship in the world but they didn't have to lose time taking on coal, as the steamers did.

Jim was the maintenance man on the ship and I asked him what the biggest problem was. He said it was leaks from the wooden top-deck floor. Although it had been renewed it didn't get enough sea water to keep it watertight.

When she was first launched they coated the wooden supports with soap and tallow to assist smooth entry into the Clyde.

Shipbuilding really took off in Scotland with the outbreak of the War of Independence in 1776, in America. It prevented ships being purchased from the States. The American Civil War created a blockade so the faster the ships, the better. We would nip in with a load of guns and come out with cotton.

At its peak there were seventeen shipyards, employing seventeen thousand men and some boys.

THE UNIVERSITY OF GLASGOW

I couldn't pass this great building without getting off and having a look. I don't know if it said that visitors were welcome, but I was here and wandering around with hundreds of young graduates. I came across a lady with some others setting up some GPS equipment and being a nosy-parker I wanted to know what was happening. The lady said they were doing a PhD.

KELVINGROVE ART GALLERY AND MUSEUM

I passed these and another 'out-of-this-world' building but hadn't got the energy to go in.

When I realised the bus was going right past my hotel I got him to drop me off. I was just about ready for the Devoncove Hotel, and although it was a bit early I could have a wash and rest my poor feet. It was just as well that I'd brought the paperwork with me as I'd booked online and they weren't a hundred percent sure about my booking, but no problems. The whole of Poland seemed to work here. I went back into town and bought a new pair of trousers in Debenhams, served by a beautiful lady from Algeria.

The hotel had given me the names of four places to eat and I made the mistake of going to one nearby.

It was quite smart, with a very polite owner and waiter, but horrible food. For a starter I had grilled cheese and salad. The cheese was like rubber and the salad was plain. The house wine was very ordinary. I then had lamb cutlets, which were overcooked and resembled an old boot. The only thing they didn't mess up was the potatoes. *'How can people mess up good food?'* I didn't pay for service. I told the man on the cash desk that if the chef worked for me I would sack him. He gulped and said nothing.

GLASGOW TO THE ISLE OF SKYE

Breakfast was another plain affair and it was good to get out of this place. I didn't want to get lost going to Queen's Station so I took a taxi. The driver was a cheerful man who wanted to know what I thought of Glasgow. He'd lived there all his life.

Queen's Street Station was inhabited by tidy people coming in to work. The station was tidy, too, with an efficient looking station master. He was an old boy who obviously took great pride in his workplace.

I bought my £24.70 ticket to Mallaig and wrote *Walkabout* sitting outside a Burger King place.

Bang on time at 8.21am the train pulled out for an interesting journey. It was a four-carriage train and it split at Crianlarich. There was hardly a soul on it, so I had a table and four seats in a warm and clean train with pleasant staff. I could sit here and read, write my *Walkabout*, sleep, eat and drink and take pictures.

We passed loads of stations and it was uplifting to be getting out of Glasgow. Slowly the character of the passengers changed from business people to tourists. The tourists were mainly grey-haired walking types and wrinkly. Just like me, I suppose.

The scenery was mainly moorland and forests. The Grampian Mountains were pure beauty.

We were now down to two carriages. We'd been lucky with the weather and the rain and wind that was forecast hadn't arrived.

BSW KILN DRIED TIMBER

The timber was all stacked up alongside or outside the huge factory near Fort William. I was watching a man load timber from a lorry onto the train using a hydraulic lift. It made the job look easy, with just a tap here and there and it was all in place. I was thinking that it was quite a responsible job because if a tree fell off it could derail a train.

We arrived at Fort William at midday and more walkers got on. Although it was only 12.30pm the sun was low and made it difficult to see out of the left hand side.

We arrived at Mallaig at 1.30pm. I'd seen five hours of amazing countryside and what a scenic morning. Who needs to travel all over the world when you have this on your doorstep?

An hour and a half later the mist had come down and it didn't look so pretty.

I went down to the ferry terminal and booked all my island tickets. Caledonian run a very smart enterprise and the ferries were as clean as the booking office. The ferry would leave at 4pm, so I went and had some lunch – a bowl of soup – in the fish market restaurant.

It was a funny little place, but no doubt it had a thriving fishing industry.

I asked, 'Is this the quiet time?'

'Aye, it's dead.'

'Have you had a good summer?'

'Very good.'

'Do you close for the winter?'

'Only three weeks in January, aye, and I need the break.'

I walked around and saw some ship repairing going on. The docks were full of boats, and it looked a hard old life.

There was an ice factory on the jetty and a man repairing nets. *'I'd get in a terrible muddle with all those nets.'* The Heritage shop was shut and the pub was being renovated, so I went back to the ferry and carried on with *Walkabout*.

A load of very smart shooters wearing all the right gear came off the ferry. They'd been to Muck, shooting geese and ducks. They really seemed to have enjoyed themselves and all looked very determined. I was amazed at how clean their gear was. They told me that they had a long journey in front of them going back to North Yorkshire, but it had been a real experience for them. And they really didn't like talking to a cocky little hitchhiker. *'Fuck you, too!'* as they sped off in their Range Rovers.

MALLAIG TO THE ISLE OF SKYE

Only four cars were loaded onto the ferry and they had to reverse on. Half an hour later I was waiting for a bus on Skye.

'Where do you want to go, mate?'

'I haven't a clue, but somewhere where there are hotels.'

'Aye, Crawford.'

I couldn't find Crawford on the map then suddenly found Broadford, not Crawford.

The bus driver stopped in a village and got out for a fag and I found him for a chat.

'Can I get a bus to take me round the island?'

'Don't know. All the timetables have been changed for the winter. You'll have to start early and go with the schoolchildren. What kind of hotel do you want?'

'Neither a palace nor a doghouse!' I replied.

I got dropped off outside the pub and didn't see the 'No vacancies' sign in the window. I went in and had a beer and thought that although I'd said I didn't want a doghouse it was now 5pm. There were about five locals drinking. They were so inbred that I couldn't even say hello. The publican struggled as well.

'It always amuses me how the local drinkers sit on the bar stools as though they're their own thrones and talk about fuck all, all evening.'

I never feel comfortable asking about accommodation in front of drinkers. I suppose I'm frightened of rejection.

The ladies in the kitchen seemed more human than the men and I wondered what they thought of those jerks. I was quite pleased, in a way, when the man said they had no rooms. I said I might come back for a meal. He told me it might be a bit noisy as there was a big match that night: Rangers v Barcelona. I told him that that wouldn't matter as it was a pub, not a crematorium.

I started walking into town. It was dark and raining and seemed dead.

A taxi pulled out of a housing estate and gave me a lift. I asked him if he was born here.

'Nay.'

Then I never did understand where he came from. He said he'd worked with the mentally handicapped for twenty-seven years. He looked a kindly old boy.

He dropped me off at the very smart-looking Broadford Hotel. JA thought this looked a bit smart for him.

When they found the manager he said it was normally £75 but he could offer £65.

I said, ' How about £50?'

'I don't go no lower.'

I said, 'I don't go higher,' and walked out. *What a dick to turn down £50.*

I found another B&B. The lady opened the door and offered me a room for £35.

'Have you had a busy summer?'

'We don't know yet, as we've only been here a year.'

'Have you enjoyed it?'

'Yes, we have. Busy, yes, but we have enjoyed it. What time do you want breakfast?' She asked if I wanted cereal or porridge, and did I want a real breakfast, and so on and so on.

Then I was shown the complexities of the room as if I was running a power station.

INSTRUCTIONS

1. Don't touch that switch or you'll have a cold shower.
2. Please fill in the form.
3. What to do if you are cold.
4. Where the keys to the front door are and how to shut the front door.

5. Touch lamp, which is apparently so technical as to be beyond the understanding of the human brain: one touch to dim, two to brighten, three to have full brightness, and four to turn off.

'Now if you get cold...' *'Please, spare me!'*

GUEST NOTICE

'EVERY DAY MILLIONS OF TOWELS ARE WASTED IN HOTELS AND GUEST HOUSES AROUND THE WORLD UNNECESSARILY. IF YOU WOULD LIKE TO BE ENVIRONMENTALLY FRIENDLY, PLEASE ADOPT THE FOLLOWING PROCEDURE - BY LEAVING YOUR TOWELS ON THE TOWEL RAIL YOU ARE LETTING US KNOW THAT YOU WOULD LIKE TO HAVE THEM CHANGED.

THANK YOU FOR YOUR CO-OPERATION.'

There were also low-energy light bulbs and a table lamp on each bedside table. I was told that one was unplugged so that our environmentally-aware friends didn't waste electricity.

I walked out and across the road to a recommended place to eat. It was good value. I ordered fish and chips and a pint of John Smith's and sat down in anticipation of another big match. A continuous stream of hardened smokers came out for their fix and then went back in to watch the game. An ignoramus stood in front of the screen blocking my view. I would've loved to have told him to fuck off, but I didn't.

I left the boring lot behind and went to bed. The view from my room was of a hideous building. *'Who could build something like this next to the sea?'*

I didn't sleep well and so wrote some more *Walkabout* in the middle of the night.

At breakfast I met Yosuke Shiozuka, a Japanese man, who was so refreshing after the deadheads of the night before. He was a young world traveller from Japan who lived in Tokyo and earned his living as a photographer for a magazine company. He said he liked travelling to Europe most of all, although when I asked him he told me that he'd also been to Cambodia twice, Vietnam and Bangkok. We enjoyed the shared experience of talking travel. He had been staggered by the cosmopolitan nature of London. 'It is good.' In Japan they don't like foreigners. He still expected London businessmen to be wearing bowler hats and was also surprised how few children there were at train stations.

Yosuke's face was a picture when his full English breakfast arrived! He got out his dented camera and clicked away.

When I got my map of Scotland out he was amazed at the size of it and out came the camera again. We talked about how expensive it was in the UK and he asked about the prices in Africa. I told him you could buy the whole country for a couple of hundred dollars!

By 8.40am I was on the road and walked for three and a quarter hours at a hundred steps each minute. I walked past a graveyard facing the loch and wrote down dozens of ages of people who were buried there; they ranged from thirty-one to ninety-nine, with the average age being sixty-nine. I was feeling good after that big breakfast. The cod liver oil pills must have been working.

The road was so busy and it was only in the evening that I realised that I was near the Kyle of Lochalsh and the bridge to the island. The traffic sped by. I ducked behind a tin shed to phone Mark to find out how the deal on the new tractor was progressing. He told me the figures and I said I was happy with that.

I came across an old iron bridge on the old road. One of the joys of walking is that you see so much more.

The forecast had been for rain and 80mph winds. I was making good progress in my wet-weather gear and had to put the hood up to keep the wind out of my ears. The only down point was that if I put my hands in my pockets to keep them warm the water ran down my sleeves straight into them.

By 10am I decided that if I was to get round the island I would need a lift so I started hitching selected vehicles. I couldn't get a lift even after about thirty-five cars and all the buses seemed to be going the other way. There was one with a blonde driver. I waved at her in case she came back the other way later.

Luib was another funny little hamlet with an old Bamford Trip Action Rake, which came from Utoxeter – patent number 135887! I stayed here for five minutes as there was room for the bus to pull in safely and the art of hitching is to find safe stopping places. I had just walked on fifty metres when the blonde bus driver came along, ignored me and roared past. *'Bitch!'* It didn't seem to be my lucky day, but that was soon to change.

Within a minute a huge Citylink bus, which I was convinced wouldn't stop for me, did. After three and a quarter hours of being on my feet I was ready for a seat.

I was to be taken to Portree Square.

MEET MRS HENSHAW

She was chatting away to the driver, talking nineteen to the dozen.

'Amazing hills,' I said.

'Aye,' said the driver.

'You born and bred on Skye?'

'No,' replied Mrs H, 'I come from Derbyshire, and before that Wales. I'm used to the hills. Came up here to be near my daughter; just the one.'

'Do you know how many people live on Skye?'

'No, you'll have to ask my son-in-law, he'd know. Terrible weather and they say it's only going to get worse. Don't know whether to go to the square tomorrow but I have to go to the post office and newsagent. It's definitely getting worse and all my flowers are black and frosted. In Wales we used to get snow, lots of it, aye.'

'Any grouse on Skye?' I asked.

'You'll have to ask my son-in-law. He knows all about that. Don't believe in rearing birds to shoot. Aye, it must be for the upper classes, I suppose.'

I said to her, 'We run a small shoot and it does help the smaller birds if you keep the vermin down and it helps the habitat in the woods.'

'Aye. Is this your first time on Skye?'

'Yeah, I've been to Islay.'

'I love Ireland!' *'You silly old ...!'* 'Family used to go there every year.'

'Dublin?'

She asked, 'Ever been to Donnelly?'

149

PORTREE SQUARE

An 'in-keeping' extension (vandals)

The planners and the architects have destroyed another ancient square by modifying it. This is a lovely old Scottish square now complete with three bus lanes and a large aluminium bus shelter. It has yellow lines for walkways and some really weird looking lamp posts. I wonder at times just where these educated idiots come from.

I went to go to the loo but didn't realise it was under reconstruction and a snotty builder said, 'And where do you think you're going?'

Funny attitude, but I laughed and walked off.

I had two and a half hours to fill before the next bus to Uig. I'd decided to stay another day here, or I wasn't going to see anything of Skye. The trouble was that the days were so short. Three hours walking might get me fit but I wouldn't see anything of Skye.

One surprising thing was that this small town had a really good outdoor clothes shop. They had a hat that I really wanted but I couldn't bring myself to pay £35 for it.

'Have you made a mistake with the price on this?'

'No.'

'Lot of money for a little hat.'

'It's waterproof.'

'So is a plastic bag,' I replied.

'Well, if you want to go around with a plastic bag on your head all day, that's fine. This is Gortex.'

The price of some of the coats like mine was extraordinary. One cost £225. When I saw that I couldn't even bring myself to make them an offer. No wonder the place was empty. Even a pair of gloves cost £17. I just walked away and wondered when they would go bust.

I went back to the bus station and it was incredible how many buses came and went. I'd hardly seen a bus all morning and now they were like flies.

'Is there a bus to Uig?'

'Do you want to go the long or the short way round?'

'The coastal route, please.'

'Then get the 57a at 3.25pm.'

The first stop was to pick up the schoolchildren, and yes, this was the school run and all eleven buses were parked outside the school. I was in the back with about thirty of them. Schoolchildren are the same the world over, noisy but a healthy looking lot, and in years to come there will be some pretty girls on Skye. The last thing they were interested in was the scenery and the bus had steamed up, but the reason for *me* being here was to see the countryside.

There are some unusual mountains; some are pointed such as you might see in Arizona and some have flat tops like a table.

When all the children got off I went and had a chat with the driver. He was an ex-lorry driver. All the drivers seemed to be sixty plus years old. I told him what a responsible job he had carting all these youngsters around.

It was now getting dark and I could just make out where they may have been peat cutting. I noticed how many people smoked up here. They could compete with Liverpool and Cornwall.

The bus driver slowed down as we passed some B&Bs. They didn't look very accommodating, with dark, empty streets and hardly a flicker of light.

We got to Uig pier and there was another B&B, but I couldn't stand the idea of being stuck here so he took me to the Hotel Uig. It turned out to be a good move.

At least there was some life here and it was run by a South African family, who'd moved from Durban about thirteen years ago.

'How much for a room for a poor man?'

'£40, including breakfast.'

'Would you take a bit less as it's the middle of winter?'

'I don't bargain.'

'OK, I'll take it!' (Remember, it was pitch black and I was in the middle of nowhere.)

I had a beer in the bar and then a wash up and then came down for dinner. The food was probably the best I've ever tasted.

Today I was to discover Skye. I decided to stay two nights as it was a nice hotel. I sat having breakfast and watched the only bus go flying past at 8.20am. I wondered how the day would turn out.

The furniture in the hotel was fairly basic and so were the pictures, but the fire kept the bar area warm. Bill used to be in IT and Penny ran a restaurant in South Africa. She had four children and he had three. When I told him that I had none he said that at times he wished he was the same.

Penny was a little worker and was looking forward to a winter break.

Today I was going to see the island and I couldn't fart about walking for three hours like I had the day before, so straightaway just after 9.00am I started hitching. It was strange because there were long periods with no traffic and then suddenly it got busy. Only when it's safe do I try to hitch.

JA'S GUIDE TO HITCHING

1. Never try to hitch in a dangerous place, such as on a bend or where there are fast cars, or one with loads of cars behind it, or one that's full!

2. If possible try to be in a position where the car can safely draw in.

3. Never try to hitch a lift with fast lorries, the Royal Mail, HGVs, ambulances, or dustcarts. They're not allowed to pick people up. Also don't try to stop young drivers with young passengers.

4. Never ask for a lift from people on a ferry, because you're putting them under unfair pressure, or at any other place such as a petrol station.

5. Always face the vehicle and SMILE. People want to see how ugly you are before stopping.

6. When a car stops, give them the option of opening the window first. Don't just open the door straightaway. Sometimes it's good to be on the driver's side before getting in, as it gives the driver longer to see who he's picking up. Keep smiling.

7. Be grateful, as it's a brave thing for any vehicle to stop and pick up a complete stranger.

8. Never get in a vehicle with muddy boots on and offer to take off any wet clothes.

9. Once in the car, the most important thing is to thank the driver very much for stopping. In fact, grovel and always remember that you are a walking beggar.

10. Once you've thanked the driver he/she usually likes you to put on your seat belt.

11. Be interesting/amusing. Never forget that he/she has stopped and you have an obligation to entertain. After you've finished thanking them, tell them where you're going and open the conversation. Tell them what a beautiful part of the world they live in. It relaxes them.

12. Talking. Don't hog the conversation. They have a story to tell as well.

13. After a few miles, tell them your name and ask their name. It puts them at ease.

14. Ask them if they've lived in the area all their lives and what they do for a living.

15. Ask about their car. Most people are proud of them.

16. Never get political or churchy (not for the first mile anyway!).

17. Vibes. Some don't want to talk, so be sensitive.

18. Always, even if they're smoking, ask if you can smoke. If they are smokers then offer them one as well.

19. Object of the exercise: to get from A to B and to make your driver pleased that he/she picked you up.

20. Always be aware of the potential dangers of hitching.

21. Never put your hand on the knee of a pretty girl wearing a mini-skirt! She might get the wrong idea!

22. Always refuse sex with pretty drivers. Valerie might not like it, especially if they're girls!

23. Money. This is difficult. If you've had a long lift, offer something towards the petrol. Most people won't accept, but it shows you're not all 'one way'.

24. Always shake hands when leaving and offer them a lift if ever they're in your area.

25. When leaving the car, think about giving them a card and an invitation to look you up (if you're happy with them). Give the impression you have made a friend.

I only had to wait thirty minutes for my first bus and yet again the driver was not the happiest man in the world, but at least he stopped.

These buses have plastic bags tied onto all the seats. It's a pity then, that people don't put their rubbish in them.

ANGUS: 1ST LIFT

After a few cars had gone past I got my first lift with Mr Angus Johnson. He was working as a cook on the Islay ferry. I asked him if he knew 'Chatter Box' (Fiona Doyle) and he said he would look out for her!

DONALD: 2ND LIFT

He was a retired PE teacher and had to retire early because of his knee. He had now had a replacement and was as good as new after years of pain – five years in fact. He was covered in grout as he had been tiling.

JILL: 3RD LIFT

Now Jill was not one to hang about and I soon got my seat belt on. She had a crutch lying near the gear lever, but I didn't ask what it was for.

She dropped me off outside the MacLeod graveyard where only MacLeods are allowed to be buried and no local riff-raff! It was a smart little graveyard, steeped in history and with a chapel without a roof.

I walked down into the hamlet of Dunvegan and found a 'fishing and shooting' shop and bought myself a hat for £4.20. It wasn't as smart as the other one for £30, but at least it was very warm and I was amazed at how soon the rest of my body warmed up once I'd put it on. I told the man about yesterday's cap and he said that the business was going under.

DUNVEGAN CASTLE

There was a smart woman taking the cash in this castle. I asked her if she thought I would pass as an OAP.

She said, 'No.' *'Hooray!'* She was the first person to call me a little liar.

Dunvegan has a family feel about it and John MacLeod still lives here, I think. They have one hundred thousand visitors each year. The whole place was well set out and didn't have all those old people sitting in every room making sure you weren't about to nick the family silver. There was a rhino horn in a cabinet; a horseman's sword with a bracket on it to put the reins through; and a dungeon with replica prisoners, with sound effects to match. It was all very effective.

ST KILDA

The population here fell from one hundred and eighty in 1697 to just thirty-seven in 1928. By then the population had asked the government if they could be resettled as they couldn't make a living; they were killing fulmars for their oil and for food. Finally, they were resettled in Argyllshire. After five hundred years of belonging to the MacLeod family, St Kilda was sold to the Marquess of Bute, who was an eminent ornithologist and when he died he left it to the National Trust.

Oats were the main crop and a little barley. Sheep and cows were milked for making cheese, and mutton was eaten in the winter, as well as sea-birds and their eggs. Puffins and geese were salted down for the winter months. Funnily enough, the islanders were not partial to fish and apart from a few soft potatoes, whatever they are, they had no vegetables. (Can you believe it – with sea all around them and they're not partial to fish!) The head of the gannet was used for mending shoes.

I left the castle at 1.00pm and left a note in the book saying: 'It has a human feel to it. Well done.'

I didn't want to go back the way I'd come so decided to hitch again. I wanted to go to Glendale and so started walking down the lonely road. I had a funny feeling I might end up in another Barrhill situation so I decided to do a U-turn and go back. It was getting dark at 2.10pm and I couldn't seem to get a lift, but it was my lucky day after all as another set of brake lights came on.

Glenda was a real lady and not a tiny woman in their three-door car, but she got out and clambered into the back. The car was covered in newspaper and was a bit of a mess. She was chatting away nineteen to the dozen. They had come from Cornwall twenty years ago, having sold their little end-of-terrace house and had bought a four-bedroom detached house with about an acre of land and five hundred trees. All was fine until a snotty English girl opened a riding school next door and spent all day shouting at clients. Then they got floodlights which shone into Ron and Glenda's house and they had to go out to get any peace.

She said, 'It can be windy here and it blew a house down the other year. Lots of people come up here to live and can't hack it. They sell their old house for half a million and get one here for about £130,000 and then can't cope.'

I thanked them for the lift and they left me at a junction that led to the moors. When I got out of the car I told Glenda that she was a real lady to have got into the back for me, but Ron was shaking his head as if to say, 'No she isn't!'

MR JOHN BEATON: 5TH LIFT

He was a real old farmer, shepherd's crook and all, and a lovely gentleman with an honest face. He was delighted when I asked, 'Are you a farmer?'

'Aye, I am. I'm only going a wee way.'

'That's fine by me.' His half a mile was, in fact, about two hundred metres! He wanted to know what I farmed and whether the foot and mouth outbreak had affected us. It was a shame we had to part so soon as I reckon we could have talked for a month.

MALCOLM: THE 6TH AND LAST LIFT OF THE DAY

When John dropped me off I saw it was eight miles to Portree and I was thinking that I really was in for another Barrhill. I really needed a lift and as luck would have it Malcolm gave me one all the way. His twin cab smelled of dogs and horses. He used to be a lorry driver and knew Ashford well. He didn't look like a lorry driver; more like a businessman.

He said that heating here was cheap and a peat cutter could get a licence for £5 per year and for £40 he could cut enough peat to last two years.

He kept horses and said you have to get the right breeds that don't get stuck in the bog. Galloways were the best. If you have the wrong type of horse it gets stuck in the bog and pulls its shoes off.

He said that there's a lot of resentment when southerners come up here and buy and build fancy homes.

On the bus back to Uig I had never heard such loud old women in my life. There was a young mum with her baby. She kept talking to the baby, either making it laugh or cry, and I reckoned she shouldn't own a dog, let alone have a baby. I helped an old lady off the bus and soon afterwards I was dropped off outside the hotel.

I had a shower which could have been tricky in a tiny unit. One minute the water was scalding hot and the next it was freezing. *'And why do they make shower bottoms so slippery?'*

Had an excellent meal and went to bed early.

ISLE OF SKYE TO NORTH UIST

The two guys at the hotel told me they were shooters. They also joined me on the ferry. They came from the Oxford area and both had their own shoots: 'Small and friendly, like.' They knew Uig Hotel well; they'd stayed at the hotel when it first opened and had been coming up here for three years. Bill and Wendy Pearce offered me a lift to the ferry in their £40,000 Mercedes.

We were driven from the terminal to the ferry in a minibus. It wouldn't have been a good idea to have breathalysed the driver. Christ, some of these guys really stink of booze and it was only early morning.

'Welcome aboard. This is your captain, Andy McKinley.'

First impressions are not always right in the morning. Ian had a bottle of beer in his hand and it was only 9am. He had a long whisky-ginger beard and he came up to me and said, 'How are you this morning?' He told me he was a crofter.

I said, 'I'm a farmer from Kent.'

He gave me a big healthy handshake, as though we were long-lost friends. I thought I'd got a right piss-head here, but I was wrong.

'I'm just here to get sheep, aye, and they cost a lot of money. I have bought back a black-faced ram, aye, and it cost me £600. I was lucky, aye.'

'Where is he then? I would have thought you would've had him on a lead!'

'Nay, he comes in a lorry with other sheep. You have to keep an eye on them for a start, aye, and keep them inside for a while to get over the ferry ride. You have to inject them against getting pneumonia.'

'I can see that, and you wouldn't want £600 of legs sticking in the air.'

'Don't like this SNP lot, aye, and I used to like Maggie Thatcher, but I be Labour myself. What buggered the Conservatives was the poll tax. No one liked it, but I thought it was spot on, aye, and if only they had waited a bit longer.'

'Are you a full-time crofter?' I asked.

'Oh nay, me main job is army computers.'

And there was I thinking I had a right dickhead, and it turns out that he has a very important job. I nearly fell off my seat with surprise.

'Did you see George Galloway on *Question Time* last night?'

'Och aye, he's a slimy bugger. I love that programme but people have more brains in the audience than the panel. What kind of farmer are you? Livestock, potatoes?'

'No, wheat and rape.'

'You must be making a fortune with the price of wheat. I feel sorry for the dairy farmers, aye, screwed up by the supermarkets.'

He told me the story about his neighbour who was a nun. She had also worked in some war zones: Bosnia, Serbia and Dafur, and was shocked by what humans could do to each other. One child had seen such terrible things that she became mute.

I left him having a big fry-up and a pint at 9.15am!

'Aye, I've enjoyed our conversation.'

Meet Angus, he was a fisherman – he mainly caught prawns – and he'd just come back from the Philippines with a new worker, who looked a hard-working sort of man and appeared slightly apprehensive. I hoped he would be treated well.

Young people don't want to go into the trawling industry; it's hard work.

Angus told me that there was a lot of paperwork in fishing today and many foreign boats in our seas. It seemed that factory ships were the thing of the future. He moaned about the price of diesel.

LOCHADDY

'Well, here we are. The Outer Hebrides!' I didn't even think of begging a lift and thought I'd be independent and not put people under pressure.

I saw an empty bus with no driver so I went to the checking-in office, but no one knew where he was.

I wandered about the place and photographed an old causeway for the cattle and sheep that ran from the market to the waiting ships. Duncan said it was to be pulled up soon for a new road.

'Anyone seen the driver?' I asked.

'Aye,' he said, 'I'm the driver and you can get into the wee bus. Just give the door a push. I'll be back later.'

I sat in the bus with the keys in it and it was a chance to catch up on *Walkabout*. I was a day

and a half behind and I don't like to be more than a day in arrears or it becomes hard work.

Duncan came back and told me that he was also a crofter, which seemed to be the case for everyone. He was no spring chicken being, in my estimation, nearer seventy than sixty-five.

Little did I know that I would spend the next six and a half hours with Duncan, going round the island. He went out of his way to be friendly.

They don't value old buildings up here and some lovely old stone houses had fallen into disrepair. In Kent they would be worth a fortune. And what do they do? They build a really ugly one next door and then the neighbour builds an even worse one to see if he can make it even uglier! These kind folk have no sense of taste in building at all.

I sat in the front of the bus and it was full of young people, ten to fifteen years old, and they were all going to the sports centre.

Everywhere you looked there was peat cutting, fish farming, new roads, Hebridean sheep, and an odd binder rusting away in the corner of a field.

Duncan told me that there used to be an RAF rocket base here and when the Cold War ended it all went quiet.

This was plover country and I had never seen so many. I saw some birdwatchers outside the hotel and they said that Uist had the biggest population of waders in Europe, if not the world. There were no foxes on the island and this must help. Skye was full of them. There were a few swans and the shooter told me that it was famous for the golden plover. The shooters were in the same hotel as me.

I had a bright young man sitting next to me. He was about sixteen and although his father was Dutch he'd been born on the island. His father was a vet but the boy wanted to be a surgeon and wanted to travel. I was sure he would succeed. I told him that in Kent all the vets were girls, because they work harder.

The next stop was to get diesel and Duncan pulled into an interesting bus depot. I asked him if he was putting the right colour diesel in.

'Och, aye.'

160

We started off again but didn't go far as we pulled into his farmyard. He disappeared and we sat there and sat there and I wondered if he was having his lunch or was in the loo.

I asked one of the ladies whether we might be asked in for lunch.

The farmyard was full of four wheel drive vehicles. In Kent these would've been stolen before you could blink.

After twenty minutes we were off again and all of a sudden Duncan said, ' Aye, I must just show you this.' We turned right onto a bumpy grass field and headed for the sea. I had never had a bus ride like this before! The old ladies had come alive and were chuckling away.

'Aye, this is the most westerly point in the UK.'

I took a photograph but stupidly forgot to get the bus in it.

This really was causeway country and it joined up all the little islands. We dropped the children off and Duncan gave a look as if to say, 'Got rid of them!'

The lady sitting next to me was a care worker and did night shifts. She told me she used to look after 'Old Seadog'.

'Who is he?' I asked.

'Seadog' was an old bachelor and grumpy with it. He disappeared without anyone knowing where, into the Merchant Navy. Twenty years later he turned up and had been round the world several times.

The care worker had looked after him whilst his house was being repaired and apparently he said to her, 'I've done without a woman for thirty-five years and I won't be needing one now!'

He was in the inn one night and someone had asked him if he would like a wee dram. 'Aye, a large whisky!' came the reply.

The band playing in the inn said to him that they doubted he had ever been off the island.

'Aye, I fell off the pier once when I was seven.'

Little did they know that he had travelled the world.

An alcoholic got on the bus with his boozy, smelly breath. It wasn't long before Duncan dropped him off at his home. He smelled of meths and when he staggered off the bus he said, 'Aye, I'll pay you when I come back.'

We never saw him again and the ladies chuckled once more.

Gaelic is the main language spoken around here and it's still spoken in schools and taught here. Duncan told me he speaks it most of the time. We stopped at Loch Baghasdail (also known as Lochboisdale) and the ladies got off and did some shopping whilst Duncan and I slipped down to the ferry. There were no passengers waiting.

Prince Charles had been known to come this way once or twice.

I bought a bottle of wine for Duncan for being kind. We picked up the ladies and we were off again. This time it was the butcher's shop and once more Duncan disappeared off for a cup of tea.

'You never want to be in a hurry in this part of the world.'

UGLY BUNGALOWS

'I cannot believe how the planners have let these people build such ugly bungalows in this area. For Christ's sake, they're scattered all over the place! They just look like gypsy homes and are in danger of mucking up this beautiful landscape.'

Duncan said they cost about £70,000. They seem to have no idea of doing renovation. Some of the dickheads even use red and blue tiles and they seem to be allowed to build anywhere. Maybe in this part of the world it is uneconomical to renovate.

Mamie and Agnes told me that there was a great community spirit here. They played bingo once a week and also whist. They had gone dancing, too, although Mamie didn't dance any more as she'd lost her husband many years ago. I told them not to get excited when I took my waterproof trousers off as I had another pair underneath.

All afternoon the bus kept stopping for shopping and even delivered cigarettes to someone. This really was a community bus.

Suddenly, Duncan said, 'That'll be £8, including your fare back to Lochmaddy.'

A young girl got on the bus and we started talking. She wanted to be a midwife and we chatted about where the name 'midwife' came from, but nobody knew. She was going do a four-year course in Inverness, starting in January. She was really looking forward to it. The fact that her aunt lived near the college meant that she could save on lodgings.

I couldn't help but notice the small size of the silage bales here. They were about the size of a television wrapped up; we also passed some round haystacks which I would've loved to have photographed as Duncan told me that not many people make them that way nowadays. As well as these I spotted the smallest football pitch I've ever seen.

Duncan said that the seaweed is composed of three kinds and is excellent for potatoes. We saw some when we went off-road and he said that it had been washed in the previous night.

On the return journey we picked the youngsters up again at the sports centre. They were in high spirits and started to rock the bus. Duncan told them to steady down. His old ticket machine just lay on the floor and he never really gave anyone a ticket. No doubt there was a system, but I didn't understand it. It was getting very hot and Duncan opened the door. One boy tried to open the roof vent but couldn't do so.

'Leave it alone.' Duncan told him.

I was amazed when one female parent came up the bus and started being abusive towards Duncan. *'Couldn't understand the language, except for the 'fuck' word.'*

'Duncan said, 'Aye.'

He was really getting some stick for not picking up the child, or for not bringing her cigarettes. I never could make out what it was all about. All he said was, 'Aye, aye, aye,' and when it was all over they were great friends!

I said goodbye to Duncan and gave him the bottle of wine and boarded the other bus. He was a remarkable man and I never did ask him what he'd done before he became a bus driver. He was a kind, worldly sort of man.

UIST TO HARRIS

At 8.00am the taxi arrived to take me to the ferry. The hotel was dead and I was glad I'd paid the bill the night before. The only people about were twitchers. The taxi driver was Alistair Ferguson from Alda's taxis. He told me that the population of North Uist was about seventeen hundred.

'Aye, you should see this place in the summer when all the heather is out.'

'What are the humps in the fields?'

'They're called runrigs, or lazy beds, for growing vegetables and they came about in the 1820s before the Highland Clearance Act which cleared all the crofters out.'

He was a bit weary as he'd been to a wedding the night before and had had a few. He rattled on about how many grandchildren he had. He was a large man and drove very slowly to the ferry whilst giving me a running commentary.

'See that island over there? A friend of mine lives there with his dog and comes over now and again in his boat. He's a real bachelor.'

Alistair stopped for a while for me to click away with my camera.

I asked, 'Why don't they repair that old house?'

'Aye, he's been offered £100,000 but he won't sell. See that island over there?

Prince Charles goes there for his holidays. That's a bonnie wee cottage over there.' *'Bloody ugly horrible thing!'* 'You should be here in the summer to see all the different purples of the heathers.'

'Are you local, Alistair?'

He said nothing for a while then, 'Aye, just earlier you asked if I'm local, and I am. I could trace my family back to 1300.' He laughed. 'Aye, you could say I'm local! A lot of people emigrated from here to Canada: boys as young as fourteen or fifteen and one even of eight, and when they asked their parents the reply was that it would mean one less mouth to feed. A few years ago a seventy-four-year-old came over and it turned out that he was the son of the eight-year-old migrant.'

Alistair told me the story about when the doctor had to do an emergency operation in a shed and they had to use the headlights of a car for light.

I took a picture of an 'Otter Crossing the Road' sign. Alistair pointed out a holiday home which was a boat.

The ferry was moored up and had to move half a mile to the jetty.

Alistair said, 'We have a wee bit of time, so I'll just take you down here.'

He poured out more history and the stories were so interesting, but I was breaking my neck trying to understand them because of his accent. He told me there are plans for a causeway to join Uist to Harris. The last estimate was for eighty-nine million pounds. 'Aye.'

HARRIS 'ERE WE COME!

I shook hands with Alistair and walked onto the ferry.

The ferry didn't hang about once I was aboard. I had my passport in my hands, but they were not amused.

There was no café on the ferry and I felt quite pleased with myself when I worked out how to use the coffee machine to get a mug of crappy coffee.

What a beautiful part of the world. One passenger was engrossed in his book and never looked up at all, whilst another went up on deck for a smoke. One hour later we arrived at Leverburgh on the Isle of Harris.

Today was Sunday and there wasn't one vehicle or person waiting for the return ferry trip. It was 9.45am and the place was dead. It was really eerie.

I met my first friend on Harris. His name was Fred; a sheep with great big horns.

LEVERBURGH TO TARBERT

There was a nice smell of burning peat as I walked through the village and there was a tiny building for the fire service. A car went by and the driver put his hand up to the common hiker.

The first vehicle I hitched stopped and gave me a lift. It was a twin cab pick-up. Hugh was a lovely, quiet, red-faced crofter and it took some time to get some humour out of him, but I got there in the end.

'Lovely part of the world you have here.'

'Aye.'

'Are you a born and bred Harris man?'

'Aye.'

'Do you ever get off the island?'

'Nay, there be no need.'

He said that youngsters don't want the crofting jobs nowadays. Hugh just keeps cattle and the hay costs £4 per bale or £150 per ton.

'You have to pay the ferry chaps as all the fodder is brought in by boat because the weather is against you making your own silage.' He told me he speaks Gaelic all the time.

We passed a pretty bay with houses that had turf on their roofs.

'Holiday homes?'

'Aye, cost £1000 per week.'

'If you had a few of them you wouldn't need to keep cattle.'

'Aye.'

'You get some big old crows up here.'

'Aye, ravens they are. I have to drop you off here.'

We shook hands and said goodbye. I wondered if the likes of Hugh were a dying breed.

At the bus stop there were just two sheep and me waiting. *'Idiots, buses don't run on Sundays!'*

As I went north it got colder and there was snow on the hills. There were steel pots lying everywhere that were used as weights to keep the fishing nets on the seabed.

This place must be very colourful in the summer as the knapweed heads blow in the wind.

Whilst walking I kept thinking that I should've spent more time in Uist, but getting the balance of how long you spend in any one place is never easy.

MEET MARIE AND GORDON

Once again the first vehicle I hitched gave me a lift. It was my first motorhome lift. They'd moved here from Yorkshire and had fallen in love with the place whilst on holiday. It was the beaches that did it for Marie. Gordon had been a pen-pusher for the local council and the pressure of work had got to him. He seemed to spend all his time doing other people's work. Now he had left all the pressure behind and they both worked in the Harris Hotel; he on maintenance with Marie as a housekeeper. She did all the bed changing, and room cleaning.

'I hate changing beds,' I said.

'Can't be fussy here. After all, I have got a job.'

The vehicle was the second they had had, having run the first one into the ground.

They had the weekends off. They pointed out the rocky landscape to me and it reminded me of the Ethiopian mountains. The film *2001* was filmed here.

'We never give lifts on the mainland, you know.'

We went through Leacainn. I noticed that up here the dogs don't bark at you and are friendly.

I asked them how much it would cost to stay the night at the Harris Hotel, but they didn't know.

TARBERT

I was going to go to Stornoway but I changed my plans and stayed here. It was the right move. Marie and Gordon said that there were not many places to eat or stay at and they were right.

I said goodbye to them and booked in.

Have you ever had the feeling that a whole hotel has been kept open just for you? I now had.

A cheerful receptionist took me up to a tastefully decorated, lovely room.

I had a bowl of soup and then went out to explore the area. I saw so many beautiful things as well as bad planning issues.

I had William, my brother, on the phone about farming matters. 'Where are you? John o' Groats yet?'

'No, Tarbert.'

'All interbred are they?'

'No, it's a very interesting part of the world.' *'I'm really not enjoying this conversation with William!'*

I also lost my mobile after that conversation.

I looked down and saw a man touching up a Mercedes with a paint brush. I also saw a dog kennel made out of a thousand-litre plastic spray container.

I went off-road and found the sea. This was turning into an amazing walk; the different types of seaweed and the various colours of the washed rocks with all kinds of shells clinging to them. *'Why are there no wading birds hacking them off?'*

I walked past the houses on this little peninsula and it seemed as though the Black Death had arrived as there was no one around. They definitely don't do gardens here.

I decided to cut across the fields and didn't realise how wet they were. It reminded me of walking in Cambodia. *'Am I going to walk on a landmine, or will I sink into a bog never to be seen again?'*

Having lived in a well-drained area in Kent, I find it hard to believe that here the water just doesn't run downhill. There are some really good examples of lazy beds here.

DRIFTWOOD AND RUBBISH ON THE SEASHORE

They're a lazy lot of bastards here and everywhere you go there's rubbish. The houses are just shit-holes and now there's mainly fishermen's rubbish, including a bottle that has been pissed in and thrown overboard.

Other rubbish includes nets, ropes, floats, cigarette lighters and bottles. I could spend a holiday up here just picking it up. Brandy and whisky bottles litter the roadsides.

I came across a really lovely old house that was falling down. In the garden were two Highland cattle that weren't worried by me one little bit. I was clicking away at all angles and hoped the pictures would come out.

The inside walls of the house still had some wooden panelling right up against the stonework, with no insulation. The cattle were using the building as a shelter and yet there was a really ugly new house just a hundred metres away.

I'd only just realised that Harris Tweed comes from here! *'Thicko!'*

I had the island and the hotel to myself. I did my 'poor man' act at the hotel and got a bargain. In the Harris Hotel I had supper served by a very pleasant girl, but I was irritated by another couple who whispered to each other all evening. I went into the drawing room to write *Walkabout*.

TARBERT TO STORNOWAY

Next morning I had my breakfast served by a young, tall blonde who really wanted to be anywhere but serving me. It was a healthy breakfast of black pudding, bacon and sausage! Whilst I was having breakfast the only bus to pass for the next five years went by!

A sign in the hotel said: 'Please do not remove the Hebridean liquid soap pumps, as we fill them each day. Thank you!'

I walked out of town and the first vehicle I hitched, stopped. I have no idea who it was as he had such a strong Scottish accent that I had a job to understand him. Let's call him Jim. He worked in the Scaladale centre for outdoor pursuits – rock climbing and sea caving were the most popular things. He told me that Lewis was owned by the community and pointed out a small island in a loch where some people were buried.

The next car I hitched also stopped and it was an interesting lift.

MEET MR DONALD MACKAY

He was a retired seaman and seven out of ten men living on Lewis were seamen as well. He was seventy-five years old and drove fairly fast.

'Nice part of the world you have here,' I said.

'Aye.'

'Are you retired?'

'Nay, I go fishing with my boy. He's in the fishing business, aye. Got to keep going!'

'What's the best place you've been to?'

'Aye, Vancouver Island.'

'And the worst?'

'The Philippines and Borneo. Used to go there for wood, aye, and sailed right into the woods and loaded up.'

'The worst moments?'

'The workers in Borneo would shit all over the deck when loading the ship. Aye, it was awful. We had to go to the hospital with dysentery, aye. And another job was to take the army out of Jordan. We had to load all the tanks; we put a wooden floor on the top and then another layer on top of that – Land Rovers, as well. When we got to Portsmouth they scrapped the lot. Some of the Land Rovers were brand new.'

'Why did they scrap them?'

'Aye, I wish I knew meself.'

One night in Bangkok the captain wouldn't allow any women on board and my job was to guard the gangway. Well, I went off to the toilet and when I came back they were trying to get on board. So I went round to the other side of the ship and there was a boat full of them trying to climb up the other side. I couldn't look after both sides. Och, aye.

Another time we docked somewhere and there was a group of Japanese girls cleaning the deck. By gum, they could work and the decks were bleach-white, yeah, and you couldn't talk to them and they wouldn't talk to you. I was in North Korea as well.'

170

'Pretty cold up there isn't it?' I asked.

'Aye, you're nearly opposite Siberia. I saw the injured of Hiroshima and it was dreadful.'

I tried to get him to elaborate but he wouldn't.

Another job he'd done was to lift the sunken ships in the Suez Canal. They had heavy-lifting boats and they refloated the ships. He'd been round the Cape a couple of times and I asked him if the weather was rough. He said it depended on what time of year you went. He'd also been through the Panama Canal a few times.

He didn't hang around in his car and was complaining about the lady driver in front.

'Donald, you should get to write all this down. It's a story that shouldn't be lost.'

I went to the café for a hot chocolate and to write down Donald's story.

There were some funny people around and that included me! They had big heads and some were very white and small, some were tall, some were skinny and some were fat.

I took my map out to get my bearings and it was then that I realised I'd lost my phone.

STORNOWAY TO THE BUTT OF LEWIS

Once we were out of town the countryside opened up. It was brown and wild, just like the Falklands. Peat is the name of the game here and everywhere you looked great slabs had been removed but nature had done her best to cover the scars. Not much peat is taken now and one man told me that it was because people are too lazy. It's all coal and gas and oil nowadays.

Once more there was a humble jumble of houses with the old ones in their glory being allowed to fall down and beside them were the really ugly new ones. Some of the smallest houses I've ever seen stuck out looking lonely on the moor. Maybe they were old crofts or maybe just shelters for the peat cutters.

The sheep were sheltering from the wind all in a line like a toy farm.

The further north we went the older and more miserable the bus drivers became, and the broader the accent – I couldn't understand what they were saying. This one looked like he enjoyed his cigarettes and had a wrinkly old skin.

It seemed like the middle of nowhere when the driver told me to get off. The bus shelter was shaped like a fan so that you could get shelter from the wind whatever the direction.

The whole countryside is divided up into fenced off strips about twenty-four metres wide; amazing. Some have sheep in them and some fences need repairing, but in general they're not in bad shape. One man told me that he was paid more not to graze his sheep, but to give the land over to the corncrakes for nesting and early cover.

I was at the Butt of Lewis and apart from a couple of people the place was mine. *'Wow, what a sight – The Atlantic Ocean!'*

I walked down to a small narrow cove to where a concrete ramp takes the boats. What a weird feeling; the waves seemed bigger than I was and I got the feeling that one would take me out to sea. I scratched my name and the date in the sand.

I found a little hut and it was, like all the buildings here, full of car engines and galvanised oil drums. The scrap men would have a field day here.

The lighthouse was to my left and later that day I read about some young men who had been playing football and one had fallen over the cliff and died.

ST MOLUAG'S CHURCH

My 'walkabout' never ceases to amaze me. I didn't take the easy way to the church and went over countless fences, but it was really worth it. The old collection box was out of this world and I was quite shocked that the door was open. I was told that they have a service once a month.

On the notice board was a message: 'Please pray for my son-in-law who is not well and going through a bad time – Sandra Ferguson.'

I left a note saying: 'Thank you for letting me travel the world, and for all who gave their lives for our freedom. Please don't let these beautiful places fall down.'

For the first time I saw swedes and turnips growing. I would have thought that this soil would grow anything with the right trace elements.

There was a sandy football pitch nearby which was full of rabbits and they were nearly tame.

People seemed not so keen to pick me up. I passed Ness Football and Social Club. I kept seeing redwings and snipe whizzing over me. In fact there was a field full of redwings with their ears to the ground.

As I went through the hamlet of Lional a collie dog came up to a gate and as I was talking to it the owner came to the door to see what all the fuss was about.

I popped into the local museum and met Murdo and Mary.

'Would you like a cup of tea?'

'No, thanks.'

Murdo was a serious sort of man with thick black hair. He taught singing and dancing within the community, but it was hard work getting the young away from the television. He told me that most Harris Tweed was made on Lewis. He asked me what I thought of the place. In the nicest possible way I did mention to him about the houses and why they were letting the old ones fall down. I could see that he was getting a bit prickly. He said it was cheaper to build a new one than to restore the old.

'The houses up here get a lot of weather and even my house that I built in the '70s needs £20,000 spending on it. The rendering goes and the slates wear out. The terrible winds make it hard on a house.'

'I can see that you boys don't do gardens.'

This sparked him up. 'Waste of time. I had lovely flowers and the other day they were flattened by the wind. Waste of time.'

Mary showed me some Harris Tweed that they were selling but without any pushiness. I asked old Murdo if he was sure that they weren't made in China. At last he broke into a smile. 'Nay, nay.'

I bought a Harris Tweed baseball cap for Valerie.

He told me that farms for the corncrakes were more profitable than keeping sheep. He said you can't shoot the greylag and now there's a problem as there are too many of them and they eat the roots and the crops.

He said that they weren't happy about the paedophiles and other shitheads that Social Services kept sending up from the south.

Mary kindly gave me some leaflets and I bade them farewell, catching the bus back to Stornoway.

I met John on the bus and asked him about peat cutting and he said that no one did it now as they were all too lazy. He'd been round the world a few times and in the Falklands. He was a retired fitter and said he now leaves it to the young.

'Have you lived on Lewis all your life?'

'No one with any sense lives on Lewis all their life!' he replied with a laugh.

I couldn't believe the price of hotels here and realised how spoiled I'd been on Harris. The Royal Hotel wanted £55 and I was told I was an old charmer as they refused my £40 offer. I went to a couple of guest houses but they never answered the door. The County Hotel wanted £50 and other B&B places failed to respond to my knock. I went back to the County Hotel.

The receptionist said she was in a strong position, but it still seemed a lot of money for a tired hotel. However, I was also tired so I took it. She told me the place was fully booked for the next night. The hotel had a grand staircase, but the carpets were again tired.

I had dinner in the hotel, which was cosy by the coal fire and I chatted to the bar lady. She was local and a member of the Salvation Army. Her grandmother was still alive and she told me that the fishermen's wives used to carry the husbands to the boats so that they didn't get wet or catch a cold. Her grandmother had said to her, 'I bet the young girls today couldn't do that!'

I ordered lamb chops and told them that if they were overcooked I wouldn't pay for them. The result was perfect lamb chops!

THE ISLAND OF LEWIS

I had breakfast at 7.30am. On the side of a pack of butter I read the following: 'Caution, may contain milk.' It reminded me of a supermarket in South Africa selling English tomatoes grown in South Africa.

I was glad to get out of this grubby, expensive hotel and to get back on the road for the day.

I took a taxi out of town and onto the right road. As I didn't know the town it was worth it. The road was busy and very bendy and dangerous for hiking, so I kept walking until it got safer.

My first lift was in a brand new Range Rover. *'I like good transport, thank you very much.'*

Dr Smith was a GP, but had done some anaesthetic work both in Aberdeen and Cambridge and he was now retired. He did say how many hundreds of thousands of miles per year he travels, and picking up hikers made his journeys more interesting. He had just been to Australia and New Zealand. He also kept a journal. I said to him that I was a farmer and if I had a crop failure I could replant, but if one of his patients didn't wake up he would be in the shit.

'People on these islands go all over the world, but never go to the nearby islands here. I can't make them out. Would you put your seat belt on, please, or you might get killed and I would be sued.'

MEET MR NEIL MCKIE

He was a builder with twenty-six people on the payroll. All the men who worked for him were islanders. He was looking for a secretary and his phone was ringing all the time. He didn't seem that interested in the island's history and had other things on his mind.

The BBC *Castaway* programme was filmed here, on an island just off Harris, and Neil had won the contract to do the building works. He said that the BBC really did waste an awful lot of money, but were very good to all the men. Money was no object. The helicopter they hired cost £35 per minute and he'd used it regularly. I asked him what he thought of Ben Fogle and he said he liked him and that he was a really good chap. Most of the others, he said, were arse-holes (his words) and self-centred.

I went into the Bernera Museum and Community Centre, but there was no life there so I walked on.

FRED FLINTSTONE COUNTRY

If I'd seen Bernie, Alma and Betty walking down the road towards me I wouldn't have been at all surprised – it's really rocky here.

The Hebrideans are very proud of their hard weather and like to think they're real men and women. They make a big fuss about it.

The crofters don't use hinges, just plastic rope and string and every gate is hanging off. *'I just wonder if they're plain lazy.'*

This was a lovely road and the only company I had were the Highland cattle that were sheltering behind a stone wall. The walk was good for the soul and it was very remote and quiet. I flagged down an oncoming car to find out how far it was to the Iron Age house. It was about a mile away.

I came across Chip, a friendly sheepdog who loved being made a fuss of.

There was a fish farm with the usual mess of lobster pots in the grass and there wasn't a soul about.

I passed more beef cattle, a mum and daughter, the same colour as the rocks. There was a calf suckling its mother in the middle of the road. I took what I hoped would be some fantastic photographs. I came to the end of the road only to be greeted, after those amazing views, by the loos and dustbins. Pity they couldn't have put them behind a rock.

I walked down to the beach and found a dead seal, but no Iron Age house. Then round the corner there it was.

They have made a wonderful job of the Bustadh Iron Age house and it was opened by Princess Anne. The place was locked so I couldn't get in. The entrance was clever as it sort of went underground and had a bend in it to keep the wind out.

I picked up some rubbish and started the long walk home. It's always better to have the wind behind you.

The cattle were still there and I invited them to Kent if they so wished! They were still looking at me as though I was an idiot.

I walked around the corner and in the middle of a field there was a car with its headlights flashing. *'I must go and have a look in case he's in trouble.'*

Just as I got to the gate and was worried that he might be having a heart attack, he drove out of the field.

'Are you OK?'

'Yeah, aye, who are you?'

'You were flashing your lights.'

'Nay, just starting it up. I'm a weaver.'

'Are you going my way.'

'Nay, the other way!'

'Typical! What's your name?'

'John McKinsey.'

Then I realised he was well pissed and so was glad he was going the other way. He nearly knocked me over and then did go my way after all.

I went back into the community hall and had lunch. The bowling club was in there and it's amazing how much old people eat. Also there were two nurses and when I asked them if they knew Dr Smith they did.

I was now back on the road and a lady gave me a nod as she drove past as if to tell me that she didn't take risks and didn't pick up hikers.

And I thought, *'You're too ugly to be at risk!'*

MEET MR NORMAN GEORGE MCDONALD

He had a very smart Audi and he was a quiet man in his late sixties or early seventies. He used to have a haulage business and a salmon farm.

We saw a double rainbow overhead. 'There's a pot of gold under there,' I said.

'Och, aye.'

I got him to drop me off at the War Memorial.

Lewis lost a lot of fine men in the war, apparently more than anywhere else in the British Isles when the ratio of those killed to the total population is taken into account. This huge monument overlooking Stornoway has big stones placed in a circle and the names of the fallen on the front.

I thanked them for my freedom and took the shortcut across the steep steps, picking up rubbish as I went. I felt quite guilty as I walked up someone's drive to stuff it into their wheelie bin, but in this part of the world if you stuffed a dead body in a bin no one would notice.

STORNOWAY WATERWHEEL

I went past a sign pointing to it and decided to have a look. It was just as well I did as the weather had become drizzly after a lovely morning.

'THE VISITOR CENTRE AND THE WATERWHEEL STAND ON THE SITE OF THE STORNOWAY GRAIN MILL THAT WAS BUILT IN 1816 AND BURNED DOWN IN 1890. THE WATERWHEEL TURNS IN THE ORIGINAL HOUSING OF THE 19TH CENTURY WHEEL.'

It was difficult to understand how little water was needed in the metal cups to turn the wheel. This was because the flow was restricted and came out in jets.

Milling has a long story and years ago all the crofters had a mill. Then one day the wise landlords decided that if one mill could do the lot they could be more commercial in selling the surplus. So they built the large mill and proceeded to charge the crofters.

The crofters weren't too happy about this and continued to use their own, but the wise landlords got over this little hitch by destroying the crofters' mills; in the days when you didn't get messed about by little tenant farmers!

I was going to go round Lewis Castle, but I was too tired, so once again I started hotel hunting.

'Have you any room at the inn?'

'I think we're full but I'll have a look. Sorry, we are full, but there are plenty of B&B places in 'such and such' street.'

Well, I walked for ages and found another guest house; he was only after £60 per night, but he was full, unsmiling and miserable. 'Sorry, we're full. Have you tried next door?'

I went there. 'Have you got a room for the night?'

'I'll just go and see. Yes, we have and it's £45 per night.'

'I'll take it.'

My chef for tonight came from Nepal. He told me his name was Tek and I told him that it didn't sound Nepalese, so he wrote it down. He worked through an agency and had cooked in Kuwait and all over the world.

The management soon pulled him away from our chat.

I didn't get a taxi next morning and walked out of town to the same place as yesterday and what a day it turned out to be.

I was walking along and composing my guide to hitchhiking around the UK when a large sweeping machine came down the pavement. I put some beer cans out around the lamp post so that his machine could grab them. The driver smiled and drove on.

I started hitching at 9.25am and within minutes I got a lift in this remote area.

MEET DONALD AND MARIA

This really was a quiet road and Donald was chatting away telling me which way I should go, but I couldn't understand a word he was saying! 'Pleased to be able to help. We're on our way to the funeral of my father.'

'I'm sorry about that.'

'No, he had a good life and was ninety-two years old. He'd been preparing himself for death as a Christian for seventy years.' *'I'm really struggling to understand his strong Scottish accent.'*

'Sorry, but did you say he was a preacher?'

'Nay, a Christian.'

'Is it a burial or a cremation?'

'There be no cremation on this island.' *'Don't think the guys like cremation.'*

'Any idea how many will be there?'

'Just a few. We would take you to the stones but we're short on time.'

'No, you've been very kind, thank you very much.'

As I got out Maria handed me a small book entitled *Daily Strength*: "THE LORD JESUS CHRIST SAID: 'DO NOT LET YOUR HEARTS BE TROUBLED. TRUST IN GOD. TRUST ALSO IN ME.'"

'Thank you so much for stopping.'

Wow, this is an amazing place. One minute I'm in a busy town and the next on a very quiet road.

I phoned Valerie and found out that all the usual troubles were there: no heating, no Aga, door's come off its hinges, and the sewage at Marshall's Farm is blocked. Why do all these things happen when I'm away?

Driving along I could see quad bikes sitting in gardens. In Kent they would have been stolen before you went to bed.

This was silence and it was drizzling. I could have been on the moon. I could sing and shout and the only things I would disturb would be the sheep.

This must be the most perfect place for birds, but there are none either on the lochs or the big pools of water – strange.

MEET DONNIE MACDONALD

'Always look on the bright side of life!'

Along he came and was I glad to see this big cheery man; a builder in his transit van.

'What are you doing out here? You never see anyone out here.'

'Am I glad to see you?! Not much public transport around.' Then I jumped in. I said to him that if he was a builder he could invest in restoring the old falling down houses, but he said it was too expensive so they just let them deteriorate. He was a real gentleman and took me right to the stones.

CALLANISH STANDING STONES

This is one of the most important and significant megalithic complexes in Europe. They reckon that five thousand years ago the weather was warmer and it wasn't as windy and that more cereal crops were grown.

It's a strange area round here. Doubtless in the summer it's busy with tourists, but what a mess it is. No one seems to pick up rubbish.

The lane running up to the stones looked 12th century.

There were old empty farmhouses with cattle running through them and a cow outside looking as though it was stuck in the mud.

I tried to hitch a lift and the car I stopped had the local post office lady in it from just down the road. I bought some stamps from her place which made the Lenham post office look like a supermarket.

Good old Joan was clearing the back seat for me. Apparently, she was on her way to the next attraction which was the Carloway Broch, where she was going to clean the loos.

I asked her about the old houses and told her that I couldn't understand why they weren't restored. She told me it had never been the custom for families to sell the family house; they just built a new one and let the old one fall down. The housing boom was new to them and it would be the younger generation who would sell them. Joan was born and bred in a black house. She had four children, none of whom had any intention of getting married.

She told me that the first farmers settled here in 4000 BC.

Black houses were so named not because in the early days they were smoke-filled and had small windows, but because they were compared to new houses being built in the late 1800s which were called white houses. The new white houses were designed to separate humans from their livestock.

The design of the black house originated from several thousand years earlier, as did the construction method. The building consisted of two concentric dry stalls with a gap between filled with earth or peat. The roof was either thatched or made of turfs and constructed on a wooden frame. The frames were supported by the inner wall which gave the characteristic look of a shelf around the outside of the building. As the roofing materials had to withstand quite extreme weather at times, they were often secured by netting with large stones tied at the ends.

Some of the black houses were still inhabited in the middle of the 1970s, although to be fair, some of them had fireplaces and chimneys instead of the chimney-free construction.

We arrived at Carloway Broch. Here the loos had a turf roof and blended in with the hillside.

CARLOWAY BROCH

A broch is an Iron Age structure designed to impress and defend, and they were probably the houses of the tribal leaders and important members of the community. The one at Carloway is one of the best preserved in the Hebrides and dates back over two thousand years. I love Health and Safety! Here there was none and I tried a climb that even I thought was dangerous. When I went back to the car park Joan was still cleaning the loos and I asked her if she wanted a hand. She said she was fine so off I went.

Sitting in the bus shelter I ate the sandwich I'd made at breakfast, which went down well. *'The MacDonald funeral must be over as there are many cars coming in the opposite direction. The occupants look very smart with their best black bonnets on.'*

MEET MARY MACLEAN

She was a carer and very kindly gave me a lift. She even went out of her way to take me to the Gearrannan Blackhouse Village.

'Thank you, Mary.'

The Village was opened by the Princess Royal and they really have made a good job of the reconstruction, turning the houses into youth hostel accommodation – and very tastefully done. Walking back from this area I noticed that there were a huge number of rock buildings. I walked past one with a hole in it and inside there was an owl.

MEET JOHN

He was a minibus driver and was going the other way on this road. He started to reverse in order to give me a lift. Once again I met a large bundle of cheerfulness and he told me to get in. He had a really bad cold giving him a red nose. He was so excited at having someone different to talk to and wouldn't stop chatting. It made it worse when I told him I was a farmer!

We passed the church where the funeral had taken place. Some were driving and some walking, all with the contented look of knowing that grandad was now safely in the hands of the Lord.

John's bus was small and I think he just picked up people from the really rural areas and took them to the main bus route road.

'We used to grow corn all around here,' he explained in his high-pitched voice.

'You mean oats?'

'Och, aye! That's right. I used to do it all with horses but when we changed over to the Ferguson 35 it ruined all the soil structure. I used to cut the crops with a scythe and tie it all up in sheaves; five hundred in a stack.'

'How did you dry it?' I asked.

'Always dried itself, no matter how wet it was when cut. We put hay in the middle of the stack to keep the mice and rats out.'

'Oh, it's the main road here. You'd better let me out.'

'No.' He wasn't going to let me out until he'd finished his story! We'd now got to the collection point for the big buses. 'What's your biggest tractor?'

'500 horse-power.'

'Wow!'

'Thanks for the lift, John. *It's always good to meet the salt of the earth.*'

I found all that talking was hard work and I was glad to get out and back to walking. I walked past Carloway FC and a Range Rover passed me going in the opposite direction. It was Dr Smith, so I gave him a hearty wave. As always there were people who had thrown rubbish out of their cars. I'm sure that if pigs drove cars they would be better behaved.

MEET CLARE AND HER DAUGHTER ANNA

This was the sixth lift of the day; Clare came from Chester and her husband came from Uig. It took her three years to persuade him that she was serious about moving up here. Their dog had been getting at their pet duck. The dog was only eight weeks old and they were taking it to the person who'd supplied it to look it over.

'Thanks for the lift.'

'Nice to help someone out!'

She dropped me off at the Shawbost Norse Mill and Kiln.

Well, it was a fair walk towards the coast and the path was made in keeping with the surrounding areas. I took my rucksack off and I felt like a horse that had lost its jockey.

It was well worth the walk and the place was very well renovated and I told them so in the visitor book: 'I am impressed.'

MEET JOHN AND EMMA

They were up here visiting relatives. They had their Sat Nav plugged in, but said that they really didn't need it up here. John was a little dark skinhead and Emma was rather quiet. He'd done quite a bit of travelling himself and had been to Thailand four times. He'd been arrested and robbed by the police when they found some dope on him. He was so disgusted that he came back early. *'He was very lucky not to land up in jail for thirty years.'*

They went out of their way to get me to the main road. On the way we went past a whalebone arch, but didn't stop.

MEET ALISTAIR MORRISON

The first car I thumbed actually stopped and an old crofter, Alistair – my last lift of the day – took me right to the town to do his shopping. He was a bit shaky and the more we talked about farming the more he liked it.

'Aye, retired now. My son does a bit of it, aye, and we only have fifteen sheep now, aye, and they're good for the freezer.'

'Do you grow any vegetables?'

'Used to, but the slugs eat them all. Never used to be like that.'

'We spent £14,000 on slug bait this year.'

'Oh my God!

'What did you grow?'

'Mainly potatoes on the sandy ground.'

'Did you spray for blight?' I asked.

'Nay, didn't have to.'

'Could you grow them on the moors?'

'Nay, on the sandy ground. What do you grow on your farm?'

'Wheat and rape.'

'Aye, you must be making a fortune.'

'I'm retired and let my nephew get on with it.'

'Aye, retired, never! You got a few years left yet.'

'Thanks very much for the lift. It was very kind of you to stop.'

Off went Alistair causing havoc in the late afternoon town traffic.

'Have you any rooms?'

'Nay, nay, try the next street.'

'Thanks very much.'

'Have you got a bed for the night and how much?'

'Come in and I'll have a look. The wife is out having her hair done.' Ben was a large cheerful man, who smoked and offered me a room for £27.

He showed it to me and I had to take off my rucksack going upstairs as I was frightened of knocking things off the walls on the narrow staircase. The room was a double with a sink and bathroom next door.

'I'll take it.'

'Come on down and I'll get you a drink. Tea or coffee?'

'Tea, please.'

I gave him £30 and he came back to me and said, 'Oh dammit, let's call it £25. We usually charge £50 for that one.'

He'd been on oil-rig construction and had loads of men under him, all on £1000 per week. He said they were like little celebrities. 'I tell you what, most people up here are foreigners and we're the only locals.'

'Yes, we have plenty of immigrants in Kent and if it wasn't for them the fruit would never get picked. The youngsters are just too lazy.'

'Aye, up here they blame them for taking the houses and jobs.'

'The truth is that they fuck their own lives up and want to put the blame on others.'

I decided that I should buy a comb as it wasn't much fun brushing your hair with a toothbrush.

All the guys drinking and eating in here looked like peas in a pod. They seemed to be Merchant Navy type men.

A family next door were having a night together and the young mum looked so unhappy; it seemed a really hard job for the family to enjoy themselves.

I went to bed.

THE ISLE OF LEWIS BACK TO THE MAINLAND

I put the television on early this morning and saw my friend Hugh Neaves showing someone round his apple orchard. It was all to do with pollination.

Walking on the way to the ferry I noticed all the beautiful wrought iron fencing outside the houses. It really did make them look elegant; most of the wrought iron on the mainland was melted down for the war effort. I suppose up here it was just too far away.

LEWIS CHESS PIECE

This chess piece was found in a sand dune in Uig on Lewis, in 1831. It was made of ivory and probably originated from Trondheim in Norway in the 11th or 12th century. There are eleven pieces in the National Museum in Edinburgh with the remaining sixty-seven pieces in the British Museum. A wooden replica stands in the ferry waiting room.

At 6.40am we were on the ferry and I found a quiet corner with light. It was the first ferry I'd been on that had a covered walkway and it was also the busiest I'd been on.

I went below deck for a coffee and wrote up *Walkabout* and about half an hour later I went on deck again to stretch my legs. What a sight greeted me – all the mountains as we came into Ullapool – sheer beauty.

There were only two of us on the top deck and this is where I met Donald.

'Wow, what a view! I've been downstairs and hadn't noticed.'

'It's a little similar to Korea.'

'This ferry doesn't hang about, does it?'

'Aye, fifteen knots. The destroyer I was on did thirty-five knots, but it couldn't carry enough fuel to keep it going.'

Donald had spent thirty years in the Glasgow police force. 'I can tell you that nothing surprises me anymore. They have a different mentality. When a man has no conscience you're finished, gone with the wind and have no Christian principles.'

'I suppose you learned in the end which journalists to trust?'

'Yep, none of them. They think the only thing that's important is punishment. That's all they understand. I had a triple bypass three years ago. I'm now seventy-five, aye, and it was all caused by stress.'

Donald told me of different instances of fear; once when a knife was pulled on him and another occasion when a gun was pointed at him.

'What was the worst thing you ever had to deal with?'

'The Hillsborough football disaster. It stays with you forever. Ye never forget and I was one of the first on the scene.' Donald wouldn't be pulled on this one.

'They rang me up a few years later saying they wanted to write a book and I told them to be careful not to print all the details as there were still relatives out there.'

'Did they respect your views?'

'Oh yes, aye. Sometimes we would do a drug raid and the next morning you'd read that the police had made a swoop, aye, a swoop. Just makes you laugh.'

'Would you mind taking my photograph?'

'Och, aye.'

'And may I take yours as I need more people in my diary?'

'Och, aye!'

'How would you help single families in inner cities?'

'No hope.'

It was an interesting chat with Donald. He'd now retired back to Lewis. He was a man heavy in thought and he enjoyed talking about it all.

'WHEN A MAN HAS NO CONSCIENCE YOU ARE FINISHED, GONE WITH THE WIND, AND HAVE NO CHRISTIAN PRINCIPLES.'

Wow! Donald was about right. He was very good to me; a complete stranger who kept firing questions at him. He could quite easily have told me to f... off, but he left a big impression on me.

The ferry docked and I jumped on a bus.

There were two buses and one didn't have a long queue so I jumped on that. At 10am we roared out of Ullapool with fourteen passengers and the clock still set to summer time.

The first thing I noticed was how much cleaner and tidier Scotland was. And there were more trees and forms of planning. It felt good to have got that part of the journey over, but I wouldn't have missed it for the world. In fact I could've been in another world.

GARVE

I went to a railway station, but couldn't see Garve on the timetable and there was no one in the station house. I found out later that if you want the train to pick you up you have to stand and wave a flag! I decided to hitch anyway.

I rang Valerie but got no answer, so then I rang Mark and got all the problems of rabbit damage and broken drains, and yeah, Valerie had been trying to get hold of me. *'Alarm bells!'*

I'd just seen bars on a house for security. I walked up to the A832. It was a busy road and I wasn't managing to stop anything. But if you *'always look on the bright side of life'* things will change and soon a brand new Range Rover stopped.

MEET RODDY

Three years ago he'd sold his construction business, RMA Contractors Ltd. He was a civil engineer. He'd been pleased to get out because of all the Health and Safety stuff. He still had a load of aggregate grading gear and was about to sell it to Nigeria. I told him to make sure he got his money first.

'So, now you have more time do you have any hobbies?'

'Nay, too busy building up another business.'

'Do you like eating out?'

'Och, aye! Been on several cruises.'

His business was on Harris where he was building sewage treatment plants.

'Would you ever fancy going on the Orient Express?'

'Aye, I have thought about it.'

I thanked him for the lift and told him to book up the Orient Express and start spending his money.

LOCHCARRON

I walked into the town and had to wait at the golf course whilst a foursome teed off over the road to a par three. All landed near the green and I congratulated them. As I was watching them a flock of greylags flew over them. One of the golfers, a nice old boy, said to me that he would rather be playing golf than what I was doing. I said I would rather be doing this than playing golf!

I passed a school and threw a ball back for them.

If you ask people round here which is the best hotel, they just say that they're all the same.

I booked in a local hotel a strange place mainly ran by awful staff. I was checked in by a fascinating girl, but the rest were rougher than me! It resembled Fawlty Towers and I quite liked it. In my room the cupboard drawer slid out right over the electric heater.

There was a big lazy looking chap in his trainers and slacks with a tired looking face.

'Is this your hotel?'

'No, my relations are coming from Portsmouth in twelve hours.'

'How often do you come here?'

'As often as possible.'

I couldn't really make the family out. There were young girls with children and there was one young girl with a man, and to this day I don't know if he was her father or her boyfriend. I suspect the latter. The daughters spent most of the time watching the television. *'Every hotel and pub has a bloody television blaring away all the time, even if there's no one watching.'*

Most of the chefs around here looked as though 'exercise' was a dirty word.

Jim in the bar was an ex-whaler. 'I only used to hunt the blue whale. I left the hump-backs and the bull-nosed. There used to be hundreds of them.' He had a slight shyness in his face, but told me he used to think nothing of it.

'Was it rough down in the South Atlantic?'

'No, it was a summer job, because in winter it would be dark the whole time.'

'How long would a whale last once it was dead?' *'What a stupid question!'*

'The water was very cold and the first thing we'd do was to pump them up with air so that they'd float; then we'd stick a flag on them so that the factory ship would spot them. The whales would always turn over when they were dead. Every whale was measured and weighed about a tonne a foot. Some weighed about one hundred tonnes. The first thing we had to do was to cut the fin off, because when the whale was towed with the fin on it would affect the steering of the boat. We would fish for six months of the year. It was a Norwegian company and all the meat went to them. You can get five tonnes of oil out of a whale's tongue. Two whales were used as a buffer when two ships had to get alongside each other.'

'Anyone who kills a whale these days should really have a lesson on how to commit suicide.'

When I came down for supper at 7pm the girl was behind the bar eating her supper and serving in between. A young man on the other side of the bar was eating his food. He was another sloppy yob, nearly sucking the food off the plate rather than eating it. *'A pig is more dignified than him.'*

I also met Nigel in the bar. He was retired but did some local work and had a second home up here. The love of his life was walking and he'd been all over the world including the Alps, the Andes and the Himalayas.

'In Nepal they have Sherpas and in Russia porters. The Sherpas can deal with high altitudes.' *'Well, well, well, I never knew that!'*

Nigel was having a coffee and was a member of CAMRA. He told me that I shouldn't be drinking John Smith's because it's full of chemicals, but before I could change the order they had half-filled the glass.

I asked him why he wasn't having a drink and he told me it was his once a week healthy day.

I went to bed.

LOCHCARRON TO ULLAPOOL

The waiter this morning looked as though he'd had more smoke through him than Battersea Power Station chimneys.

Once more the dining room was morgue-quiet, so I shouted out, 'What a view!' and that broke the ice and everyone started talking to everyone else.

The only nice girl in the hotel said to one guy having breakfast that she wouldn't have his job for all the money in the world.

'What's his job?'

'A driving instructor.'

'What's today's programme?'

'A girl's got a test and that's it for the day.'

'How many lessons has she had?'

'Twenty-five to thirty.'

'Do you think she'll pass?'

'Yes, but it depends on whether she gets nervous.'

HITCHING HERE WE COME

I met the following nice people this day, who gave me a lift:

1. Norma, who was a water tester and an ex-RAF engineer.
2. PO Gill on a post office bus.
3. Adam, who was a steeplejack and a nutter.
4. Mike, who was an ex-agricultural transport manager.

5. Roy, who filled NATO ships with fuel.

6. Jim, an architect.

7. Bob, a retired coal face worker.

8. Nearly forgot Diane Gillie. Just as I was thinking that nobody loved me, Diane stopped. *'On behalf of my feet I thank you from the bottom of my heart.'*

I'M IN LOVE. MEET DIANE

All good things are worth waiting for and this morning Diane was taking her Kenyan clients deer stalking.

'Thank you very much for stopping.'

'Where are you going?'

'No idea,' I replied, 'I have no itinerary. What a wonderful part of the world you have here.'

'Yes, isn't it?'

'Are you going out stalking?'

'Yes.'

'I saw a sign up in Glenmoor estate. Is that where you're going?'

Anyway it turned out that Diane was the gillie today and it was the family estate. Her client had a game reserve in Kenya and I said to him, 'Is it a smallish reserve with some game? I suppose the small park is about 100,000 square miles.'

'No, about 250,000 square miles.'

'Does your wife know you're in the hills with the gamekeeper? I bet you told her that it was raining and foggy and you've got a grumpy, alcoholic, smelly old gamekeeper! For a small fee I'll keep quiet!' *'Poor Diane, she now has this cocky little shit on the back seat!'*

We drove in to a set of old farm buildings and the car in front was also with them. I don't know what they thought when I jumped out.

Diane's clients were well-spoken, smartly dressed and polite. The driver in the front vehicle apologised for not picking me up as their car was full.

Diane told them that I was writing a book about my travels round the British coastline.

I laughed and said, 'I can't even spell, let alone put a sentence together!'

Somehow I got talking about Paul Theroux. One of the clients had read his books and a friend of his had travelled with him.

'He's a funny man but writes well.'

I asked if I could have a photograph of them all, which they agreed to and I said I was definitely booking up for stalking next year. *'I want to go stalking with the lovely Diane!'*

As I left, someone asked if I was going up into the hills.

I said, 'No fear!' and waved goodbye.

I was back walking again and this was a lonely old road but it wasn't long before my next lift came along.

Dear Norma was very kind and unloaded all her clutter on the front seat, which was full of old books and bottles.

She worked for Highland Water and went to all the water plants and got samples sent off for testing; thanks to European legislation.

She used to work in the post office, and when she left school she went into the RAF and qualified as an engineer. I asked her why she came out and she said that she was young and had to give eighteen months' notice.

'You should come to Kent and service my little plane.'

I thanked her very much for the lift and she went off in the opposite direction. She dropped me off at Torridon. There was a post bus sitting there with a miserable driver eating his lunch. I pointed to him and he shook his head and said he was going the other way. *'Fuck you, too.'*

The funny thing about hitching is that the more remote you are the more likely you are to get a lift.

Gill, another post bus driver, took me from Torridon to Kinlochewe. I'd always wanted a lift in a post bus.

'What's the worst part of this job?' I asked.

'When it's raining and horrible.'

'And the best?'

'Helping people out.'

Apparently, these buses go where there's no bus route or community care service.

A lady came out of a house. 'Can you register this for me, please, and I'll pay you when you come back?'

Gill told me that she also delivered pensioners' meals and I asked her if she went and did their shopping as well.

The lady who wanted a letter posting told a story about someone who'd hit a pothole and how the car had turned over and was covered in mud, but fortunately no one was hurt. There were tears in her eyes.

Gill dropped me off at the post office in Kinlochewe

KINLOCHEWE TO GAIRLOCH

Well, you have to take the rough with the smooth and this ride was rough. Adam drove at 100mph on some not very good roads and I mean 100mph and no less.

'You don't hang about do you? You're going to have to drop me off.'

'You're kidding!'

'Unless you slow down.'

'It'll be a ride you won't forget.'

'Well, you should speak to the doctors in casualty who deal with dead bodies whose eyes are hanging out. If you hit someone head-on their eyes pop out.'

It didn't make any difference and he continued going at a mad speed. Somehow we got talking about flying.

He asked, 'What sort of plane have you got?'

'The Robin Reliant of the aviation world, a Cessna 150.'

'How fast does it go?'

'Not fast enough for you!'

He had just come back from Kazakhstan and you'll never guess his job – a steeplejack. 'I only went to school for three years. I wanted to do a job no one else did.'

This is the guy who goes up tall steel chimneys and then comes down in a cradle. 'See that road sign, Adam? It means there's a lorry in the middle of the road.'

He dropped me off at Gairloch. *I'm alive, alive, alive! I love life! Let me go to my Daily Strength! "KEEP ME SAFE, OH GOD, FOR IN YOU I TAKE REFUGE. THE LORD WATCHES OVER YOU. THE LORD IS YOUR SHADE AT YOUR RIGHT HAND. THE LORD WILL WATCH OVER YOUR LIFE. THE LORD WILL WATCH OVER YOUR COMINGS AND GOINGS, BOTH NOW AND FOR EVERMORE."*

'Well, Adam, thanks for the lift but I think you're heading for an early grave.'

Out of nearly one hundred lifts, this was by far the worst. After that lift I felt quite ill and it was good to get back on my feet again.

'Nice part of the world you have here.'

'Glad you're enjoying it.'

At 1pm I got another lift.

MEET MIKE

He was a retired Merchant Transport Director and he'd done the buying and selling. He gave me a short lift from Gairloch.

MEET ROY

This dear old boy stopped for me in rather a hurry and had a job to get started again. He stalled his Skoda. He was an organised person and everything was packed neatly. He had a very strong Scottish accent, had very red skin and was very tall. His job was to fill up NATO ships with fuel and the lock we were passing had been full of ships during the war. The lift was short but very interesting.

I now had a fair walk before my next lift and I enjoyed watching the seals and being alive. There were lots of wrens to keep me company. *'I must make up a poem about them. 'Wren, wren, why don't you become a hen?'*

MEET JIM

He had a long goatee beard and a ponytail. He was an architect and had a very comfortable car. *'We hikers don't like silly little cars!'*

He said, 'That's the house I built.'

'Too tall. If I was a planner I would only give permission for a single storey building.'

'Traditionally they are one and a half storeys high. That's another of my houses.'

'Christ, it's got dormers and skylights. I wouldn't have them as well!'

He had a good sense of humour and dropped me off at his house.

MEET IAN

You wouldn't think so, but it's hard work hitching because the more they talk the more I have to write down. They think they're giving me a lift and don't realise that they're giving me an interview.

Ian supplied central heating equipment and he explained that heating from the soil worked, but it was expensive to install and it was usually the third or fourth buyer who'd get the benefit.

He came from Edinburgh, and like me he had come here on holiday, stopping at various vantage points. We saw a huge bird that could've been a buzzard or a golden eagle and decided to call it the latter.

Poor old Ian had a really nasty elbow; he'd fallen badly and at a nasty angle and the bone had come out of the elbow. He wasn't making a big deal of it though. Driving through Corrieshalloch forge is a National treasure. Ian dropped me off on the main road to Ullapool. He went right and I went left.

MEET MR BOB MARSDEN

I'd been lucky today with lifts and I was once more picked up very quickly. Bob was a retired coal face worker from Lancashire. He now lived on Harris and we swapped names and addresses.

He came from a long line of coal miners in his family. He said his knees had gone and he had bronchitis. His knees had been damaged by having to lie on his stomach by the low coal seams. They'd still used the canary to detect methane right to the end of the coal mining industry. The canaries were so sensitive to gas that they would just keel over and they would be taken out for fresh air and to recover.

What frights he'd had. He said that on one occasion he'd had to dig his father out – he was OK but covered in scars. On another occasion, a truck carrying forty men went into the mine but nobody smelled a thing and they were all gassed.

I asked him about mining the coal face. He said they would drill out nine inches and dynamite it. All the coal went back on conveyor belts, some five miles away. 'That was what killed it – the distance. We knew we couldn't compete with the Chinese or Russians.'

We swapped Christmas cards for several years; unfortunately Bob's wife has since informed me that he's passed away.

Arriving back in Ullapool, I popped into the tourist information office to find out about accommodation and tomorrow's buses. The gentleman had much pleasure in telling me that the bus didn't do this route or that route and I was thinking of telling him I knew a route it could go – somewhere where the sun doesn't shine! I'd rather hitch.

HOSTEL

'Q. What's the difference between a hostel and a hotel? A. One has an 's' in it.'

'Have you got a bed for the night?'

'Yes, it's £15 for a dormitory or £20 for a single.'

'I'll take the single.'

'That's up the road. Do you want to follow me in your car?'

'What car?'

'Jump in!'

She showed me round the little let. There were still three rooms for hire. A dehumidifier was working nineteen to the dozen. She said to leave the key in the door and never took my name or address.

I had the whole house to myself; very nice but lonely.

I went into another 'outdoor pursuit' shop and was seduced into buying a cap.

'Would you take £20 for it?'

'No.'

'I'll have it anyway.'

'You won't lose it if it's expensive.'

It was the best thing I could have bought as it rained the next day and it was a life-saver.

I had a beer in a funny old pub and then phoned Valerie. It was a fairly lively chat as there were plenty of things going wrong that I'd not sorted out. I had apparently tried to gas her with the central heating boiler, but I reckoned that if I had, I hadn't made a very good job of it.

ULLAPOOL TO SCOURIE

What an adventure this has turned out to be. You just don't know what's going to happen next and that's what I like about it.

I was on the road at 9.35am, later than I'd wanted to be. Time seemed to fly by in the mornings. There was a signpost to John o' Groats – 170 miles away. It was raining, but I had all the gear, so what! This is the most beautiful place in the world.

MEET BETTY AND ROGER

They were an Irish couple visiting relatives. His living was singing. It's always great to have a lift.

Just as I was getting to know a bullock, a bus turned up, so 'goodbye, sir!'

The only other passenger was a large lad with learning difficulties.

I said to the driver as we sped off, 'Have you been a Grand Prix driver for long?'

'Sorry if I'm driving fast, but I had a puncture this morning and I'm trying to make up time.'

'What's the castle like? Is it worth a visit?'

'Yes.'

'Then would you drop me off there, please?'

ARDVRECK CASTLE

I was glad I'd stopped. The old house was built in 1727. The castle itself was built in the 15th century. A few years ago this place had a private golf course and was famous for its many different types of grass.

The roads were so lonely here and I was walking and walking. I had to turn off and walk up a slight hill. A police car drove by but didn't stop; not that I'd really thought he would stop anyway.

Tony drove past and stopped in the lay-by. I wasn't sure if it was to pick me up or not, but it was. He took most of his shopping off the back seat, next to a young man with learning difficulties. So I piled into the back with the wheelchair and enough shopping for a month.

Penny was in the front and was connected to an oxygen supply with a huge bottle in the back. *'As if poor Tony hasn't got enough problems without me adding to them.'*

We started off and Tony was chatting away in the front, but as it was fairly noisy in the back and what with his accent I couldn't understand a word he was saying. I just hoped he was not asking me any questions. I thought he worked in a care home, but I found out that Penny was his wife and the lad in the back was his son. We arrived at Scourie.

Ken and Madeleine were the only people in the village who kept their guest house open all the year round; the other seven closed in the off-season. I was the only customer.

'Would you like to see the room?'

'No, thanks, I'll take it.'

'Would you like supper?'

'Yes, please.'

'Would haddock and chips and soup be all right?'

'Yes, that would be fine.'

'Would you like a dash of cream in your soup?'

'Yes, please.'

'I'll show you to your room. Supper is at 7.30pm.'

'I may go out for a walk later. Is there a pub?'

'Yes, it opens at 6.30pm.'

My room was ideal; one of the lightest rooms I've ever had, with two single beds and a little toy dog on the pillow. There were also some little china dogs in the flower garden coming up the drive.

There wasn't a spot of dust anywhere and on the way out Madeleine was still cleaning.

'Having a clean up, then?'

'Yes, while it's a bit quiet I can get on top of things.'

It was a funny place and there was no one about at all. I passed the community ladders with a sign saying: 'Please put them back in the evening!'

'Yes.'

I walked out of the village and saw two llamas high on the hill looking at me as if to say, 'What are you doing here?' It was drizzling and overcast. I decided to go to the pub, which, in fact was the Hotel Scourie. Again it was very clean and very unwelcoming. That's an understatement, so I had a pint and got out.

I went back to the B&B and thought to myself that I mustn't be horrible to Madeleine, who no doubt is a hell of a hard worker and a good cook.

In the bedroom, on the tea-tray there were exactly two milks, two tea bags and two hot chocolates.

Her husband Ken was not that well and was waiting for surgery on his knee. They used to have a bakery and tea rooms, so he was on his feet for long hours.

I was a happy bunny and I spread the contents of my bag all over the spare bed, hoping that I wouldn't get ink on the yellow sheets.

It always seems strange having supper on my own and dear old Ken was doing all the waiting. I felt rather spoilt. Even the sugar had a film over the top. To bed.

SCOURIE TO KINLOCHBERV

'THIS GUEST HOUSE IS COMMITTED TO THE PRINCIPLES OF THE WALKERS AND CYCLISTS WELCOME SCHEME AND HAS BEEN APPROVED BY UIST, SCOTLAND, TO CATER FOR THEIR NEEDS.'

Breakfast was again served by Ken. I said to Madeleine, whom I could imagine was a slave driver, to go steady on him; that he needed a rest and that if they needed help to get a young lad or girl from abroad to work for them. Old Mad gave me a sideways look and Ken said she looked after him very well.

I said my goodbyes and buggered off.

It was now 9.05am on Sunday morning and although overcast the weather was OK. I was walking with just my shirt on and it amazed me how quickly I got fit. I was walking at a good pace, about 110 paces per minute, but nobody loved me. I just couldn't get a lift. In four and a half hours there were twenty-five cars and I missed about four of them because I didn't hear them.

An hour and a half into the walk and it was starting to rain and for the last two hours it poured. In fact it was the heaviest I'd experienced on my 'walkabout'. My new cap was a godsend and worth every penny.

A car pulled up and he thought I'd broken down as there was a car on the opposite side of the road. He couldn't make out what I was doing out in this weather, and I was, he thought, a deer stalker. I asked him for a lift and got chatting about shooting and all that shit, and that we had a pheasant shoot in Kent. I thought I might get him interested in me but to no avail. He was overworked and full of himself; he was a keeper. He had a three door car and the front seat was full of deer stalking clothes; all very smart and he kept looking at them as if to put them in the back, but then decided not to and said the classic: 'I'm only going as far as da-de-da,' and drove off.

Apart from Mr Old Deer there was still beauty in this countryside and for the first time on my 'walkabout' I had stags staring at me and hinds running across the road. Some were peering down from well above and the stag had his little group of girlfriends. He looked so majestic. A sight like this made it worthwhile getting wet. *I couldn't get a big thrill from shooting you, sir.*'

There were two stones perched up on a mountain, with a tourist board sign nearby saying that they got there in the Ice Age and when the glacier melted they were left there.

MIRAGE

How could your fellow countrymen drive past anyone in this sort of weather? I managed to pull my jumper on without getting too wet and suddenly saw a sign: 'HOTEL – OPEN ALL YEAR ROUND'.

As I got closer and closer I could see a light on, but I couldn't see anyone. At last I was here. I opened the door and walked in.

What I expected was, 'Oh my God, you poor thing! Have you been out in all that rain? Come in by the log fire and warm up. Have a double whisky on the house! My God, you're lucky to be alive. I'll get you some soup and warm clothes.'

What I actually got was, 'We're shut. There's a hotel down the road.' She did manage to phone the other hotel. 'What's your name?'

'Boyd. John Boyd.'

'Down the road, four miles.'

I'd been cursing all day. All the estate car drivers drive past you and it's always the little three-door banger, where you have to squeeze in the back, that stops.

Just then the brake lights of a brand new Saab estate came to a stop!

'Thank you so much for stopping and I'll take off my wet clothes.'

He just couldn't believe that I'd walked the twelve miles and he took me the four remaining miles to the hotel. *'If this person had been a woman I would've given her a big kiss!'*

THE KINLOCHBERVIE HOTEL

Well, this one was much better and once more, bar one, I was the only person staying there. I think the other one was the local paramedic.

'I must remember on wet days to put all my clothes in a bin liner in my rucksack as these are all wet.' Luckily, the radiators were hot and there was a good towel rail.

Although there was nobody in the hotel rooms the bar had a fair sprinkling of locals.

'What would you like to drink?'

'A double whisky. Famous Grouse, please.'

'Afraid we don't have that. Would MacKay's do?'

'That's fine, thanks.'

I gave a toast to all the buggers who'd passed me by!

I shoved my boots in front of the fire and stuffed them with newspaper, only to grab hold of them a while later to find the sides had melted and I burned my hand. I had to hold it in an ice bucket for three hours. Stuart, the barman, also worked as an auctioneer in the local fish market, which was near the hotel in the busy harbour, and it had an ice-making machine.

Three trawler men were in for a drink. They would start fishing at 5am. Sometimes they would go out for six days at a stretch and fill the boxes up with fish and salt them. The salt was already mixed with the ice. Sometimes they were boarded by officials and they were tracked by GPS. They hated the foreign fishermen in their waters. They said that they were for ever dragging up the rubbish the others chucked overboard. *'Bastards.'*

One of them told me I must be well-qualified to write a book. *(I didn't let on too much.)*

I decided to have another whisky and had to work hard to stop them buying it for me. Instead I bought them a round. *'I'm beginning to be happy and I wonder why?'*

I had a rare fillet steak. It was great and a little kindness thrown in really helped.

The hair dryer was very useful for drying things, but it did tend to overheat and then switched itself off – it didn't help that I'd sellotaped the trigger to 'on', especially when I left it in my boots.

KINLOCHBERVIE TO THURSO

Stuart was a bit like me when it came to getting breakfast and he never did bring the milk for the cornflakes. But he really wanted to please and I had a huge, four rasher breakfast.

As always in remote places they like to say, 'There goes the bus!' just as you are having breakfast. Then they go on to tell you that there's only one bus every ten years! I've learned not to worry about the little bus and to hitch instead.

David was a young Elton John lookalike and he took me all the way to Durness, about fourteen miles away. He was interested in shooting and I told him that if he wanted any pigeon shooting to come to Kent. He was saying that up here is the only live bombing base in Europe and over by Cape Wrath is the air traffic control which looks after the bombers.

He dropped me off at Durness and it was a nice feeling to be at the top of Britain. I couldn't get to Cape Wrath, but turned left down the road and saw a beautiful sight of barnacle and grey geese coming in, and some lovely stone walls. I met another walker who said he came up here to get away from people.

I popped into a little shop and was again amazed just how immaculately clean they are up here in the north.

I really did slip up walking and had to do a huge horseshoe turn, but all was not lost because I went past the house where John Lennon, the Beatle, used to come for his holidays.

This really was some coastal road and I could taste the salt. The roads were so quiet.

I sat and had my bacon sandwich on a bridge. I was pleased I'd made some lunch, but was wondering if I'd ever get a lift. I walked on for another two hours.

At last I saw brake lights, and Lynne, with her two girl friends squeezed me in the back with Sally. These were some well-dressed ladies who were just sightseeing.

'Ooh, look at that lovely house!'

'Ooh, look at that loch!'

'Ooh, look at the sun on the mountains!'

These girls were very good to pick me up and sit me with the slow-talking Sally. They dropped me off at Tongue. 'Ooh, ooh, ooh!'

A big thank you, Lynne.

'Who could say they live in Tongue? I live in Monaco myself!'

I popped into the local pub. The landlady said I would have no problem getting a lift and wanted me out ASAP. The feeling was entirely mutual.

Castle Varrich loomed in the distance like some old master of the area in better times. I made my way out of the village and was surprised at the wide road going out, but it didn't take long before narrowing.

Chris gave me a short lift. He was a plumber and had done work for David Bowie. He had hitchhiked himself, so he knew the story.

I said how lovely this place was and he replied, 'This isn't countryside, but a wilderness.'

The plan was to get to Thurso tonight, but it was forty miles away and at this rate it wouldn't be possible.

I sang, *'Always look on the bright side of life.'*

POST BUS

I flagged it down and he said, 'You do realise you have to pay, don't you?'

'No trouble.'

It cost £5 and was the best money I've ever spent. We were mainly picking up post office mail at the post boxes.

The driver, Dan, was also a crofter in his spare time and being in a less favoured area helped. I think it was his wife who ran the business. We went from post office to post office and also filled up with diesel. He told me that the bus was famous as Griff Rhys Jones had been filmed sitting in the back of it. It took three or four hours to get the shoot right and then it only lasted two minutes.

We picked up another post lady who declined to sit next to me in the back seat. She wasn't very happy as she'd been sitting in the cold for an hour.

Dan kept going on about how he was replacing his Massey-Ferguson 815, or whatever it was. 'Can't have anything too heavy or it marks the moors. Can't get a Massey-Ferguson for love or money up here.' Then he had a rattle on about his five and a half percent pay rise and a backdated lump sum.

He let me out as I wanted a pee. The silence of the place was amazing; just a few little humans and their vehicles troubling it from time to time. The bus took me all the way to Thurso. I was dropped off at Thurso Railway Station and if I'd wanted to I could've caught the train to Glasgow in a further twenty minutes, but I decided not to.

Thurso is a funny place at night. I'd decided to try a proper hostel, the Thurso hostel, Ormlie Lodge.

The entrance took a bit of finding as the builders were in, but a very polite one showed me the way. I found the reception after walking up a corridor, which looked like a prison, and met a charming, polite young lady who looked fascinated at seeing me, wondering why a posh git like me was in here.

It cost £10 per night with an extra pound for a duvet and towel. It was a self-contained room with a little bed and a sink and all the things you need. She showed me where the loo and bathroom were. I asked for another duvet which was just as well as the bottom sheet didn't look that clean.

I went to eat at the Royal Hotel, not sure that the Royals would like this place being named after them! It cost £30 per night; the bar filled with young workers; and the food was cheap.

A really mouthy woman with a Chinese-looking girlfriend was working the men at the bar. It was the older man who was going to buy her services. I could see it in his eyes. He was a young man really, but damaged by hard drinking and smoking. He was red and craggy and had bad teeth. I'd never seen such young men look so old.

I had a pretty crappy meal and went back to the hostel with my baseball cap down and avoided eye contact. I didn't think it would be a good idea to get involved in the hostel social life.

I didn't sleep well. It was time to get home.

THURSO TO LENHAM

I was first on the platform for the 6.50am train. Most people on the train didn't even look out of the window. They were more interested in reading *The Sun* or the usual load of shit papers.

One minute we were in the countryside and the next minute the sea was beside us and we were nearly in it. We overtook a lorry. Now it was back to farming country.

Two ladies were opposite me gossiping and talking about sod all.

'Och, aye, I get free travel. My husband worked on the railway all his life,' one said.

'Do you get free bus travel if your husband worked on the buses?'

'Don't know.'

'Did you marry him for love or because of the free pass?'

GLASGOW

I felt I was coming home and I knew a little more about the place. I told the rubbish man that the station was a credit to him. I checked at the station that I had an 'open' ticket.

I went for a meal.

'Everything all right?' the waiter asked.

'Pretty ordinary.'

'And the main course – was that ordinary?'

'No, it was below ordinary.'

'Would you like a dessert?

'No thanks, I don't think I'll risk another.' *'After all he's managed to fuck up two courses.'*

I had a lump in my stomach for hours. (Later I was to write to them but never got a reply.)

I waited on Glasgow station and was getting cold – I'd put all my clothes in my rucksack. The girls were coming in to go clubbing, but they more or less had nothing on. One girl had high heels and could hardly walk. I thought it was funny, but no one else did. *'Maybe I'm an old pervert!'*

I found the sleeper train and was told that I had to share.

'But I'm a pervert and a murderer!'

'Too bad for them!' came the reply.

The blinds were down and it was still dark, so it wasn't easy to write *Walkabout*. I didn't realise we'd been sitting in the station for ten minutes.

And this time I didn't meet Princess Anne and she wasn't knocking on my door saying, 'I am poor'.

It had seemed very strange to have been in such isolation one day and then on a packed underground the next.

And so I got to Lenham.

'I'm home, Valsy!'

CHAPTER SEVEN

Orkney and Shetland Islands

Spring had arrived and it was time to get back on my 'walkabout'. This time I was going the easy way and flying back to Edinburgh; an hour later I'd arrived.

I went to Waverley Station to buy a forward ticket. 'Single ticket to Thurso, please.'

'Can I ask you your age, please?'

'Very old.'

'Are you over fifty?'

'Yes, ma'am, just a bit.'

'The fare is usually £50, but you can have it for £15.'

I had to pull my finger out as the train was to go in ten minutes.

I boarded the train and wondered if it was first class. 'Can I sit there or is it for someone special?'

'Nay, sit there and be y'self.'

We were soon over the Forth Bridge. I could see what they meant about the painting job; some of it was newly painted and some was quite rusty. I'd heard on the radio that there's now a paint that lasts for twenty-five years, so maybe that means an end to the continual painting.

Horses were wrapped up in huge Barbour type coats in their untidy waterlogged fields. The farms were neat and tidy, but the sandy-type soil looked sodden in places. Carrots were tucked underneath straw and the odd farmer was working on the land. Rabbits were plentiful up here and came out of the railway embankment. Sitting in the train gave me a bird's eye view. There was even the odd black rabbit. In some places you could look down on the birds of prey.

I decided to stretch my legs and went for a walk.

There were many young people on the train. A group of girls were on their way to a hen party and they were dressed to kill. The bar was closed, thank goodness.

As we went through Pitlochry I decided to give my friend, Colin Hales, a ring. He has a holiday home nearby. Today he's in Kent and is very sad as he's just had his faithful dog, Brama, put to sleep.

This beautiful countryside had changed colour since November, and as I travelled through the patchwork landscape a herd of stags could be seen with their antlers sticking up like antennae. I was the only one looking out of the window. There was still some snow hanging on in the shadows of the mountains. Another field was covered in geese and the old cock pheasants were in the stubble, somewhat fewer in number than in November.

We arrived at Inverness and I'd travelled for over four hours for £15. I had four seats and a table and somewhere to put my feet up when no one was looking. I went to the ticket office. 'Could you tell me the time of the first train to Thurso tomorrow, please?'

'6pm.'

'None before?'

'No, it's Sunday.'

I then went to the bus station and booked in.

I walked into the Clansman Hotel, which was a bit scruffy as the builders were in but it was family run and had a nice atmosphere. I rang the bell and the lady seemed to appear from nowhere.

'I didn't see you. Have you a single room for the night?'

'Yes, £38.'

'May I have a look?'

'It's not quite ready. We've only just opened for the season. Would you mind waiting for a few minutes?'

'OK.'

When she came back I took the room. It turned out to be a great little hotel.

I decided to go for a walk and felt quite fit with all these piss-heads around. Once again, I've never seen such young people look so old. I named them FFB: Fags, Football and Beer.

I went out to eat and at the restaurant everyone kept going outside for a smoke, so I joined in as it's a good way of meeting people. Afterwards, I went for another walk, but as it started to rain I ducked into a porch where a group of youngsters were milling around.

'I'll tell your dad you're taking shots,' said one.

'I'll tell your mum you're with Lizzie.'

And so to bed at the end of another long day.

INVERNESS TO THURSO

I had a quiet breakfast in the usual hush-hush breakfast room.

'Why, if the sea is that way, is the river going the opposite way?'

'No idea.' (I got in a muddle)

Standing by the river I could see eight churches, including St Andrew's Cathedral. It was Palm Sunday and the vicar was giving out crosses. It was funny watching the punters putting their heads to one side to show how much respect they had for the vicar.

Whilst I was packing at the hotel there was a test going on at the University to compare organic, free range and intensively reared chicken for flavour and tenderness. Much to my delight the intensively reared chicken won, because the Professor said, 'They were grown quicker and therefore were more tender.'

I was now on the bus for Thurso after leaving a very clean and friendly bus station at Inverness.

Some of the farmers' storage silos had fort-like tops to make them blend in with the environment.

Alness is the storage centre for two huge oil rigs; Sedco 711. I could see them out in the distance in the North Sea. Going by bus really does let you see the countryside at your leisure, with oyster-catchers, geese, jackdaws and stone walls which on the whole looked in pretty good shape. I also saw an old steam roller that had ended its life in a children's playground.

At Dornoch the driver said that we could have a five minute 'smoke break'.

I met Greg with his golf clubs. He was returning from a weekend of golf, drinking, playing pool and smoking. 'I am knackered.' I reckoned he was another FFB, but I was to meet him again on Orkney.

We drove past a derelict mill which looked as though it wanted someone to love it. It had an intact wheel and a river flowing past. The area here is marshy with some forest consisting of a variety of trees.

The schools resemble those in Cornwall with integration of boys and girls now.

Dunrobin Castle flashed by, so maybe on the way back I might stop off and see it.

Strip farming's back in fashion here and some interesting old farm machinery was rusting away in farmyards: old hay mowers, balers, potato diggers and a few Butler sinks.

Ancient stone barns, which to me have the 'wow factor', went by and in the distance there was a wind farm gracefully generating electricity.

Thick gorse hedges adorned the countryside and there were some fantastic stone bridges.

I saw my first lamb of the season and some sheep on one farm had already been shorn. There must've been a good reason for it, because if anyone had taken my coat off in the middle of winter I wouldn't have been very happy!

We passed Wick football stadium, and like the one at Thurso, it wasn't quite a Manchester United, but give them a chance.

Rooks were busy nest building whilst the hum of life in Wick went on beneath. The farmers had made a mess by letting their plastic bags fly into the fencing where they blew about like a line of washing.

PAVING SLABS FOR WALLS

This was quite extraordinary and the slabs stood like tombstones all round the outside of the fields.

It took three and a half hours to arrive in drizzly, dull Thurso. When I turned the corner I saw the Hotel Royal where I'd had a meal the last time I was here. Somehow it seemed much smarter, so I went in.

'Hello. How much is a room for a poor man?'

'Should be £40, but I'll do it for £35.'

I left and walked up the street. I thought the Royal seemed to be a good bargain so I went back and checked in. Life is much more fun when people are polite.

Paul couldn't do enough for me and I'm sure it helped that I was the only one in the hotel. I had a shower and watched a little of the Dundee v Rangers game which was a good match. I left at half-time when Dundee was leading 1-0. At the bar in the evening I found out that the result was 2-2.

It was too early to sit about so I walked out onto the road and back to the slab walls we had passed. I wandered past two very young parents pushing their new baby in a pram. A farmer on his quad-bike was checking his ewes and new-born lambs, and a water trough was leaking through a pipe. I wondered if he was on a meter.

I found the slab walls and took my photographs. I wandered up a farm track to a sign that said: 'Stainland Farm'. It was a very smart tarmac drive with recently clipped hawthorn hedges on each side and a slab wall as well.

The farmyard was full of animals peering out of every building. One of the buildings was stone with fantastic curved archways, which were very low with a bull looking out. There were sheep with their lambs in the house garden, but not a soul about. I said hello to some very contented mothers-to-be. They lay there chewing the cud and were in excellent health.

I walked down another track where a tractor and plough stood abandoned. I couldn't find the farmer to tell him about the water leak.

I returned to the hotel where I asked the cheerful barmaid what the main employment here was.

'BT Call Centre,' she replied.

I had my meal in the main restaurant and was served by Paul. The food and service were excellent – nothing was too much trouble for him.

THURSO TO ORKNEY

My 'walkabout' never gets boring and I was to have quite a day today.

I'd had a dreadful night's sleep as usual and kept sliding off my anti-piss mattress. I made up some sandwiches at breakfast.

When anyone tells you how long it's going to take to walk somewhere always add on 25%. The supposed half-hour walk took fifteen minutes longer and I could see the ferry coming in. When I arrived at the ticket office I was told that the bus had left for the ferry, so I had another five minute walk.

'D'ye live on Orkney?'

'No, not that stupid!' I said.

'That'll be £16.50.' *'Idiot! Next time I must say that I do live on Orkney as locals get a reduction.'*

Well, it was a brand new boat. *'These Scottish MPs certainly know how to spend English taxes.'*

The crossing would take two hours. I thought it was going to be a nice peaceful journey, but when Mrs Fulloflife asked if I wanted to chat that was an end of it. She was a short plump lady who had just sold a third of an acre for development and had bought a hundred acres, a house and farm buildings on one of the smaller islands. She was a divorced fifty-one-year-old and full of enthusiasm and ideas, but not a listener.

She was going to start 'The Good Life' with pigs, sheep and vegetables. Power was provided by the wind. She was going to learn the lot. But how she was going to find the energy, I didn't know. She was so fat that her legs were touching and then she offered me some chocolate she had bought on the ferry. The ideas kept pouring out: she was going to build a house into the cliff, learn to fly, buy a speed boat, and even buy a pony and trap. She wanted my name and address so that I could help her farm. She said it had all cost her £150,000, so if it all went wrong would it be the end of the world?

This was her second journey with the removal boys, and goodness knows, they were different.

AID RUNNERS

Yet again, I have to say that it can be very easy to underestimate people and the following two were classic examples. They were slumped in the seats like plastic bags, but when they started talking they made my life seem rather boring.

Jake was a petrol technician who'd worked all over and was now retired, or as he put it, he pottered.

They were into everything. They had bought Russian army lorries that could run on any fuel and had sublet them to Kenya Aid Companies so that they could run supplies to the Sudan. They had tyres on them that could run even if they'd been shot out.

They'd been in Romania and had bought land on the first day of the New Year after it had joined the EU. They'd bought seven hundred acres, some of which was allocated for housing. They were also good friends of the beautiful housing minister.

His mate, Jim, was older and had led Jake into all these adventures. He was covered in tattoos, had seven children and seventeen grandchildren. He'd had two heart attacks and he still smoked – he was a man with no fear.

Jim had driven the first truck into Kuwait and had been the only lorry driver to go through the Mont Blanc tunnel (for some reason or other), telling the police that had they stopped him they would have been infringing his human rights.

These guys were into bio-diesel made from old chip and waste oil.

When they found out I was a farmer I got the usual shit about the fact that they'd never met a poor one. 'How much did you pay to come up here?'

'£100 return.'

'You must be fucking mad. Ryanair do it for £15 return. Fuck me, we go to Spain for three days for £10. We always look for the cheapest flights.'

Mrs Fulloflife had bought the lorry and it really cost nothing as they'd already sold it in Orkney. It seemed a 'win-win' situation with them. I said that my life seemed boring compared with theirs and one of them replied: 'Life is what you make of it.' *'Funny bloke.'* He hardly had any sense of humour; and I hardly got any writing done.'

ORKNEY

I jumped on a bus which took me round the industrial area. Half an hour later we were in Kirkwall. I found the Kirkwall Hotel. The receptionist barely looked up, let alone smiled. The price was £60-80 per night and would be going up in April. I had a cup of coffee and thought better of it.

I asked an FFB having a smoke outside what he thought of the hotel. 'Don't waste your time. They're a fucking rip off. Go to Pomona just around the corner.'

He'd moved up from Boston as he was fed up with all the fucking Lithuanians drugging and pissing in his garden. He'd had £2000 worth of Koi carp stolen from his pond. *'Fucking bastards!'* He'd sold his place three years ago at top rates, had bought an old church in Sanday and was doing it up. The council was the problem and he was working for someone up here to earn money. He told me that now he was up here he never even bothered to take the keys out of his car.

I was grateful that he'd put me in touch with the nice family-run Pomona B&B-cum-café round the corner. It was to be my home for the next five days.

I managed to get a huge room with three single beds and a bathroom for £22 per night. The place was run by Colin, who used to be a crofter, a fisherman and a builder. When he came to show me the room his hands were covered in flour.

'Hard life being a fisherman,' I said.

'Nay, not really. Lobsters are easy, but to get scallops means being away for four nights. The local Orcadians don't work so I have Polish girls working for me.'

I had a shower and then went out to discover Orkney. I walked a fair way out of Kirkwall and then started hitching. A car stopped and Annabel, a very cheerful lady, gave me a lift. She told me she was 'just a cleaner' and I told her not to put herself down. She whizzed me past the airport and dropped me off.

I had another lift from June. She had a huge Shogun type vehicle and had come up from Lanarkshire. She'd bought a redundant school and she and her partner were doing it up. When she dropped me off she asked if I would like to look round and meet her partner.

June was business-like, shortish and in her late fifties or early sixties. Her partner really didn't want to know me at all. He had long grey, hippy-type hair. They didn't seem to be a good match and I took a dislike to him.

She asked him if he would like to show me the rest of the building but he never did.

Someone had pinched the school bell and unfortunately they'd installed new white PVC windows.

I went into Deerness stores for a bottle of water. All the stores here are clean and run by locals.

With all the scattered houses there seemed to be nobody about. It was very strange.

I saw a really old and rusted International tractor with spade lugs. *'Must be a scrap-merchant's paradise.'*

I turned round and walked back along the same road. One man told me that years ago there'd been no geese on Orkney, but now it's full of them and the farmers aren't too happy.

I slipped into the St Ola Hotel for a pint before going back to the B&B. I chatted to a couple of chaps, George and Duncan; one was a harbour worker and the other a professor. One thing you don't want to be here is a teetotaller or a vegetarian.

They told me about the sheep out on North Ronaldsay which only eat seaweed and are very small and taste different from normal sheep. Seaweed has a high pH level and is spread on acid ground. It's used a lot in the growing of potatoes. The seaweed-eating sheep number about two thousand and are wild. When they're sold off – usually going to fancy London restaurants – several of the crofters share the bounty. Three pints later I came out quite merry.

I had a shower and went to the Kirkwall Hotel for dinner. I was served by a young girl who didn't smile at all and walked along like an old farmer. I told the head lady that the food was good, but that the girl who served it had no passion for her work. She said, 'No passion?' I should have said interest. She told me that the girl was only sixteen and I was being hard on her. Perhaps she was right.

I needed some sleep so went to bed for a dreamy old night. I dreamt I was down the chimney at New Shelve Farmhouse and it was falling in on me, and I couldn't scramble out. I then dreamed that I had a crawler tractor stuck on the railway line in blue clay and a train was coming. Once more I was glad to wake up.

I had breakfast with Mr Spark who worked for the lighthouse board as a technician and went around maintaining lighthouses. Yesterday, he'd slipped off a ladder and cracked a rib. Most of the lighthouses are being converted to solar energy and if one goes out they are all connected to a central supply in Edinburgh. He said there are twenty-four technicians working on about 240 lighthouses around Scotland.

I went to the bus station and asked for a bus to St Margaret's Hope. When I asked a lady driver if it was her bus she said, 'No', so I went back into the bus station and asked the station master if I had time to go to the tourist office.

He said, 'Your bus has just gone.'

I couldn't believe it. Now there were only the two of us in the station and the station master was doing fuck all except chatting to the female conductors. I told him he was a stupid idiot for not telling me as he knew where I was going.

'What do you want me to do? Tell the driver to come and pick you up?'

'No, but you're not doing anything, just fucking about and you knew where I was going.'

I now had to make new plans, so I started walking out of town. 'Is that the A961?'

'Don't know.'

'The road to St Margaret's Hope?'

'Turn left at the top.'

I couldn't make this walk out and even though I'd walked the same road yesterday I didn't recognise any of it.

George gave me a lift. He used to live down south, but had retired on medical grounds as he had angina. The doctor told him that either he could keep on working or move to a stress-free environment, so here he was. He used to live on the island of Sanday, but what with a large garden and being so far away, if there were medical problems he wanted to be near the mainland. Sometimes the fog would come down and they couldn't fly and sometimes it was too rough for the ferries. He used to manage a building society and when he wanted help he couldn't get it. They said they couldn't afford it, but when a new manager took over and said he didn't know how George had coped, they gave him an extra four people. George dropped me off at the Churchill Causeways, having gone out of his way.

THE CHURCHILL CAUSEWAYS

These causeways were built after a German U-boat slipped into the harbour and sank the HMS Royal Oak on the 14th October, 1939. One and a half miles were built, mainly by Italian POWs, using 250,000 tons of rock and 66,000 locally cast concrete blocks. They were opened on May 12th, 1945, four days after the end of the war. Most of the causeways are now used as roads connecting the various islands. This is where I came across the Italian Chapel.

The Italian POWs were captured during the North African Campaign and were sent to Orkney to work on the Churchill Barriers. They lived in many cheerless huts, but the active Italians made concrete paths and planted flowers. The one thing that they lacked, however, was a chapel.

In 1943 two Nissen Huts were made available and these were placed end to end and joined together. They used the simplest material available and turned it into a mini-cathedral.

After a fairly long walk across windswept causeways, dear old Tora picked me up. She had retired from dairy farming and her husband and son were butchers. Every Tuesday and Friday she did deliveries and the back of the car was full of meat.

Her hobbies were gardening and the WI.

We drove onto the ferry and I helped her offload. She told me that Tora was a Viking name.

I found a pub and had a coffee. The landlady said, ' Hope you don't mind me doing some painting?'

She was painting away and chatting and was positive, active and attractive, although her non-existent breasts didn't bulge the boiler suit out at all.

'Anything I should see over here?' I asked.

'Yeah, go to Windwick and see the rocks.'

I saw a grey pussy cat and called it over to me. It came running and lapped up the attention, purring all the time.

I asked the landlady if the busy time started at Easter, and she said, 'May,' and had her fingers crossed.

My next lift was with John McKenzie, a retired crofter and bus driver. He was a bit shaky, but it was a welcome lift. He told me that he really didn't give lifts, but said I had a nice face! He'd once given two Germans a lift and after a while he'd dropped them off. Later in the day his friend went past them and didn't stop, so they threw a stone at his car.

He also told me about a couple of guys hitching and when a car slowed down but didn't stop, they lashed out with a bike chain. A few miles up the road he stopped for some petrol and found the bike chain hanging on his wing mirror with two fingers attached!

He told me that during a bad winter a lot of hares had died off.

'Do you have grouse?'

'Just a few.'

'Wild deer?'

'No.'

'Do you have foxes?'

'No, although there was a big hoo-ha on the radio because one had been found dead by the side of the road.'

'Do you have footpaths?' 'What a stupid question as all of Scotland is open access!'

'Do you speak Gaelic?'

'No, only in the Western Hebrides.'

WINDWICK AND HESTA ROCK

He went on his way after dropping me off in a lay-by. I made my way to Windwick by following a sign that pointed down a farm-type track. I should've turned left but went through the farmyard and carried on down the track at my peril. Thirty barbed wire fences later I found Hesta Cliffs, but it was an interesting walk. I disturbed all the geese and found some pheasants and a wild cat, and some strange country byways. I kept thinking that at any minute someone was going to turn up and tell me to 'get off my land' but no one did.

At Hesta Rocks a sign said that 188 men had perished on HMS Narborough and HMS Opal. On the night of 12th January, 1918, the two destroyers left Scapa Flow to join the light cruiser 'Boadicea' to patrol east of the Pentland Skerries in the Pentland Firth. A fierce blizzard blew up and the destroyers requested permission to return to Scapa Flow as they could not maintain their radio contact with Boadicea. They went off course and both struck the rocks at Hesta Head near Windwick on the east coast of South Ronaldsay. The only survivor was William Sissons who climbed the rocks to a ledge and stayed there for thirty-six hours.

Jane took me as far as St Margaret's Hope as she was going to take the ferry back to John o' Groats. She was a funny girl with great big fat legs and with nothing about her save the fact that she stopped for me.

I went back to the pub, but it was shut. He had gone to pick his daughter up from school.

It was a wild old day with showers and a bit of hail and snow chucked in.

I had another lift from a neat German lady who worked as a genetic scientist in Edinburgh. Apparently, she'd seen the advertisement in *The Guardian* to work in the Orkneys. I asked her if she was in favour of GM farming and she wasn't sure. She dropped me off at the Churchill Causeways.

I walked through the village and again marvelled at some of the old buildings that were unused and unloved.

My last lift was with Brian. He took me all the way to Kirkwall. I asked him if he had lived on Orkney all his life. 'I hope not,' came the reply. It broke the ice and I roared with laughter.

ST MAGNUS CATHEDRAL

This is the most outstanding building in the Orkneys. The Vikings started building it in 1137 and parts were added over the next three hundred years. It's the only wholly medieval Scottish Cathedral and the best preserved building of that era in Britain. The original spire was struck by lightning in the late 17th century. Major work was undertaken in the early 20th century. The building looked impressive from the outside and even more so inside.

I was glad to get back to my nest at Pomona's; food and bed.

I had thought I knew my way about this small town but I kept going up the wrong way and was given a load of awful instructions. So it turned out to be a three and a half hour walk day; nobody loved me and they made me walk miles. I saw lots of oyster catchers, sheep and lapwings.

At last I got a lift from Margaret, who'd come here ten years ago and really loved the islands. She'd retired on medical grounds with a dicky back and had to drive bolt upright. She'd worked for Customs and Excise doing the booze and cigarette bit, but she got fed up with all the red tape involved. She went out of her way to be helpful and dropped me off at the Houton ferry terminal, where the ferry goes to and from Hoy and Flotten. It had a very ugly hotel next door to it which was shut.

I stepped into the lonely booking office and ended up, unplanned, taking a ferry to Hoy. I didn't have long to wait either. *'If you'd told me forty minutes ago that I'd be on the ferry I wouldn't have believed you.'*

The ferry was small and if you wanted to take a vehicle you had to book early. It had no fancy café and only a few seats.

Half an hour later we were on Hoy. On the way I got chatting to an interesting man who was on his way to Flotten. He worked on the oil refinery and his job was to x-ray pipes for wear. He worked twelve hours on and twelve hours off for three weeks and had worked all over the world, on and offshore. He didn't really like the work, but it paid the bills. He said that one hundred miles offshore he'd once seen a sparrow hawk take a racing pigeon.

Scapa Flow is one of the greatest natural harbours in the world, and is no deeper than sixty metres with an average of thirty metres. It was used by the Vikings a thousand years ago, but it is best known as the chief naval base during the First and Second World Wars. It was closed down in 1956.

Following the German defeat in the First World War, seventy-four ships were interned pending a decision of the peace treaty in Versailles. After nine months of waiting, on June 21st, 1919, the German officer in charge gave the order to scuttle the fleet. With little communication, he didn't realise that the Versailles Peace Treaty had been extended. The Germans had been preparing for this day for some time, welding bulkheads open and quietly dropping important keys and tools overboard so that the valves couldn't be shut. The Royal Navy tried to prevent them but only saved eighteen of the fifty-two ships.

A few years later tenders went out for the biggest marine salvage operation ever. Forty-five of the fifty-two ships were raised and cut up for scrap. It wasn't an easy job as fierce storms often sank the ships again when they'd been raised.

LYNESS MUSEUM

There was some history here. It was a naval base in the two wars, with storage for a hundred thousand tons of oil to supply the warships. They had many warship guns and propellers, but when I tried to get in the door of the museum I thought it was locked. I then met Lewis Munro on the ferry going home and he said it was open but the door was stiff. Lewis had been looking after the museum for twenty-two years. He told me about the troops coming home from the First World War: they'd escaped the trenches, only for the ship that was bringing them back to hit the rocks. Two hundred men died and there were only about eleven survivors.

It started to rain so I sheltered in a huge ex-naval building that was left over from the war. It had farm machinery and animal feed in it and it wasn't long before Valerie and Eric wanted to know what I was up to. When I told them that I was also a farmer we all started talking farming.

Eric had lived all his life on Hoy and had never been out of Scotland. He worked for Valerie who looked about sixty, but according to Eric she was nearer eighty. She was a very smart lady who had been heavily into horses until she moved to Hoy.

Eric told me that there are two kinds of weather up here. 'Rain and wind; and wind and rain!' Valerie said that on one occasion they were about to combine the barley when the wind took the heads off. Sometimes they get to combine the barley but are lucky if they get the straw. Eric hates farmers who use the straw on carrots and he said that even in Aberdeen they chop it.

LYNESS NAVAL CEMETERY

This really does shock you to walk round here and to see just how young these men were; one was just sixteen. I signed the remembrance book saying thanks for our freedom.

I found some farm buildings with lovely architecture and wondered how people could fill such a place with rubbish and fail to give it the respect it deserved.

Hoy Hotel across the road was the saddest and ugliest building you could ever wish to see. Later on I discovered that it was an old naval building.

'I know I haven't seen much of Hoy as I didn't have enough time but the few hours I've been here have been very interesting, especially meeting Valerie and Eric.'

On the return journey all the passengers were construction workers, who were building an extension to the school and I felt a real skiver walking off the ferry as the only non-worker.

I took the bus back to Kirkwall and said goodbye to Lewis and went into St Ola's pub for a pint. The professor chap was there again, but although I'd had an interesting chat with him a couple of days ago he barely acknowledged me.

I went to the nearby Ayre Hotel where I had a shitty meal. I returned my chips as they were lukewarm and when they came back they were undercooked, so when I went to pay I knocked off the price of the chips.

BREAKFAST

I spoke to Mrs Muir, the owner. 'And how are you this morning?'

'I was all right.'

'What do you mean?'

'We've got a weeeeeeet beeeeeeeeeed this morning!'

'Sorry, a what?'

I couldn't understand a word she said and she looked so down in the mouth. I found out that what she meant was that they had a 'wet bed'. One of the oil workers had been on the piss and had wet the bed.

'We've had this trouble before, and we always charge them for a new beeeed. Colin rings up the oil company and tells them we've got trouble. The company man says that if we have trouble he wants to know about it because these men represent the company. They always pay for a new beeeeed.'

While I was having breakfast an oil worker came in, a man of about thirty-four.

'Oh, Mrs Muir, I have a feeling you're not very happy with me. This has never happened to me before. I just had four pints'

I felt so embarrassed to be in the same room that I left them to argue the toss.

Dear old Mrs Muir, when she says 'toooone' she means 'town'.

Poor old Orkney has sixty-eight cruise boats visiting her each year. The good news is that they get a little dosh, but everyone's happy when winter arrives and they stop coming.

I caught the bus for a trip around the west end of the island and it was just right as it was a wet and miserable day. Every field had a lake of water in it and there once again we met Mr and Mrs Greyleg Goose.

The odd passenger got on and off.

I changed buses at Stromness and I hardly had time for a cigarette. However, I met a couple from Nigeria who had such big honest faces. I asked the gentleman what he was up to here and he said he was a petrochemical engineer student.

'You must be clever.'

'Why?'

'Because you are!' I replied.

Scattered everywhere there were brand new ugly houses which looked bloody awful in this beautiful countryside and yet there were also some lovely old farm barns which were falling down.

There were no trees up here but there were rabbits and hares.

The bus driver wasn't hanging about and would've made a good racing driver.

A farmer had put up loads of empty plastic fertiliser bags to scare the birds away and the geese were grazing underneath them.

Back in Kirkwall I had some time to spare, so I went into the FWAG office and met Kay Sims who used to work for Scats of Robertsbridge – she was made redundant when the Grain Farmers took it over. I had an interesting chat about conservation around Orkney.

I went and booked my ferry ticket to the Shetland Islands that night. I asked the pretty receptionist if she would like to come with me but she declined!

There was a gale warning but there was a chance it wouldn't arrive.

I went and squared up with Colin and had to force the money on him for staying in the room until 10pm. He let me keep the key as he said that the ferry might be cancelled. He said the room was £20 and not £22!

The pick-up point was outside the hotel at 10.40pm and I was the only passenger. Even the bus was rocking in the wind, but the ferry was still running. I couldn't believe how many people got off the ferry – there must've been just under a hundred. It departed from Aberdeen.

I could've shared a cabin for £18.50 or had a single for £48, but didn't bother, and it worked out OK.

I found a sofa and tried to make myself comfortable for the night. When the piss-heads left to get more beer I switched the television off and when they came back I heard them swearing and they were too stupid to switch the thing back on.

Now we were in the middle of the storm and the yobs became less mouthy. Luckily, we had a smart security man who kept an eye on them.

There was a big bang and I thought we'd hit a rock, but in fact it was just the big waves. The ferry was very neat and tidy and the staff were pleasant as she creaked her way to the Shetlands in the howling wind. Those people who weren't drunk looked drunk as they staggered about the ship. I tied my rucksack to the table leg and kept wondering if it might smack one of the noisy folk in the face, but it didn't. I continued to catnap. The drunks were now asleep and the smell of disinfectant came wafting through the ferry.

GOOD MORNING!

'Now, John Arthur is like a little boy, looking out of the window at the huge waves in this 50-70mph wind.'

Seagulls trailed the ferry and I wondered how they avoided getting caught by the massive waves. It was strange because there seemed to be little ponds in the middle of the waves and it was like sailing through the Alps. *'Oh well, if the dear old 'Horrosey' goes down, at least death will come quickly.'*

On the boat I met Cynthia and her husband and two young daughters. They were up from Lancashire and had never been on a ferry before, or even to Scotland, and they were going up there to live full-time. They had swapped council houses, white goods and all. I admired their spirit.

After seven and a half hours we arrived in Lerwick and the police were waiting to arrest a druggy type.

I had no idea what I was going to do. I also needed to get my thoughts together. I walked outside the ferry terminal building and couldn't believe the strength of the wind. It nearly blew me away and the only time in my life that I've experienced anything like it was in the 1987 storm in Kent.

The hotel was directly opposite the terminal, but a prison would've had more atmosphere. I had a crappy expensive breakfast.

Please meet Jose Francisco; he was a delightful young waiter from Ecuador.

'What do you most dislike about this country?' I asked.

'Racism, such as I experienced in Brighton.'

'And what do you like about it?'

'It's an organised society.'

I've never seen street lights dancing before. I went into the Co-op to get some cigarettes.

'What's it like here on a bad day?'

'Aye, it's not going to last.'

'Yes, but what's it like on a bad day?'

'Aye, this is just a breeze.'

FORT CHARLOTTE

I went for a short walk to get into the town centre and before I booked in I was watching an elderly couple walking down the street, bent double and struggling in the wind. It had got even stronger and they gave up and turned round.

Again, I've landed on my feet with a three-star guest house right in the middle of town. I even had my bed made up when I went out on the second day. I would've left the room much tidier if I'd known she was going to go in.

Really, this wind wasn't safe to be out in and it was difficult to stay on the footpath and not be blown in front of a car. But they obviously knew how to build here as there were no slates off the roofs; dodgy roofs had blue netting on them.

I went and checked in at the tourist office and if anywhere wanted three-quarters of its staff laid off in winter, it was here. But they were very helpful.

I battled my way into the Queen's Arms for a cup of tea in a really tatty old public bar. I met Ewa from Poland; she had a degree in metal engineering and this was her second visit to Shetland. Her sister and brother-in-law were here as well. She really appreciated me asking her about her career and we were on the same wavelength.

The man picking up rubbish today with his tweezers had an easy time as the wind blew all the rubbish out to sea.

People didn't seem that bothered about the wind, as if to say it was just another day. The rubbish bins out of town have a weighted mesh in them to stop the litter blowing away.

I walked out of town, past the pitch and putt and the cemetery, to the cliffs. The rubbish was flying past me.

Back in town I had a huge hot chocolate and met a curly-haired chap who was a director of the National Theatre. He was quite flamboyant and was trying to get to a production on Unst. He was wondering if he'd had a wasted journey.

I went back to the guest house for a rest and to write and then went to the Grand Hotel to eat. The only thing 'grand' about it was the name. It was freezing cold and the food was cold as well so I sent it back. I don't think it was any warmer when it came back. The dining room was huge and there were just three of us huddled round the imitation coal gas fire. It gave as much heat as a lit match would've done. When I went to turn it up I pulled a muscle in my shoulder. *'Pathetic? Yes!'*

Ewa, the Polish girl I'd met at the Queen's Arms was working here tonight; both places were owned by the same company. I met three offshore guys who were all engineers. They were waiting for the wind to drop so that they could get out to the rig. I asked them if they knew that

Ewa was a metal engineer. I was a bit naughty really but I wanted them to realise that she wasn't just a stupid waitress. The next moment they were chatting away in technical engineering terms and I didn't understand a word they were saying. Ewa was now two feet taller, with a big smile on her face. I think she enjoyed the evening.

After that I went to bed.

It was Easter Saturday; there was a layer of snow and it was the coldest day I'd experienced at any time on my 'walkabout'. I even had to buy some gloves.

I wanted to go south so I rushed out of my bedroom to catch the 9am bus, only to find that it didn't leave until 9.30am.

I watched the bus drivers washing the salt off while I got myself organised. I took the bus to Sumburgh Head.

Walter Scott set part of his 1821 novel, *The Pirate*, in the Old House of Sumburgh during the 17th century, which he named Jarlshof.

Well, hotel extensions don't come more out of place than this one in a beautiful part of the world. The planners need shooting. Planners? What planners?

I went into this dead-looking place just by the Jarlshof ruins. I think I was the first customer for three hundred years.

'Cup of tea, please,' I said to a rather dumb girl.

She came along with it and said, 'Was it tea or coffee?'

'What have I got?'

'Coffee!'

The first coach of the season had turned up and the dumb girl looked horrified.

The coach guide asked, 'Do you do sandwiches?'

'No!'

It was time to get out of here. There was a T-shirted girl with big boobs and the shirt read: 'Peak Performance'.

I walked along the beach hoping to get some shelter from the snow and marvelled at the large seaweed that had washed up – it looked like human bones.

JARLSHOF

I didn't know what to expect here and I was the first official customer as it opened for the spring. Davey was the manager and I made him jump as he was outside and didn't see me coming.

Jarlshof is the best known pre-historic archaeological site in Shetland. It lies near the southern tip and has been described as one of the most remarkable sites ever excavated in the British Isles. It contains remains dating from 2,500 BC up to the 17th century.

The Bronze Age settlers left evidence all over the place, including the Iron Age ruins, decorated bone objects and painted pebbles.

Later digs in the 1950s found evidence of fishing and farming: sheep, cattle, pigs and ponies were kept; Atlantic cod, saithe and ling were eaten, together with whale and seal; a few dog bones were found but chicken bones were absent.

OLD SCATNESS BROCH

This site was discovered during the construction of the airport access road. Excavation started twenty years ago and eleven summers later they found an iron broch. Barley that they found showed that it was built between 400-200 BC. Old Scatness therefore gave the archaeologists the rare opportunity to understand Pictish-Viking transition in Shetland.

Another broch site and it was still being excavated. I had to shelter here as another snow storm blew in.

The Vikings introduced flax to this area and when they arrived they burned their boats for firewood – the rivets out of the clinker boats were discovered and apparently they also used eggs to bind the mortar.

MEET MARY

This was the first time I'd ever been stopped on the road to let an aeroplane land. Mary had her radio and I got some pictures of the plane landing. If you were to fly in the other way or if you didn't get it right when taking off you would land right in the bay. Unfortunately, some years ago that happened and many passengers were drowned.

Meet Shirley she gave me my first lift. She was a school teacher and she gave me a much needed ride. It wasn't quite as easy to get a lift here as in the Hebrides.

I stopped hitching as in the distance I thought I saw a field of Shetland ponies. With the snow it took ages to find them and when I got there I found that they were cattle.

Another lovely young mum, Annie-Marie, and her daughter stopped in their camper van. She put her daughter in the back and off we went. She was an art teacher and her husband did outdoor pursuits, rock climbing and kayaking and things like that. They were from Lanarkshire, but thought one day they might return home.

We passed several stone walled enclosures in the middle of the fields, about half the size of a tennis court. Apparently they are called 'Planty Grubs' and were used for growing vegetables.

Back to Lerwick and it was bloody cold.

Ewa had said that the food was better in the Queen's Head and how right she was.

To start with I had Queen's fish soup with dill, then Shetland lamb-leg steak with shallot mash with mussels and rosemary jus. The vegetables were stir-fried with asparagus, courgettes and mangetouts, and boiled potatoes. The waitress was called Parvis and she was from the Czech Republic. She had a smashing 'open' face.

'Would you tell the chef that this isn't good?'

Her head went back in horror.

'Tell him it's excellent!!' *'Go to bed, nutter.'*

'I must be mad! It's Easter Sunday, there's been snow overnight and I still want to discover Sandness on the west coast.'

I decided that I must wear more clothes so I put on three shirts, one jumper, one waistcoat, one waterproof top, two pairs of trousers and then waterproof trousers as well, one pair of pants, three pairs of socks, one pair of boots, a hat and a pair of gloves! In fact all the clothes I had. And it was still cold.

I had another super breakfast, but suddenly a cutting saw started up and Lynne sent Jim to sort them out.

'It's a bit much at 8.00am on a Sunday morning,' she said, 'when I've done a night shift. And I'm ready for a fight!'

'What do you do?'

'Four others and myself do the Coastguard Centre weather report and all that.'

'Did it record the wind on Friday?'

'84mph, but we have recorded 200mph.'

The idea this morning was to go west from Lerwick, but there were no buses. I greeted the gang of men who were erecting scaffolding round the guest house ready to repair the windows on the first of April.

Lynne was a bit uppity. 'Why do they have to put it up so early?' *'Well, it is the first of April next week!'*

The ganger was pleased to talk. He knew Kent and had lived in Gillingham, but had followed the work and ended up owning a scaffolding business here.

To get a lift I had to walk out of town and find my road. I could've taken a taxi but that's against my principles. *'I am walking it!'*

MEET BECKY

What a lovely sparkly young girl. She was about twenty-five to thirty years old and if you think about it, she was pretty brave to pick up a complete stranger – dressed in black – in the small space of her car.

She ran a wing in a care home for dementia. She had six clients and the house took a total of twenty. Apparently, the pay was good. She loved her job and said she had more trouble with the staff than the patients. She told me how she had been to Kyrgyzstan and had promised herself that when she came back she would never complain about anything again, not her house or her job, as she'd realised how lucky we all are. I told her that I'd also been to Kyrgyzstan the previous summer and so we chatted away about travel like long lost friends.

Her parents had moved up here from Norfolk ten years ago. She and her brother had always said that there was no way they'd ever move up, but now they're all in the Shetlands.

She was on her way to a friend's baby's christening and the car was full of presents. She said she was early and wanted to take me further, but I made her chuck me out. What a breath of fresh air – I felt good as she dropped me off. She told me to write about her in my book.

I must be mad; it wasn't a good day for walking and hitching. I really needed a balaclava, but it wouldn't have done much for my hitching image!

Things went steadily downhill and nobody loved me. Even in a blizzard they drove past. I took shelter in seatless bus shelters several times along the route. I thought, with all these clothes, that I would overheat, but I was cold. The wind just blows into you and even when I got back to the hotel my ears hurt for ages.

I checked my bearings in Bixter, a village with nothing open and not much to open to tell the truth, and then I went back into the open countryside.

A snowplough appeared out of a side road and after a while another snowstorm came up. I legged it across a field to a roofless croft.

When I went inside there were two girls. I don't know who was more startled, them or me.

'Excuse me, but have you room for one more?'

'Yeah, come in.'

'Many thanks. I feel quite guilty eating in front of you girls. If you're ever in Kent, look me up.'

'What have you got in that rucksack? We're hungry.'

'Sorry girls, I've got some cigarettes.'

'We don't smoke. It's a filthy habit. D'ye want sex?'

'No, I have a full-time partner and it's a bit cold!'

'Suit yerself.'

I thanked them for their hospitality and continued

on my way. They came out to see me off, then went straight back inside. *'It's a pity they were sheep!'*

Meet Tim Fraser, who was a project manager for ferry or oil terminals. He asked me, 'What are you doing out here?'

'Just having a look around. You probably think I'm a nutter, but I'm not.'

'There isn't much to see out here in this weather.'

'I keep finding something.'

'Where are you going?'

'Sandness.'

'I'm going to Walls.'

'That'll do!'

We arrived at a windswept and snowy village. He dropped me off and told me that he didn't think he'd done me any favours.

'Is there a pub or café out here?'

'No, there's fuck all.'

He went off to visit his mother.

The sign to Sandness was up a narrow snow covered road. Well, it might've been the road – with so much drifting snow it wasn't easy to tell.

Tim had said there wasn't much there and if I wasn't careful I'd get stuck, so I decided to cut my losses and walk back to Lerwick.

Meet Jim. 'I can't really give you a lift because I'm not insured.' He worked for Lerwick County Council as a plumber and was on call today. He'd done three calls and had two to go. He wanted to watch the Manchester United v Liverpool match, but was too busy.

Anyway I got my lift all the way to Lerwick. *'Funny really, as one minute I thought I was going to perish in the middle of nowhere, and now I'm in a sunny Lerwick.'* It was certainly a good decision to turn back.

By early afternoon I was tucked up in my little bed; warm and with the television on.

Later I went past the fish and chip shop and was amazed to see Jim from the guest house serving behind the counter.

I found out that he owned the shop and had done so for thirty years.

Three young lads outside the fish shop said, 'Want to buy a fag?'

'No, thanks.'

'Have you got 50p to spare?'

'Not to buy cigarettes?'

'No.'

I ended up giving them a pound as I couldn't find 50p. *'Sucker!'*

LERWICK TO THE ISLE OF UNST

It was cold and windy with snow showers; a three shirt day. Jim kindly made me sandwiches, because in the early morning I wasn't that hungry. I paid the £75 for the three nights' stay – it was the best bargain of my 'walkabout' – and then he drove me to the bus station.

The bus driver was going too fast for my liking on these snowy roads. I was in the back seat, strapped in. I was surprised by how few houses there were, but the roads were busy. Through Brae we passed several fish farms. There always seems to be a tarmacked airstrip somewhere. I wondered if they were something to do with the refinery. We passed BP's Sullom Voe Terminal where the oil is pumped from offshore.

We arrived at Toft at 9.10am where it was the end of the route for the bus. I had a short wait for the ferry to the Yell. I couldn't believe how luxurious the ferry was for such a short crossing with so few people. Apparently, it was supplied with oil money and not only that, there were two of them.

Thomas Edmonston at the age of eleven wrote his first list of Unst plants. In 1845 he wrote a book on the plants in the whole of Shetland. In the same year he was made Professor of Botany at the Anderson University in Glasgow. Three months later he went on an expedition and was accidentally shot as he stepped ashore from the boat in Ecuador. He was only twenty.

I was glad that Jim, from Fort Charlotte, had booked me into a B&B, because it was snowing and windy. Unst only has a population of five hundred – plus one holidaymaker!

YELL

There were no buses here and transport was by means of a 'people carrier'. Our driver was Jim Jones, I think, and I had to work quite hard to get a smile out of him, but did in the end.

As we came north we had more snow and Jim was a careful driver. He didn't really have much choice as the two vans in front were having a struggle to get through, and in the end got stuck. Jim sailed past them. I felt quite guilty but Jim just carried on driving.

He dropped me off at the ferry terminal for Unst where the Wind Dog Café was. I said to the manager that I had heard the wind and seen the café, but there was no sign of a dog!

Jim apologised because we would have to wait for an hour and then he drove off. He had said that we shouldn't worry as we would be collected.

The café was a little piece of heaven in the middle of nowhere, where I could have a drink, get warm and write *Walkabout*.

'Would you like tea or coffee?'

'Coffee, please, and black.' I got tea! *'Never mind, John Arthur, you're at the end of the world, so just drink it.'*

I ordered another: 'Coffee, please, black.' I got another tea! 'This is tea.'

She tried it. 'Ah, got mixed up.'

The café had a sign saying: 'THIS IS NOT A BURGER KING. YOU DON'T GET YOUR WAY. YOU TAKE IT MY WAY OR YOU DON'T GET A DAMN THING!'

The owner, Margaret, was a tough, cheerful shortish forty-year-old. She was always on the phone. Another sign said: 'DO I LOOK LIKE A PEOPLE PERSON?'!

'Well, we're on the ferry with one car and two passengers, heading for snowbound Unst; Britain's most northerly island.'

In no more than fifteen minutes we were in Unst. This time our taxi was a Discovery, with a very shy driver. The taxi, or bus as they call it here, had just three passengers and the snow was thicker than ever. We ploughed through it and I wondered why I was here.

The countryside was bleak and snow-swept, but we didn't get stuck and we arrived safely.

Tony and Irene's B&B really was different; just a working home with a few spare rooms. The living rooms were stacked full of televisions and bed linen and there seemed to be enough ironing to last for years.

'Well, someone has to be the first of the season,' I said.

'We had a South African here a few days ago who turned up in shorts!'

Tony was a handyman who'd built his own house, very much in the sixties' or seventies' style. I've never seen such tall doors and they must've been seven feet high. It was very noisy; you could hear every footstep and light switch and every time Tony got up for a pee in the night.

The curtains and paintwork were very seventies. In reality it was a warm place, but atmospherically it was cold. It was a two-storey house which was unusual up here. The best part of the house was the kitchen, which had a panoramic view.

Tony spent a lot of time looking through his binoculars to see what was going on and if the roads were blocked. Something about this place reminded me of Canada.

I walked back past a hotel, which had gone into private hands although the sign was still there. A car came out of a driveway and got stuck in a drift, quite unnecessarily, and the driver got tetchy with his wife when he pushed and she drove. Someone said he was a Red Arrow pilot without an ounce of common sense.

I had to take shelter behind a stone wall but I wasn't lonely as a ringed plover, a curlew and a grey curlew-type bird with orange legs sat nearby. None of them seemed one bit worried by me.

I found another abortion of a hotel with blankets hanging outside. I tried to get in the door and the place had that damp smell, like Leysdown-on-Sea, on the Isle of Sheppey, when coming out of winter.

'Any chance of a coffee?'

'Yeah, in the bar. Go out and round the side.'

On my way back I went into the shop and bought my supper. It was two cheese rolls and a pork pie, and I ate most of it on my way back to the B&B. Eating places up here at this time of year are pretty thin on the ground.

I got lost on the way back and then I saw a man walking towards me – I couldn't believe there was another idiot like me out in this weather.

'Is this the way to Tony and Irene's?'

'No, it's the other way.'

'Am I pleased to see you!'

After this walk in the blizzard I realised that houses were there to keep you warm. 'Who cares a damn what colour the walls are or what pattern the curtains have.' It was just good to get back and go to bed.

After breakfast at the kitchen table, where we competed with *Breakfast TV*, Tony took me round his vintage machinery.

I never thought I'd see a threshing machine worked by pedals and having a handle and its original wooden seat.

Tony had an Aladdin's Cave here, including vintage Lister generators, some of the only ones in the world. He told me that the building for the machinery had cost £20,000.

They were renovating another cottage, the oldest on Unst. They'd completely taken away its entire character; the only thing of interest left was the old swing fire pot holder. *'Quite honestly it makes me feel sick, but Tony's so proud of it and Irene's wallpapering it.'* All the timbers in the roof were a kind of varnished pine.

I thought Tony had a sad streak in him and wondered if it could've been war damage, but he told me that his son had been killed in a car crash when he was twenty. He'd missed the bus and taken a ride as a back seat passenger, a week before joining the army, and that was that.

Tony said it had knocked the stuffing out of him for two years. His son had been an engineer and was keen on the vintage machinery, so they built the museum as a memorial to him and he would have wanted it to carry on. I congratulated Tony on looking after our heritage, as so many farmers were selling such stuff for scrap.

Tony drove me to Ordale tarmacked airfield. He told me he'd had ten flying lessons but had then had to give up because of family commitments, so he'd taken up hang-gliding instead. He never ceased to amaze me. He'd had a nasty accident in the Merchant Navy, when a sliding door banged shut on his arm during a storm in the Bay of Biscay; he was lucky not to have had it amputated.

He drove me to the other end of the island, told me where the odd cafés and places of interest were and then dropped me off.

'Now I realise why sometimes I can't get a lift. When you open the car door and get out, the wind is so cold and it's even worse in a howling gale. If you're driving in a nice warm car you have no idea how freezing it is outside.'

There were some amazing old croft houses that were mainly empty; some had tar roofs and some had roofs that had fallen in and porches in a similar state.

SHETLAND PONIES

I thought I'd better go and introduce myself to these little short-arsed excuses for horses. *'No, I shouldn't be rude as they're very friendly and today they're hungry.'*

Willy Lawson was just about to feed the horses and was pleased to chat. He was very quietly spoken, born and bred on Unst and had never been further than Edinburgh. He'd been a storeman for the RAF and was now retired. He was seventy years old and said that there were fifty-three registered studs on Shetland. He said that the other day it was so windy that his hat had been blown away, never to be seen again. I told him that he should get one like mine that never blows away. Just as we said goodbye and shook hands my hat blew off and went into the ditch! I couldn't believe it. This is when you really get to laugh at yourself and Willy had a good chuckle, too.

I met two girls walking the other way; they were up from Cumbria doing self-catering. It was good to meet some other people and to know that I wasn't the only tourist on Unst.

CHOCOLATE FACTORY

There was a deserted RAF building which Tony had told me was now a café. I asked a guy in the snowy car park if he knew where it was. He said, 'Yeah, I own it. Come on in.'

Aaron and his wife, Cassie, had come up from Sussex about three years before. He used to have a toy model shop and his wife had been a landscape gardener.

They now trade under the name 'Foords Chocolates'. To begin with they didn't know anything about chocolate making and it was all done by trial and error. The best chocolate ingredients come in pellet form from Belgium. On a good day they can make 8,500 chocolates and on an ordinary day about 4,500.

Aaron kept on about his chocolate factory but in reality it's just a kitchen and all his sales are done on the Internet. He told me a story of the time he'd made a batch of Tia Maria chocolates: he'd washed up at 11pm and the next morning found that the chocolates were all sticky and had to be thrown away. Apparently the steam from his washing up, although invisible, had ruined the lot.

In the walking business it's better to have the wind up your jumper than in your face!

A car stopped with the two girls in it. 'Would you like a lift?'

'No, thanks.' *'I think the girls were in love with each other.'*

Another car stopped. 'Would you like a lift?'

'No, thanks, I need the exercise.'

I couldn't resist popping my head into this small rock quarry. Ashley and Wally told me that the rock was going to make a new pier, but their real love was being crofters. They said that there was nothing more satisfying than feeding the sheep in the snow and that they didn't look on it as being work.

THE MOST NORTHERLY CAFÉ IN BRITAIN

Just the job here! There are no other places to eat and I met Charlie, Pat and Lorraine.

Most Northerly bus shelter in UK

All these shops are spotlessly clean and well stocked, and even though far from anywhere, the vegetables are fresh.

Last night I'd thought that being stuck up here would be hard work, but I'd had two good days.

I did ask Tony if, for payment, he would take me around the area but he couldn't, so I asked the local taxi service and they couldn't either. It was suggested that I could go around with the 'Meals on Wheels' people, but that didn't materialise either.

I phoned Pomona to ask if they had a bed for tomorrow as I was coming back. Colin said, 'We're fully booked, but we can let you have the sofa if you like.' I accepted!

SHETLAND TO ORKNEY

It was my last breakfast with Irene and Tony. I said my goodbyes and Tony dropped me off at the bus stop just outside the most northerly post office in Britain.

There was one other passenger, John Davidson. He was a quiet shy seventy-year-old who looked a bit down on his luck. He'd come from the Midlands many years ago and had lately been living on a shoestring. I found out that a couple of weeks earlier, and for the second time, he'd had a huge operation for a hernia. The hospitals up here, like the schools, were very good and he'd been in for ten days. He told me that he'd lost a stone and was going to keep it that way. We talked about the fat youngsters and he called them the 'Lost Generation'.

He wasn't a bitter man and I agreed with him that the young don't work and eat rubbish.

I never did get to the bottom of what he did and when I asked him if it was connected with the sea he just said, 'I'm an armchair reader.'

He used to cycle a lot and when I suggested one with an electric engine he said, 'Why can't they make one that recharges when going downhill?'

The oil storage depot serves both Atlantic and North Sea oil and when it was being built it employed 4,500 people.

He told me about the burning of the waste gas. 'It's better to burn it than let it into the atmosphere, but maybe there should be a better use for it.'

We said goodbye at Lerwick. 'Look after yourself, John,' I said.

'Don't worry, I know how to do that!'

I had a £10 salad and a drink in Ola's café, but it wasn't comfortable for writing and it was cold. The place was busy and a young mum phoned her friend in the High Street and the next moment there were hundreds of young mums with the fruits of their loins in tow.

I felt dirty and hungered for my little room in Fort Charlotte Guest House. The ferry was leaving at 5.30pm. I passed the chip shop and thanked Jim for the contact in Unst.

I spent the waiting time in the spotless North Link Ferry Terminal. Specsavers had an advert showing a farmer who was shearing his dog instead of his sheep!

They always check your name getting on and off. The ferry was spotless and I found my usual place and was soon joined by others.

I thought one chap would turn out to be an idiot and that thought was confirmed when he asked if he could turn the television up when *Emmerdale Farm* came on.

Back in Kirkwall I felt I was coming home and Colin picked me up with his new stray dog, Bobby. Someone had cancelled so I was given a room.

ORKNEY TO SCOTLAND

It was sunny and there was no wind. I said goodbye to Colin and his family and waited for the bus to Stromness. I met a young man called Richard who'd failed all his exams at university and had taken a job cleaning buses. He'd now been offered an apprenticeship in mechanics and was enjoying it. His father had come up here years ago and had got a job as harbour master. Richard, like me, loved trekking because you meet people.

The greylags looked really happy munching away with the sun on their backs in the tightly-grazed waterlogged fields. *'Goodbye, geese.'*

At the ferry terminal, as on *I'm a Celebrity*, I said, 'Get me out of here!'

Pam replied, 'Don't be like that. It's a lovely day. Are you a student OAP islander?'

Everything is so smart on these ferries and I simply can't fault them.

Back at Thurso, I found the road to John o' Groats and started to thumb a lift. The first car stopped. *'My big smile has worked again.'*

Don was taught engineering and only retired when he reached eighty. He was now eighty-seven and a very smart professional man. The last job he'd done was setting up a kitchen manufacturer's computer system. He dropped me off at Castletown.

I walked through Castletown under a huge rookery in the tallest trees around. I walked past a gatehouse and then on to Castletown Mill.

I couldn't get over the size of it. Some of the roof had fallen in and some of the huge pulley wheels were still rusting away. A sign said: 'DANGER-KEEP OUT' and they weren't joking. *'This place needs someone with loads of cash and love.'*

Walter Smith was walking towards me.

'Do you know the history of this place?'

'Yes, it used to belong to my grandfather, but he went bankrupt in the 1920s. The farmers never paid him.'

'Steady on,' I said, 'I'm a farmer.'

MY SECOND LIFT

Frederick Richards, or Rick as he liked to be called, was on his way to pick up a big gas bottle in the little trailer where I put my rucksack. A bottle would only last a fortnight and cost £70. He lived in a mobile home and with no insulation it was freezing cold, so he would leave an electric blanket on all night. He'd retired from Peterborough. He asked me to guess how old he was.

Playing it safe, I said, 'Sixty-seven.'

'No, I'm eighty-one.'

MEY CASTLE

It was closed and as all the best castles were closed I carried on walking up its long drive. I met Yakie walking the other way, who came from South Korea and was at Wolverhampton reading media studies and business, and loving every minute of it all.

I walked into the gardens and all the gardening tools were out. I went round the outside of the castle feeling like a naughty schoolboy. I never saw a soul. It was a funny looking castle.

Back on the main road to John o' Groats I walked for an hour and was just about running out of steam when I got a lift from John Crickley.

He'd come up from Lanarkshire and he reminded me of Fred Dibner. He was on his mobile talking to his son for ten minutes before I could thank him for picking me up. I've never known anyone talk so slowly.

'Aye...son,...take...the...A299....Keep...off...the...motorway,...better... views....Aye... son.'

John took me all the way to John o' Groats.

JOHN O' GROATS

What a dull and uninteresting place it is – just like Land's End – and there isn't even a sign post that you can pose next to for a photograph!

I got John out of his car to take his photograph and then he took mine.

A group of Chinese tourists wanted me to take their photograph.

'Do you think China will take over the world?'

'Yes, without a doubt.'

'Are you all from one-child families?'

'Yes, all but one who has a brother.'

I said goodbye to John Crickley and walked up to a nearby hotel. *'What a dump for all the tourists to come and see.'*

'How much is a night for a poor man?'

'£45.'

'Wow!'

She came back and said, '£35.'

'I'll take it.'

I had a chat with a drinker who used to paint all the radio masts on lighthouses and he was well on his way to being pissed.

The evening meal was a pretty crappy one and when they came and asked if everything was OK they never waited for a reply. *'Never mind, the views here are terrific. Just go to bed, you fussy little git!'*

It was raining. I decided to leave at 8.00am before breakfast to try to catch the 8.40am train from Thurso. I signed the comments book and I gave 10/10 for the room and 2/10 for dinner. (When I returned a couple of months later they had altered the two into an eight!)

I never saw a soul when I left at 7.30am. The only two days of good weather had given way to rain and as I walked along the road to Thurso I was glad of my wet-weather gear.

The only traffic on the other side of the road was a bus and with luck he would return. He did. 'Glad to see you,' I said.

'Eh?' said the dry old stick.

These bus companies are smart up here; they deliver you to the rail station at 8.50am and the train leaves at 8.40 am! The next train wasn't until 1.00pm.

So I then had to rush down to the centre of town to catch a bus to Inverness which would take three and a half hours. I was lucky to get it.

It's not very often that I ride on a bus which fills up. The bus went from freezing to warm and I stripped off my wet-weather gear.

Every 'walkabout' has a 'Miss Lard' and she got on the bus with her boyfriend. She had the usual striped slacks and trainers which were not done up. She had greasy hair with more grease on it than in our workshop. She wore glasses and had a large bandage around the head, from which I imagined they'd just taken out her brain, or perhaps tried to put one in!

She nearly fell onto my seat as the bus took off, but fortunately slumped into her own, slipping across it like a plastic bag full of water.

Then Miss Greasy Lard put her seat back and I was pushing my knees into it to make sure she couldn't do so. *'I don't know if she's simple, but if not then she should be!'*

A young mum with two children and a stupid looking father in a baseball cap got on and it encouraged me to take mine off. One had a T-shirt on saying: 'I'm with Stupid' with an arrow pointing sideways. I think that was dead right.

One passenger moved to the back seat so that two ladies could sit together, but they never thanked him.

Three and a half hours later we were in Inverness.

Next morning I walked around Inverness trying to find the train station to Edinburgh, only to realise that it was only a hundred metres from the hotel.

Three hours and twenty minutes later we were in Edinburgh. We'd passed more stunning countryside; with horned stags and hinds with their young having an early morning suckle.

There were plenty of police around for the big Celtic v Rangers match.

I booked in at the hotel and then I walked to the top of Scott's Monument, all 287 steps of it.

The castle was full of tourists and although I was one as well I didn't like being with them.

Later, I jumped onto my open-top bus and it was cold. We passed the Scottish Parliament building. *'How could they spend so much money on such an ugly place?'*

I rang Sarah Richards, Katie's daughter, who was working in Edinburgh. We arranged to meet that night. I was a bit nervous about the evening and didn't really know whether I'd done the right thing. She rang me when I was on the open-top bus to see about the arrangements for the evening.

I wondered what they could want with an old wrinkly on a Saturday night.

Not long after 7pm, Sarah and her now husband Will picked me up. She had a huge smile, gave me a kiss and put me at my ease.

We drove back to their flat which they shared with three others. Laptops and large plasma screens were the order of the day here. They were engrossed watching sport. It was a brand new flat right on the river. I watched the reflecting light on the river whilst having a cigarette on the balcony after a lovely meal. I must say I felt really old with these whizzy young people. They didn't hang back on the drink so I took a taxi back to the hotel.

EDINBURGH TO LENHAM

I crept out of the hotel early and caught my flight home.

My friend Tibor picked me up and took me back home. Another end to a very interesting couple of weeks.

CHAPTER EIGHT

Thurso to Newcastle

It was 'walkabout' time again; time to return to Thurso after a two month break. It was not long before I was back at King's Cross Station, peering in all the windows trying to find a seat. The train was full and the only empty seats were first class ones.

I walked back and sat in a first class carriage. I couldn't fiddle about for too long as the train was due to leave in a few minutes. I felt quite guilty sitting here as most people were standing and all the more so as I was served with coffee and biscuits. I got rid of the 'Reserved' ticket on the seat and sat there wondering how much it would cost.

'Tickets, please! You realise this is first class?'

'Well, it cost me £133.'

'Well, it'll cost you another £25 to stop here.'

'OK, here's another £25.'

I didn't argue with him as the rest of the train was 'standing' and it is a long way to Edinburgh.

'Excuse me, but is the first class ticket I've bought a return one?' *'Cheeky shit!'*

'No.'

'Does the ticket take me to Inverness? It has Edinburgh on it.'

'NO!'

'Thank you.'

My neighbour told me it was still cheap and it was the best £25 I've ever spent.

I was just thinking how miserable he was and then he started to chirp up. He was a train-spotter on his way to Carlisle to see some steam trains, then coming back to London tonight.

'Pretty crowded this train,' I said.

'Yes, weekends are always busy and being a Bank Holiday it's worse. And the real problem is that the Western Line to the North is closed.'

We had an apology for the fact that as the train was so crowded they couldn't use the food trolley, except for first class. *'How sad it is how the other half have to live, is it not?!'*

Stevenage had some lovely black soil growing sugar beet and linseed. We reached Doncaster at 9.30am and my train-spotting neighbour noted down all the train numbers. He wasn't alone and as we passed the different stations other 'spotters' were there with their cameras and notebooks.

NEWCASTLE

Only now could I find a seat facing the right way and a table and three seats to spread myself out on. There was another gentleman who'd been standing all the way.

'About time you got a seat. You've been standing since London,' I said.

'Yes, they've given me permission to sit in here.'

'I had to pay £25 for the pleasure.'

'Afraid I'm too mean.'

'I wonder why Calor Gas has to be in red bottles. Every bottle at the caravan site we passed stood out like a sore thumb.'

The guard announced that on the following day, and under Bye-law 3 there would be no alcohol served on the train, or consumed on it. Anyone breaking the law would be in deep trouble.

We arrived at Edinburgh just over four and a half hours after leaving London and I didn't have to wait long for the connecting train to Inverness. In fact there was just long enough to go out of the station for my first cigarette and to chat to a beggar. I thought if I gave him a pound I might get a story, but I didn't really get my money's worth.

'Hi, how are you?' I asked.

'All right.'

'Been on the streets long?'

'About three years.'

'Any work in this area?'

'Nah.'

He was a real no-hoper and I regretted giving him the money, but I did get a photo.

Perhaps I shouldn't be as hard on these guys as I know that most of them have mental problems.

EDINBURGH TO INVERNESS

Once again the train was nearly full and I was with ScotRail and not National Express. I had no first class ticket and had to lower myself to sit with the standard people. *'It's hard!'*

I was joined by a couple of thirteen-year-old boys who were going to Kiltarlity to see their grandparents. Their mother, who was behind us, got blocked in with some very fit looking hikers. One of the boys was a nephew and they came from Nottingham, and what with their accents and the noise of the train I had a job to understand them. But they were both enthusiastic listeners and I enjoyed their company.

The boys were doing a crossword and kept asking their mum how to spell this, that and the other. I gave them my pocket dictionary, saying, 'I can't spell.'

One boy said, 'I'm dyslexic,' to which I replied, 'So am I.'

Opposite us there were a couple of people going hill walking and they looked unhealthily fit. I saw some snow in the sheltered places on the mountains, but no deer.

The train was so full that it was the first time I'd ever seen the staff stressed. They nearly 'lost it'.

A sign came up saying: 'Alight here for Edinburgh Airport'. *'Why not just say: "Get off here"?'*

I've always said that the train journey from Edinburgh to Inverness is one of the most magnificent you can make, and all the more so on this lovely sunny day. *'But it's not grabbing me as it usually does. Maybe I'm tired, or maybe I've done it too many times.'*

In Perth we saw the Royal Scotsman parked up. 'Can't we get on that one?' I asked. 'Yes, for a few thousand!'

I arrived at Inverness only to have a pigeon shit on my head and all over my glasses. I booked in at the McDougall Clansman Hotel.

'You must be Mr Boyd,' they said.

This really is a lovely family-run hotel. As the grandmother told me what it would cost I didn't have the heart to beat her down and I paid the £42 in cash. I got a huge room with a double bed. The place is just a simple, clean hotel with a family atmosphere.

I showered and then went for a walk. There were drinkers even at 5pm and the police were buzzing around interviewing one of the locals.

The Waterloo Bridge over the River Ness was originally a wooden one, but was replaced after ninety years by a lattice-girder structure in 1896.

I looked at lots of different restaurant menus but ended up going into dear old 'Rooms'. It didn't disappoint and I had South American cottage pie, kidney beans, peppers, mashed potatoes topped with melted cheese with a big parsley leaf on top, and salad and sour cream. The whole thing was given a kick with Mexican chilli sauce. *'Great hotel and great food, and that's an excellent way to start 'walkabout' number eight!'*

I went to bed.

'YOU HAVE NOT CHOSEN ME, I HAVE CHOSEN YOU. THUS SAITH THE LORD.' This was written outside a church.

INVERNESS TO THURSO

After breakfast I went for a walk for an hour round part of Inverness. The alcoholics were looking for a place for a nice, cosy, early morning drink and we exchanged friendly 'good mornings'. They always have their own special swinging walk.

Domino's pizza shop looked disgusting with all the Saturday night's rubbish outside. I passed a burnt-out hotel and loads of backpackers' hostels and B&Bs. I had no idea there were so many in the back streets.

I checked out, said 'goodbye' to the owners of the hotel and got onto ScotRail's two-carriage train to Thurso. It wasn't crowded so I took up eight seats. It was pure luxury.

'We are now approaching Alness. This is a request stop.' *'Please throw the anchor out!'*

BRIDGES

Some of the old stone bridges have had concrete ones put on top, leaving the original ones underneath. *'What a great idea.'*

It really was a treat to sit on a sunny day in late spring watching the countryside unfold. Gorse in flower was scattered throughout and cheered things up.

By now we were just metres from the sea and seagulls were lazing in the sun. Farms and crofts littered the land and the sea was nearly turquoise. There were a few holiday caravans tucked under the sea wall, just far enough from the high-tide level. The yellow gorse, the green fields, the brown bracken and the heather made it a painter's paradise. As the train continued to hug the coastline, sheep ran away from the train as though they'd never seen one before. Mummy sheep were proudly showing off their newly born lambs in the sunshine and herons were sitting on the rocks waiting for fish to make a mistake. Fishermen's rubbish littered the beaches.

There really was no room between us and the sea as we came into Helmsdale. Railway stations with their beautiful ironwork flew by like something from a bygone age. Some were newly painted and others were in need of it. There were also stone walls that needed to be repaired.

'I reckon I should get all the drunks out of Inverness and camp them here until the walls are repaired. One could stand outside the pubs like the old press gangs, hit them over the head and they'd wake up on the middle of a moor, chained by the legs so they couldn't run home!'

It was serious deer country and very wild. The snow fencing was no longer maintained and was rotting away. There was new forestry, too, with its smart new fencing to keep out the greedy deer.

As we approached Thurso, pylons, electric poles and telephone masts reminded us that industry and people always have to be served, even in this beautiful part of the world.

The spring barley planted at this altitude was just managing to push through the ground, and in all the low places the soil looked like a battleground. The wet soil had competed with the tractors and there were no winners.

The guard announced that we were going to reverse into Thurso. We saw some cyclists who looked so fit they could cycle round the world without a rest.

THURSO AGAIN

Paul got off the train; he had been cycling from Land's End to John o' Groats, but unfortunately his bike had broken down in Tain and couldn't be repaired, so the next day he was going to walk and push his bike the rest of the way to John o' Groats.

He told me it was the people who made the trip for him and he'd learned not to worry, but to take things as they came. He had a good attitude and I took a photo of him, and suggested he should try the Royal Hotel. I wished him luck for the next day and said goodbye.

James' was the second vehicle I thumbed and he took me all the way to Castletown in his large red van. Once more he had such a strong Scottish accent that I couldn't understand him. I asked three times what he did for a living but still couldn't understand. He was a quiet, shy man and went out of his way to drop me in the car park.

The first car I flagged down stopped and Ella took me to Dunnet. She was involved with horses and tourists. At the time, though, she was on her way to Dunnet Head to check out a walking route, as she was intending to take a group of Girl Guides there.

It had been a good start to hitching, but I never got another lift and had to walk all the way to John o' Groats. It wasn't difficult to understand why there were no buses on a Bank Holiday and it was a Sunday. In this part of the world they don't do Sunday work. *'Well, fuck the motorists! The wild flowers are coming up and I'm enjoying looking at them.'*

The funny thing about this walk was that I could barely recognise any of the roads, and even wondered if I might have veered off the correct one. A signpost showed that John O' Groats was nine miles away and I never thought that in a million years I would have to walk it. It was strange because motorists coming the other way looked at me as though I had two heads and then roared past me. *'The sooner they run out of petrol the better.'*

I startled a buzzard, watched the swallows working the hedgerows and dreamed of having a beer – I'd run out of water. I passed a pub but decided to carry on walking. It just went on and on and I was sure a big yellow bus would turn up, but nothing came. After four hours of walking, not counting the hour I'd already done that morning, I was nearly clapped out.

I had a chat to Gill, who had a ninety-acre farm and was just about to feed her horses; one of which was a huge farm horse. We both agreed that if the price of oil went up much more the 'large lady' might have to come out of retirement.

'How much further to John o' Groats?'

'Three miles.'

'I'd better get going then, so goodbye.'

JOHN O' GROATS

After nearly five hours of walking I arrived at a local hotel.

The food was about what I'd expected. They forgot my order, so I went to the bar to get my own drink, where the girl was just about alive, but all I could think of was a Polish replacement. The restaurant was busy with people enjoying themselves and there was the odd loner like me.

They tried to be posh but never quite made it – still, I hadn't the energy to find anywhere else.

JOHN O' GROATS TO WICK

I had the usual crappy breakfast with toast that could've been used as roofing tiles.

I wrote in the comment book: 'EVERYTHING IN THIS PLACE IS CHEAP- EXCEPT THE BILL.'

I needed to get out again to find the road to Duncansby Head. I passed a couple of motor homes, one called 'Compass Drifter' and the other 'Auto Trail'. It was two miles to Duncansby and I passed a pebbledash prefab in ruins and the usual ugly houses they build.

Nobody wanted to give me a lift so I ended up walking there and back. I tried cutting corners across the grass but that caused my knees to play up walking downhill. I met a young Swedish couple who'd converted their red van so that they could live in it. They'd heard that Duncansby Head was the place to see, rather than John o' Groats.

I was now on the very bend of Scotland. It was a lovely warm and sunny day and there were loads of seagulls and flowers.

Raynor was a German marine chemist who taught at Aberdeen University and he was a keen bird watcher. He told me that the dark seagulls were Arctic skuas.

After taking a picture of the Stacks of Duncansby, I flagged down a car that stopped. He told me he was only going about another 400 yards to do some bird-watching, but he offered to give me a lift anyway. I thought it wasn't really worth it but as soon as he drove off over the horizon I regretted not taking the lift.

SOUTH, SOUTH, SOUTH!

'We've been west, we've been north, we've been east and now at last we're going south. Hooray!'

This was new country; the wind was at my back; there was some Scottish sunshine – what more could I ask for?

A cyclist whizzed past me from behind and made me jump. 'Hello there.' I said as I jumped a foot.

'I did ring the bell,' he replied.

By 11.30am I was hungry, so I sat down and ate my bacon sandwich made from this morning's roof tiles, putting in another packet of butter to help it go down. A handy dustbin took the wrappers.

I saw this amazing little plant called the cotton flower which looked like a rabbit's tail blowing in the wind. I was told that they used to make cotton from it. There were orchids starting to push up as well on the verges.

Not many people loved me this morning and Caroline was the only one to give me a lift for ten minutes to Keiss beach. She was an artist and used any medium. I asked her if she could make a living at it but she said she couldn't so she taught art to supplement her income. Her mother lived in Ashford, Kent.

By now we were in castle country. They seemed scattered in all shapes and forms defending the east coast. I chatted to Alan, the farmer, over the fence. He was trying to encourage his cows and calves to the water trough, as they'd only just been turned out. He got out of his truck and splashed the water to encourage them.

'How's the beef job?'

'Pretty good.'

'I'm a farmer from Kent.'

'Whereabouts is Kent exactly?'

'The bit that sticks out near France.'

'I've nothing against the English and two of my best friends are English and came up from the Isle of Wight. That's them repairing the water trough over there. I'll phone them and tell them you're coming. They'd like to see you.'

'I'd better get going then. Goodbye.'

Meet Richard and John. 'Hello there,' I said, 'Alan tells me you're from the Isle of Wight.'

'Yes, been up here a couple of years now and love it.'

They were adjusting the water-cock and were responsible for the fencing. They looked as though they knew how to work. They said there was a month's work just getting the gates in good order.

After the long walk the day before I was hoping to have an easier day, but it turned out to be the longest walk I'd ever done. It took seven and a half hours and I was pleased with 'Mr and Mrs Legs' that I could do it.

Alan said that his neighbour was a corn farmer but that it didn't look very well. I actually thought it looked fairly good and the barley was just coming out in ear. It seemed too early for spring and too late for winter. There was only one field growing wheat that had some bad wheel marks in it.

The rock cliffs had given way to sand dunes and a narrow golf course was tucked between the farming and the sea.

MR AND MRS SMUG

They were two Rotary Club members and had cycled all the way from Land's End to John O' Groats in twenty days.

'Nineteen and a half, actually,' said Mrs Smug. They'd raised £2,500 for charity and they were now cycling back to Wick to catch the train home.

As usual, just about a mile before Wick the bus turned up, but at least he did stop.

'Thanks for stopping. Not many of you guys around today.'

'No, I saw you earlier. £1.30, please.'

'There weren't many buses on the Thurso to John O' Groats' run yesterday...'

'Nay, wouldn't have been. They don't run on Sundays.'

'Can you drop me off in the middle of Wick?'

'OK. There's a good café just on the right.'

Morag's café used to be two shops but when Tesco opened up it killed the high street trade, so she turned it into a café. She said it was the best thing she'd ever done. She gave me directions to a B&B and told me to tell Brenda that she'd sent me.

'Can you tell me the way to the quayside?'

'Dunno!' *'I think Wick has its fair share of 'Dunno's.'*

All the shops were open on this Bank Holiday and the timber lorries were unloading in the dock. The only places that were shut were the banks.

At the B&B I rang the bell, but there was no reply. Brenda was gardening in the front. She said, 'I have a small room for £25.'

'I'll take it.'

She had a spring in her step and I was soon tucked up in my tiny comfortable room. I had a snooze and at 5pm went to discover Wick and more.

There was something about this place that I liked. It was still a working town, with old-fashioned shops and not mucked up with tourism. The old warehouses were made of stone and the docks were amazing. Timber was being unloaded in the dock for export and a fisherman was taking crabs off his boat. They were bound for France and he said that some of the big ones were twenty-five to thirty years old. Most of the fishermen were touchy old buggers and it was always hard work to get a conversation out of them.

I stumbled across Argyle Square with an avenue of lime trees which went through the middle of it. Apparently, it was designed by Thomas Telford. I noticed here that they still had coalmen delivering – in Kent they would be classified as a rare breed.

Like most Scottish towns Wick has a fair number of churches and the Minster has its own rookery and ancient tombstones. It was a dirty old church with rubbish all over the place, but it still had character.

The town of Wick lies around the bay where the River Wick enters the North Sea. Linen spinning was established in the town by 1749, but it was the growth of the herring industry that most facilitated Wick's development. The new quay was built in 1768 and the British Fisheries Society promoted the area heavily.

Harbour improvements were designed by Thomas Telford. By 1862 over 1,100 fishing boats operated out of Wick, which now had a population of 8,131.

By the middle of the 19th century secondary industries included ship and boat building; also barrel making and grain milling.

The farmland around Wick underwent considerable improvements in the late 18th and early 19th centuries, which involved the proper enclosure of fields, land reclamation, redistribution of land among tenants at fixed rents, extended tillage, improved drainage, liming and a new six-year rotation. The staple crops were oats, turnips and potatoes. Some farmers also provided peat for fuel. Among the livestock reared, cattle were either of the pure Highland breed, or crosses between short-horned bulls and Highland cows, while sheep were generally Cheviots crossed with the Leicester breed. By the mid-19th century, fishing had a more significant impact than farming on the economy of Wick. The statistical account notes that 'from immemorial vast shoals of herring have frequented the coast', but cod fishing was preferred earlier in Wick's history, and the development of the herring industry occurred relatively late. Both white and red herring were caught off the Caithness coast, the former in the greater quantity. White fishing was also carried on to some extent, and the river Wick supported a small salmon fishery.

Walking out of the High Street to the new out-of-town Tesco was like a big vacuum cleaner sucking everybody in; staff, motorists stopping for fuel, and shoppers for 'Buy-One-Get-One-Free', and on this Bank Holiday Monday it was a hive of activity.

I passed a field full of Ayrshire cows that really looked good grazing on the lush grass. They looked at me as though again I was a bloody idiot.

ACKERGILL TOWER

This was turning into an amazing evening. I saw a huge castle-like building from the bus and farm buildings with two tall chimneys. I was drawn to it like a bee to a honey pot. It had a very smart entrance with a large grown hedge each side. It had mown verges and rabbits, including a black one. The 'Private' sign made it all the more interesting and as I walked down the sweeping drive a Toyota farm truck crossed in front of me and with my guilty conscience I thought he was going to tell me to 'Get off my land,' but he disappeared. I reached the main entrance and there was still no one about.

As I got nearer I started to wonder who lived here. There was a golf range in the front and a croquet lawn, and there were two strange buildings. I thought I would come across His Lordship sitting drinking his Pimms and asking me to join him. I peered over the Tower sea wall and saw their private boat moored up. As the Tower windows were open I thought it was time to make a hasty exit.

I passed through the scruffy farmyard, with beef-cow machinery all over the place. I didn't have the nerve to poke my nose into these fascinating barns. The road went straight through the yard and after turning right joined up with the main

road. On the way I saw some amazing Aberdeen Angus beef cows that were bristling with health.

Alan was gardening and I asked him who owned Ackergill Castle.

'Mr Bannister. He came up from the West Country after he sold his travel company and he did a complete renovation.'

'What are the two strange buildings in front of the castle?'

'Dovecotes.'

'Why do the farm buildings have the two high chimneys?'

'They used to be for the steam threshing engines.'

He was mowing the grass and answered all my questions. He worked for Scottish Water and covered a huge area. He was fifty-four and had lost his wife two years earlier with cancer.

I told him that when I was on the west coast I had hitched a lift with a girl who used to work as a mechanic on aircraft and was now collecting water samples for Scottish Water.

'Oh, that's Norma. I'm seeing her next week.'

'Well, give her my regards.'

Alan was a mine of information and told all. His house was right in line with Wick Airport and it was called 'Airstrip'. His brother-in-law was an air-traffic controller. Apparently, Madonna had thought of buying Ackergill. It also hosted operas; the 'Discovery' was launched there and Land Rover/BMW uses it. The previous night they'd had a firework display, but the place was so clean that I saw no evidence of it.

I walked back into town and by now I was ready for a beer. I went into Wetherspoon's newly renovated post office restaurant. It was now ultra-modern. On the menu it said the beef came from South America.

'It's a wonder these local beef farmers don't lynch you!'

'We're trying to change the policy, but it takes time for things to work through.'

The television was blasting away reporting that the Americans had just landed a probe on Mars, 174 million miles away. It's an amazing achievement, but no one seemed interested as they tucked into their chips.

It's not often in my life that I've gone into a restaurant, had a beer and a nice meal, paid for it and then come out with more money than I went in with. They'd let me have my meal on the Chesterfield sofa and when I checked to make sure that I hadn't left anything behind, I lifted the cushion and found £1.20. I lifted the next and found a £10 note. The next one had another load of small change under it. I walked out feeling a little bit 'up-my- own-jumper'.

Today I'd walked for eight hours and I'd never done that before. I went to bed.

'Please note, that I'm writing this in the B&B after a pint of beer and two glasses of wine and it's now 2.30am, so expect some rubbish.'

WICK TO PORTMAHOMACK

My hips were aching the next morning as I read the 'No Smoking' policy in the room. It said that if that wasn't agreeable to their guests they would suggest moving to other accommodation. *'What's this country coming to when you can't have a cigarette in bed?'*

Breakfast was fun with five of us sitting round a table – two lorry drivers, a motorcyclist and a Scottish salesman.

It took ages to eat my food because of the conversation. We eventually sorted the world out and went our separate ways.

Two police officers were coming towards me so I put my hands up and they said, 'Not today!'

I caught the bus, the Inverness one. I didn't have to wait long to Brora. On the way down to the castle the barley crops looked awful and the farmyards were a disgrace. Most of them looked like agricultural bombed out sites. A young teenage girl got on and sat there with a dead face. She just sat there texting with an iPod in her ears.

The driver dropped me off right outside the gates of Dunrobin Castle. The castle is a stately home in the Highland area of Scotland. It's the seat of the Countess of Sutherland and the Clan Sutherland. Its origins lie in the Middle Ages but most of the present building is the work of Sir Charles Barry, the architect of the Palace of Westminster. He greatly extended the building in 1845. It's now owned by Lord Strathnaver and with 189 rooms it is the largest house in the Northern Highlands.

I enjoyed sitting down and watching the falconry with forty others. For the first time I had to put my wet-weather gear on and then the sun came out. He flew the birds low across our heads and then threw them cut up chicks to eat, saying that they were yesterday's naughty children. Andy, the falconer, said that falconry was really the sport of the rich and sometimes wars were prevented by trading birds. He said that the birds never fly off as life in the wild is very hard and by staying they know they'll always get fed.

Owls are lighter and can hover and some of the diving birds use their weight and kill with their claws. Tawny owls hoot, whilst barn owls squeak. He said that when they see a crow or heron they try to make it spew up its food, only for them to eat it. Some of the birds can see a mouse from 285 metres and the hawks have a kind of reinforced nostril to enable it to breathe when diving.

I walked inside an outbuilding and met Eric who was looking after every sort of stuffed wild animal from Africa. I spent most of the time talking to him as he was an interesting old boy. He'd trained as an engineering structural draughtsman and had come out of it when everything was electrified. He loved golf and was going to play in a competition the next day.

I met some Irish ladies who were also over here to play golf. One was a doctor with a good sense of humour. I said to her that she looked like a seventeen handicap; she said, 'Fifteen.'

It was time to get on the road again, but I had no idea where I was going to, so I decided to go with the wind.

Dunrobin is well connected with a road and railway running right past it. It even has its own little station, which I'd admired earlier when going north. But the down side is that there are only about two trains each day. A lady was flapping about on the station and the train was due to arrive in a few minutes. I couldn't believe my luck. The woman told me it took about an hour to get to Tain, which wasn't far down the road, but the train went the long way round. I nearly changed my mind but as I had a ticket I thought I could sit and write *Walkabout*. The train arrived and we had to flag it down. It was the first time I'd ever hitched a train!

I met Bob and Monica from Canada. He was a retired teacher, only fifty-five, but now that his pension had kicked in he was OK. He said, 'We've got a nice home and one in the country and we have a nice motor car.'

They just seemed a little too comfortable with life. I asked fat Monica if she had ever been to Africa.

'No, no, Africa isn't for me.' *'At least if the Africans or the animals fancied eating her they'd get a good feed.'*

The train was running five minutes late and the conductor was asking passengers about their connecting journeys, explaining that the driver was trying to catch up.

I wondered quite what I was doing in Tain. It was the tiniest station I'd ever seen. When I got off at the station and walked behind this old boy going up the steps into the town I thought what a slow creeping old geezer he was, and then realised I wasn't catching him up.

I went into the tourist office. 'Could you tell me the next bus to Tarbat?'

'Not many go there.'

Miss Lifeless kept fiddle-fucking about with timetables and I could've walked there in the time it took for her to look it up.

'Thank you very much for all your help.' I should've asked her to wiggle her pretty little behind to check she was still alive.

When walking out of town I was watching an interesting blonde training her dog, with I presume her thirteen-year-old daughter. She had tattoos over her arms and wore tight-fitting trousers and had a firm round bum with leather-type, knee-high riding boots. She had a little face that said she had got some history. She had now crossed the road and was walking behind me.

'Oi, STOP!' she yelled. 'Oi, you!'

I thought she was calling the dog. I turned round.

'Do you want a cigarette?'

I didn't really want one but thought it rude to refuse. 'Oh, thank you. Nice part of the world you have here.'

'Yeah.'

'You got horses?'

'Yeah, me partner hasn't paid the rent and we've got to get out.'

Then out in front she went, shouting instructions to the dog.

'Any buses round here?'

'Na, don't bother. I just stick my thumb out.'

I tried to hang back a bit as it wasn't helping my hitching. I couldn't believe how quickly they walked. Thirty minutes later she offered me another cigarette.

'Would you like one of mine?' I asked.

She wouldn't take one but insisted I had another of hers.

'I can't give you anything.' She gave me a big smile, or that's what I thought! *Dream on!*

This was a straight fast bit of road and after feeling unloved and twenty-seven cars later, Tommy stopped. He was a painter and decorator. He went out of his way and dropped me off at the Castle Hotel.

'Have you got a room for the night?'

'I think we're fully booked. Yes, we do have one. £35 per night.'

'I'll take it.'

One thing about having a smoke outside is that you meet the locals. I met Duncan who really didn't want much to do with me, but didn't have much choice as we put the world to rights. We even touched on politics, especially when an old left-winger joined us.

Duncan and I had a lot in common. He said that the modern generation would rather roll over and die than go out and pick fruit. He said he was helping to renovate a building and invited me to have look in the morning.

The pub was full of construction workers drinking and eating; some were staying here. They were building a new water pipe through the village. The girl behind the bar had her work cut out serving everybody.

I had a haggis with whisky sauce and lamb – it was beautiful. And I had three sorts of spuds – chips, boiled and sautéed.

I tried to give Duncan a fiver to buy Tommy a drink, but he wouldn't take it.

To bed. I had just got to sleep when suddenly, with a hell of a bang, my door flew open. I thought 'Blondie' had tracked me down.

'Sorry, mate, wrong room!'

The lad behind the bar had given him the wrong key.

PORTMAHOMACK TO CROMARTY

Duncan had invited me to see his work, but I walked up the wrong way past the golf course on the way to the lighthouse. I met Hugh on the way and he was shutting a gate with his JCB. He had worked on the farm for forty years with three generations of bosses. They had 250 sheep and grew 'tatties', as he called them. He had a rotten old limp, but said he had no pain. The farm was run by Gordon O'Brien.

There was some quality farming here and it was the best I'd seen in Scotland, with free-draining, fertile soil, growing wheat, barley, rape and peas.

'A seagull overhead is talking to me and won't go away. It's amazing and I think it fancies me!'

There were a couple of agricultural sprayers working in some windy weather and one was just pulling out of the gate, so I flagged him down. *'Meet Mr Douglas Gill.'*

'I'd like to congratulate you on the standard of your farming. I'm a farmer from Kent.'

'I don't know about that but my parents are in Kent at the moment, near Romney Marsh.'

'Who do they know down there?'

'Stephen and Valerie Furnival. They used to farm nearby.'

'They're good friends of mine.'

On the way to the renovation I stumbled across the Tarbat Discovery Centre. This was another fantastic looking old church and the lady in the garden said it was open. It had been converted into a museum and was opened by Prince Charles in 1999.

8000 BC	MESOLITHIC PERIOD
4000 BC	NEOLITHIC PERIOD
2000 BC	BRONZE AGE
700 BC	IRON AGE
0 BC	ROMANS IN BRITAIN
300 AD	PAGAN PICTS
500 AD	CHRISTIAN PICTS
700 AD	VIKINGS (NORSE)
900 AD	MEDIEVAL
1100 AD-1500 AD	EARLY MODERN
1800 AD- 2000 AD	MODERN

Until 1800 barley was the main crop and then it made way for oats for the first time. Oat husks are called 'sowans'. They suffered famine in 1784 and potato blight in 1851. In 1778 Parliament passed the Recruiting Act which allowed local JPs to force into the army or navy those who were disorderly or had no apparent trade, those who demanded extravagant wages, or those who left the county or country in summer at harvest time to find better money. *'Those were the days.'*

The fishing industry has all but gone. *'If fish is so healthy, why are most fishermen overweight?'*

The Education Act came into force in 1872.

At last I found it at the end of a long unmade track. Duncan failed to tell me his so-called renovation was only a 'castle. Ballone Castle was built in the late 16th century and in 1623 came into the hands of the Mackenzie's clan. The fortress was later abandoned for more luxurious dwelling and became ruinous by the 1700s. Now, it has been meticulously restored and is in good hands.

I asked another man on site whether he was the builder or the owner. 'I'm the owner.' He then roared with laughter and said, 'Wish I was!'

He showed me around. He was a modest man and a stone-mason. I couldn't tell the difference between the original stone and the new. There were just three men on site and Duncan fashioned all the stone as he went along and was renovating the top of a well. He told me it would take about three or four hours to make a curved stone.

The night before he had told me he was helping to do some renovation, but he failed to tell me that he was an expert stonemason. I nearly didn't come here, but what a fool I would've been. There were no youngsters on site to help with mixing and humping stones and learning the trade. The cold wind whipped off the North Sea with the castle just feet from the cliff top.

I congratulated them on their skills and carried on my way. I didn't have to walk far before I got a lift.

Charlotte was going shopping and Gladys, who was a real old Scottish farmer's wife, didn't look happy at her daughter-in-law's decision to pick me up. Charlotte was a caterer in the converted community centre and went a long way out of her way to drop me off at the right place.

I was standing at a dangerous junction on the A9 and after fifteen cars Richard, a taxi driver, stopped.

'Thanks for stopping. How much will it be?'

'Nothing, it's my day off. I'm going to Cromarty so I might see you later.'

He told me that although taxi driving was very competitive he managed to make a living – but the price of fuel didn't help.

My next lift was with Gary who was a real gent; he jumped out of the car, shook my hand and treated me like royalty.

His father was a very keen football fan and was sitting in the front studying form. Gary was an oil engineer and hitchhiked himself. He kept saying, 'Good on you, good on you!'

The good Lord was shining on me today; David White stopped in his fancy orange sports car, took me right to the Cromarty Arms and enjoyed showing me the sights. He was an interesting man, now delivering parcels. He'd just had a marital break-up and was trying to get his life back on course. He'd been a medic in the navy and was now doing a degree in surgery. It sounded as though he was a nurse as he was talking about instruments being handed to the surgeon. He'd also done a lot of travelling. When I saw the landlord at the pub I left David a drink for when he next came in.

When I arrived in Cromarty I went into the first pub which had been recommended by my driver. It had a big roaring fire. It was £25 per night with no en-suite. I was going to look elsewhere but couldn't be bothered. I really was put above the shop and the bathroom was the family bathroom, complete with waxy cotton buds lying on the floor. My wardrobe was full of someone else's clothes.

The landlord and his wife weren't a happy couple and he was covered in tattoos and had a pot belly. He was busy playing the one-armed bandit, whilst she was busy working. There was no contact between them at all.

CROMARTY COURT HOUSE

This was a splendid museum, built in 1773, and it won the museum of the year in Scotland. It had animated figures re-enacting a trial in the courtroom; it must have been good because it made me jump when I walked in there and they started talking. This place is well worth a visit.

I went into another hotel for a drink and met an Australian farmer who told me that they had had a big drought in Western Australia and that the first two weeks in June would make or break the harvest.

He had the look of Mr Disappointment on his face. After he packed up farming he went cray-fishing for ten years and then got his fingers burnt on a mussel farm, in particular. Now his mother-in-law needed care in the suburbs of Perth so they'd moved there and he hated it.

This was his first time in the UK and he was with his wife and son, who was a bright spark and worked for Rio Tinto, travelling round the world. He was an unassuming man and I liked him. He told me that Mongolia is stuffed full of minerals.

Willy was the local village character, very short and stooped. He was so short that he had to be helped to put his money in the fruit machine. It was rather touching to see a young lad helping the eighty-eight-year-old. When I got up for breakfast the next morning he was the only person around and apparently he'd only recently stopped walking for charity.

CROMARTY TO ELGIN

I went for a walk at 6.00am before breakfast. I walked up the hill and found the tradesmen's tunnel entrance to Nightingale's family house. They are also near neighbours to us in Kent. It said: 'Private', but I couldn't resist the tunnel going up to it; with light shafts guiding me the seventy-five yards to the entrance of the house. I poked my head out and felt like a rabbit. I didn't have the cheek to go any further, so went back and found the main driveway with a sign saying: 'Private – Keep Out!' I wound my way along it and *'Wow, what a house!'* The only sign of life was a noisy peacock. I didn't push my luck and returned to a nearby wood because nature was calling.

I found a quiet place, dropped my trousers and then heard dogs barking. I never did see them but got out pretty quickly. Later on, I thought it must've been a 'barking dog' burglar alarm.

I walked to a messy dairy farm with another beautiful building which had its roof falling off. I had a chat to a calf and I saw a deer jump over a fence as though it wasn't there. There were still elm trees around here. In the wood was a pigsty with a sign on the fence: *'Henrietta, the pig, has passed on and we would like to thank everyone who fed her and adored her. Thank You.'*

I said to a lady walking up the street, 'Quite a place you have here.'

'Thank you. I came here from Germany over fifteen years ago and I wouldn't go back if you paid me.'

I had breakfast with Val and Dave, the only other couple here. They'd come up from Liverpool. She was a sweetie and worked in the caring business and he was a press photographer. They were so nice and polite and we had a quiet laugh about the hotel.

I walked round Cromarty Church and what a lovely place it is. I put a comment in the book saying: 'Cromarty is a gem of a place. Please keep PVC out of the windows.' If you like churches or old buildings you have to come here. I couldn't get over what a beautiful place Cromarty is with its amazing architecture.

Richard gave me a lift and this was to be my only one of the day. He was a local fisherman and also owned a gun and tackle shop and did some deer shooting. He gave me an update on all the farmers as we drove along.

'See that farm? Two sons run it. Wait till you see the farmyard. It's like a graveyard.'

'Are they dairy farmers?' I asked.

'No, beef. There used to be four or five dairy farms but they've all packed up. The last farmer had three sons but none wanted to milk. The farmer couldn't get a cowman so he sold out. See that farm? It's the best on the island, but the farmer died last year. Would you like to come back to my home for a cup of tea?'

'That's very kind of you, but I have to get on.'

I walked into Fortrose and asked a young fifteen-year-old whether there was anything worth seeing and he said, 'No.' But just round the corner was the Fortrose Cathedral, which was cared for by Historic Scotland. The outbuilding was used for the Borough Council Chamber and the bottom half was a prison after the Reformation. A couple of builders were struggling with a rock in a barrow, so I gave them a hand. They couldn't believe it and thanked me very much.

I missed the bus to Avoch, which was another ex-fishing village and had to walk as nobody would pick me up.

Eleanor was waiting at the bus stop.

'Hello, is there a bus coming?' I asked.

'Should be one at 12.20pm.'

'Would you like a cigarette?'

'Thank you.'

A man came over and said that the bus had gone and another was due in half an hour.

She said to me, 'Come on, and I'll buy you a drink.'

We went into the pub and had a cup of tea. Eleanor was a Yorkshire girl and a very special person who looked after people with brain damage. She told me all about Health and Safety and that when people tell her not to touch the patients she tells them to bugger off as she knows more about caring than they do!

After half an hour of talking we felt we had known each other for years as we seemed to have a lot in common.

When we came out of the pub I left my rucksack behind.

At last a bus turned up. 'Can I get to Nairn without going to Inverness?'

'Only if you can swim.' said the driver.

'In that case I'll go to Inverness.'

Eleanor chatted away behind me and told me she had walked seven miles that morning with her little dog. When I asked her how long it had taken she said it was about an hour. As it had taken me about four and a half hours I took that with a pinch of salt.

I never thought I would be back in Inverness again but there I was. I decided that Nairn was a bit close so bought a ticket to Banff instead.

We went past some intensive farmland growing carrots and potatoes.

I couldn't believe what a scruffy, rough-looking lot were at the bus station in Elgin. This country is just full of degenerate 'no-hopers' in every town and city and they must slowly drag the country down. But to be fair some of the poorer people in life tend to hang around bus stations.

I had a cup of hot chocolate and a bowl of soup that stuck in my stomach like a bale of hay. I found a rather smart B&B but it was full, or maybe I was too scruffy and she sent me round the corner to Southbank.

I rang the doorbell but couldn't make anyone hear me, so I phoned them up. 'Have you got a room for the night?'

'Yes, £35. I'm three-quarters of an hour away so just walk in and in the drawer you'll find the key to Room 4.'

'What if you don't like the look of me?'

'Too bad!'

One half of the house was a converted chapel; it had no character left but the room was brand new and light and had oak doors. I didn't have the nerve to have a shower before I'd paid my money and I felt more like a squatter than a paying guest.

After walking up and down past the fast food places I settled on having an Indian meal which was very good. After seeing all the scruffy people around, the staff members here were very smart and polite.

I said hello to a man selling *The Big Issue* who came from Romania.

Next morning I saw him again.

'Have you got a pound?'

'You have to work for a pound,' I said.

'No workie.'

'Try picking some fruit.' I walked away and thought, *'Fuck him!'*

ELGIN TO FRASERBURGH

I had breakfast and made for the bus station. I had forty-five minutes writing *Walkabout* and the time flew by. An explorer ticket cost £15.

Mrs Lard got on the bus with her miserable crying child. She was too lazy to get her out of the pushchair and had a 'fuck it' look on her face.

The sea mist was coming in and there were ghost-like wind turbines which looked redundant. After passing intensive carrot and potato farming we arrived in drizzly Banff.

I went into a little café and had a chat with the mother and daughter owners. They told me to watch out for the druggies in Fraserburgh and they also told me about the places of interest. The mother worked-out and looked more like a sister than a mother. Apparently, she'd wanted to join the RAF but had been turned down. Meeting a family like this makes my 'walkabout'.

I found Duff House which was built between 1735 and 1740 and widely thought to be one of Britain's finest Georgian houses. It was built for William Duff of Braco who became Earl of Fife in 1759. The story of Duff House didn't get off to a happy start. Disputes over its building reached such intensity that Duff never lived here. So acrimoniously did this end that it is said that he never even looked at the completed house and had his carriage blinds drawn whenever he passed.

When I entered Duff House I felt a bit scruffy. I hadn't shaved since I'd left home and my homemade anti-leak boot protectors didn't look that professional. The security staff watched me like a hawk. As I put my bag in the locker I said, 'How am I going to get the family silver in here if I can't take it with me?!'

Louise was a large lady with a matching character. I asked her if they did weddings and she said, 'Why, do you want to marry me?'

'Yes, of course!'

A couple of minutes later I saw her again and said, 'I've found the bedrooms.'

Some of the paintings here are huge and I asked one of the 'Dunnos' how they had got them up. 'Dunno!' I asked Louise and she said that they put the frames up first and then unrolled the pictures into them. *Don't ask me about the massive mirrors, though.*'

Rose was in charge of the library and was cataloguing what was in the books to encourage people to read them rather than them just sitting there. She was a sprightly, oldish lady with a big smile. I told her she had a sparkle about her.

I had to laugh at two old stuffed shirts going around; both with grey hair and long faces. They were just so miserable as to be funny, and Louise thought so as well.

Gordon was the caretaker. He did sixteen hours a week and earned £90 for the work. He also supplemented his income by fishing and the boat cost him £50 per month. He told me the sea had been fished out and he was worried about the cost of diesel.

There was another chap in the garden picking up rubbish, who had learning difficulties. He said, 'You shouldn't drop your rubbish but put it in the bin.'

'Quite agree with you, mate.'

I stopped to get a Mars bar before walking across the bridge into Macduff and before starting my unforeseen long walk. At the bus station they'd told me that you had to go to Aberdeen to get to Fraserburgh, but big head knew best!

The fog was coming down and it was a fast and twisting road with no lay-bys. I found out that Fraserburgh has the highest drug problem in the country, so any hiker is probably looked on as a druggie. I probably walked for eleven miles. I stopped in Macduff for a horrible pint of John Smith's. I asked three people how far it was to Fraserburgh. 'Dunno!' And it's their next door town!

In Macduff a young lad told me that the next bus was in two and a half hours so I said to him that I'd better start walking.

I talked to a miserable old farmer on his Renault tractor. 'You a dairy farmer?'

'Aye.'

'Price of milk gone up?'

'Aye, so has everything else.'

'Yeah, I'm an arable farmer from Kent so I know all about that. I'd better let you get on.' *'Poor miserable old farmer. He has enough assets to sell up and get a new life or retire, but he probably knows about nothing else than moaning and milking his shitty cows.'*

I walked through Longman Hill and if there'd been a B&B I would've taken it, as after walking for three and a half hours I was now the miserable bugger.

The cars seemed to be getting faster and the mist thicker, but there was always hope. The 5pm bus from Banff could be somewhere and would I be in the right place when it did arrive? I couldn't believe it when I looked round and saw the bus. I quickly flung my arm out and it stopped. I could've kissed him as there were still fourteen miles to go. I was the only person and I went out like a light and was amazed to wake up in Fraserburgh.

'Could you recommend a hotel?"

'There are only two,' and he burst out laughing.

Fraserburgh was not what I'd expected. It looked like an old gold mining town when it had run out of gold. It was so different from Cromarty. It has a population of 12,360 and is heavily dependent on the fishing industry, which provides 60% of the employment. It also has the seventh oldest golf course in the world. The town has had a local lifeboat service since 1806 and has suffered three lifeboat disasters: one was in 1918 with the loss of several lives; another in 1952 when six crew members died; and a third in 1970 with the loss of five of the six crew, whilst on service to a Dutch fishing boat.

The Royal Hotel was a grand name for a dead looking place, but I couldn't be bothered to look at the other hotel, which maybe I should've done. When the guy finally came to the reception desk I think he was suffering from shock at seeing a customer. One night was £45 and non-negotiable.

The room had a bathroom bigger than the bedroom and the bed had see-through sheets.

I had a nice hot bath and went to the Railway Hotel for some food.

'What's Fraserburgh famous for?'

'Doing nothing! Will you be eating?'

'Just looking.'

'Are you ready to order?'

'Give me a chance!'

I had an above average meal. As I went out the youngsters were in the doorway.

'You a smoker?'

'Yeah,' I replied.

'You a boozer?'

'Yeah.'

This must be the home for boy racers. There were little sporty cars with huge exhausts and screechy tyres roaring around all night showing off. Even ear muffs and double glazing couldn't keep out the noise they made.

I had an early morning walk and what fun it was. I knew the old town was a bit of a shambles, but there was something about it I quite liked. It was not an 'up-your-jumper' place but one where people were just trying to survive. I don't think I've ever seen a town so down and out. One hotel was boarded up, as was a taxi office. Gilbert and Noble Home Start had closed down and the Pizza Takeaway looked as though it had had a brick through the window the previous night.

The notice on the church door said: 'All welcome', but had no notices on it. The shops that were trading all had 70% reductions on stock. Most were charity shops: Shelter, British Heart Foundation, the Salvation Army, and Barnardo's.

Even the mortgage advice office was boarded up, as was Craig Allan, the baker, and if you really wanted to fuck off out of this shit-hole for a holiday, Duncan's Travel Agent had also called it a day.

I was now walking along a road called Dennyduff Road and this had a mixture of dog shit and human blood on the pavement.

I went back to the Royal Hotel where two cheerful girls were cleaning the entrance. They asked what I wanted for breakfast and then dropped everything and went and cooked me an excellent one.

Let's buy a car and sleep in that, we will walk to the garage.

Perhaps not!

Let's book in a hotel, not a good idea.

Let's buy a house, 'Oh a little late.'

That's better.

Let's get a mortgage. 'Too late'.

279

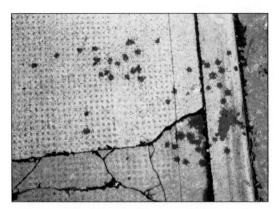

Mind last nights punch up!

Mind the dog shit!

I am hungry. Lets go to the bakers,
Oh too late!

Let's see whats on in the church, not a lot.

I think we need a holiday. Oh too late.

I love you Fraserbrugh but time to get taxi home. Oh to late!

FRASERBURGH TO STONEHAVEN

The 9.55am bus was full. Everybody always seems keen to get out of dear old Fraserburgh.

Duncan was sitting next to me, who was about twenty-eight to thirty, and didn't have the happiest face in the world. We got talking and he opened his heart to me. He'd trained as a joiner and had worked in Holland. All was going well until the company had gone bankrupt. They didn't pay him and he had to get himself back home. Back in the UK, he had done a private job which took three weeks and on the last day he went out and all his tools had been stolen, including the wooden box he'd made to hold them all.

Then he split up with his wife and four children and moved back in with his parents, who've since asked him to find new accommodation. He was now on his way to Aberdeen to meet a friend and live in a bedsit.

His phone rang and his friend, who was going to help him move, said that his van had been stolen the previous night. 'I just don't know what to do,' he said. I told him that when you reach rock bottom there's only one way to go.

CND AND VEGANS

These people had their tables set up so I had a chat with them. I asked them what would happen to the Scottish hills if there were no sheep on them and they said they'd just let them go wild. I didn't really get through to them, although the man was very nice and argued his point of view. The CND girl just closed up.

THE VENISON SELLER

He was in the farmers' market and told me he got fed up with taking Americans and Germans stalking deer. One German had had forty-two shots to get six deer and the venison man said, 'No wonder they lost the war!' All the Americans wanted with pheasant shooting was quantity, not quality.

Aberdeen seemed very grey, dull, misty and miserable. *'Keep moving south.'*

I went past Aberdeen railway station and decided to use the train. Some Polish guys were getting stuck into a drink before boarding. I wrote my diary sitting on a leather sofa and couldn't resist looking under the seat. No luck this time!

A lady was waiting with her dog.

'Do you have to pay to take your dog on the train?'

'No.'

'Would you put a lead on me?'

'You're terrible!'

Trains don't fuck around going into every housing estate looking for a passenger who isn't there anyway. *'And it has only gone up the street because it's subsidised by the taxpayer to pick up someone on the dole.'* Cut the crap and get the train.

We were hugging the coast line and passed a field full of rare breeds. There was an interesting golf course right on the coastline just before Stonehaven and it looked as though it could be fun.

Stonehaven train station was very smart and freshly painted, complemented by the beautiful Victorian ironwork.

The Railway Hotel was fully booked and that turned out to be the case for the next hour.

For the first time on my 'walkabout' I couldn't find a bed, and people always get great pleasure in telling you that they're full, so I ended up going to the tourist office.

'Could you get me a single room?'

'There's not a single room in Stonehaven.

'Well, there's one at £65, but they're not in.'

'Well, I would take it then.'

It was tempting to say, 'Thanks for fuck all' but I didn't.

ROOM AT 31

I got a room here. *'If a big fat person stayed in my room they wouldn't fit in the shower.'* The place was so different. It was really contemporary;

in fact it was nearly brand new. It did a 'help yourself' breakfast, but none of the owners lived in; they just gave you a key.

I'd had such a lovely trip round Scotland, more or less having the place to myself on previous 'walkabouts', but now I came up against 'people'. The types I mean are those big fat things with feet on them, and arms that look as though they're pumped full of water waiting for the next drought. If you're really lucky they may be in shorts and even have their favourite football team tattooed across their backs.

I didn't quite know what to make of this place. It was a bit like crossing Margate with Rye. I walked along the beach and kept looking out for a nice restaurant. I went to the harbour and all the pubs were overflowing onto the pavements; all except the fancy restaurant which won the 'fish restaurant of the year' award. I looked at the menu and sushi cost £25. I wondered whether or not to give them the pleasure of telling me they were fully booked.

I must have walked for an hour round this place and ended up having fish and chips on a seat by the sea. I enjoyed watching the beauty of the rooks and the black-headed gulls with their mauve feet. Paul Theroux describes black-headed gulls as 'Hangman Gulls'.

I went to bed.

Next morning I found out that there was a restaurant right next door to where I was staying. *'Nutter!'*

STONEHAVEN TO ST ANDREWS

Waiting for the bus I watched a boot fair being set up. It cost £10 for a pitch and happened every Sunday. *'What a load of cheap rubbish.'* A fat ugly woman and her husband didn't have the brains to have brought any change for their first customer. The only thing I would've bought for a fiver was a leather rule. Her grandfather had travelled the world as an engineer, but neither she nor her children wanted it. I told her she shouldn't be selling her heritage.

The bus arrived bang on time. There was only one other passenger and we whisked down every street looking for another old git but there was nobody.

I thought of stopping off at one of the villages we went through, but abandoned it and it was probably the right thing to do. Tesco continues to dominate this part of the world, and indeed the whole of Scotland.

I didn't realise I had to change buses so had a rush to do so. A drunk downstairs shouted at me, but the good thing about a double-decker is that you can get away from them.

There were some really good farms in this area, mainly growing wheat, barley, rape and daffodils.

VOTE FOR JA

'WE WILL PROVIDE FREE BUS TRAVEL IF YOU ARE UNDER A CERTAIN WEIGHT. WE WILL SET PASSENGER FARES ACCORDING TO HOW HEAVY YOU ARE!'

'In other words, fat fuckers can walk.'

ARBROATH

I noticed that they seemed to have white fire engines up here, and also their fair share of fat, tattooed guts with vests talking on their mobiles. 'Hello. Hello. How are you? I'm all right.' *'Let's talk a lot of fuck all!'*

I couldn't stand the idea of staying here too long and stayed just long enough to get the bus to St Andrews. I had a couple of rolls in a railway café run by a beer gut.

I arrived at St Andrews and couldn't believe I was actually here on a drizzly Sunday afternoon. They'd just finished the Ladies' Curtis Cup between England, the USA and Ireland.

St Andrews, known as the home of golf, started life in 1754 on May 14th and to this day they still have problems with equality, where women cannot do this or that or enter here or there... Myself, I'd much rather play with a pretty girl than some old fart. The club house at St Andrews is so ugly. Perhaps they should have employed a female architect.

I had a job to find a B&B and once again ended up going to the tourist information office. They take a percentage and as it turned out the place they got for me was more or less next door; Hoppity House. It was another 'help yourself' type of place and after a warm welcome from Ian I had a walk around the town and arrived at Royal St Andrews – the home of golf.

I took a picture of a bunch of Irish girls standing under the Curtis Cup banner. I shouted to them and asked who the greatest golfers in the world were? I said it was the British and that made them laugh.

I walked down to the 18th hole and watched all the Japanese having their photos taken on the famous bridge. I had mine taken as well! OK, I know I'm sad!

Women golfers all look just the same; like peas in a pod. They're very brown and thin and have their heads held high, like people on a mission to the moon and all are totally focused on getting there. *'Don't interrupt them or you break their concentration, you silly man.'*

'We're very important people and have been chosen by God to follow this little white ball from one hole to the next and to one golf course after another, even if it means going round the world to do so.'

Christ, there are some large ladies walking about in the streets. Like a farmer friend said, 'If I could fatten cattle like that I'd be a millionaire.'

I walked for miles around the town and ended up at the Thai Restaurant which was near my hotel. I was given a huge welcome so I ordered a beer and flicked through their expensive menu. 'Does that include rice?'

'No, that's extra.'

I paid for my beer and fucked off out of there. Even in the reception area they had the nerve to say that the service charge was not included.

I ended up in a funny restaurant where the rocket was yellow. After a beer and a large glass of red wine I felt quite merry as I staggered back into the Thai Restaurant to find my room key – only to find it in my back pocket after all.

To bed. I dream about shitty papers.

VOTE FOR JAB

'In order to broaden the mind of the average thick-head, each must read two pages of current affairs. Only then will the paper open to reveal the smut and other crap contained in it! Do I have your vote?'

I had my serviced accommodation breakfast and made my sandwiches with fruit and cheese and still had some left over.

I felt rested and better and pleased with myself for getting out really early at 7am. I shut myself out of the hotel and then realised that I'd left my faithful map behind. I couldn't believe what an idiot I was and I rang the bell but no one came.

While I'd been waiting for the hotel to open I watched the builders laying huge granite paving slabs. The slabs were lifted by suction by a mini-digger and then painted with cement to make them stick.

'Nice to see craftsmen at work,' I said.

'Aye, but we're not craftsmen.'

'Oh yes, you are.'

Derek the dustman was ex-Navy and used the chat lines to keep in touch with his old friends all over the world. The students were leaving and putting out huge amounts of rubbish and if the lids wouldn't close they would pull it all out. There was a strike on so he wasn't sure if the rubbish would be collected.

On the bus, the man in front was, of course, reading *The Sun*: *'KATIE'S LOST HER PANTIES!'*

We went past the turf farm and left dear old St Andrews and its fine gentlemen behind.

ST ANDREWS TO BERWICK-UPON-TWEED

I want to summarise my visit to Scotland but where do I start? Scotland probably has some of the most stunning countryside in the world. I met some lovely people who were very kind. When hitching, some folk went miles out of their way and I was even asked in for a cup of tea. I give big thanks to all the islanders, including those in Orkney and Shetland, and to all the bus drivers who stopped and picked me up. The family in Kirkwall treated me like Royalty.

For £8.50 I got to Edinburgh. I phoned Neil and he gave me a farming update.

Every now and then a couple of stuffed shirts would get on the bus and it was clear that they found it hard to lower themselves to sit with the common people. They would sit there so well-dressed and so uncomfortable with their surroundings. It was funny really. *'We don't normally travel by bus. We have a Rolls Royce, a house in London and another in Monaco.'*

EDINBURGH

I went to the train station and found out the times of the trains to Berwick. I had a chat to the same beggar I'd seen at the same place before, and to whom I had given a pound. I tried to put it as politely as I could. 'How are you? Do you remember me? We had a chat about a week ago.'

'Aye.'

'What's the weather been like?'

'Pretty wet.'

'Have you ever thought about cleaning shoes? You could make a fortune.'

'Nay!' *I think a lot of these guys have blown their minds away with drug abuse.'*

A tattooist was having a smoke outside his shop. He looked weird and had blond spiky hair and looked so yellow it seemed he was dying. I didn't dare make eye contact but would've loved to have had his photograph.

THE SCOTTISH PARLIAMENT

I didn't realise that it was so easy to get in; there was no charge and you could go right into the Chamber. Enric Miralles, a Spanish architect, designed it and if you think the English can design some ugly buildings, try the Spanish. They did an excellent job here! I wondered if the Scots were sticking two fingers up to the Royalists as the Queen's Palace is right opposite. Alex Salmond is the First Minister and wants a separate Scotland. What a great idea; they can pay their own benefits instead of them coming up from the south.

Two very polite security guards told me Parliament was not sitting at the time, but I was amazed just how close you could get to them. I asked if they got any hecklers and they said that if that happened the police just chucked them out. I was pleased I'd paid the place a visit.

QUEEN'S PALACE

The Queen comes to Scotland every year at the end of June and in July. Security is tight and they have a huge barrier across the entrance. Some fancy looking boys in a Range Rover came out. Some tourist ladies were having their photographs taken with a guard who was all dressed up in his Scottish gear.

I found the train and an hour later I was in Berwick.

Berwick's strategic position on the English-Scottish border during the centuries of wars between the two nations, and its relatively great wealth, led to a succession of raids, sieges and take-overs. Between 1147 and 1482 the town changed hands more than thirteen times and was the location of a number of momentous events in the English-Scottish border wars. One of the most brutal sackings was by King Edward I in 1296. It set a precedent for bitter border conflicts in the Scottish Wars of Independence. In the 13th century Berwick was one of the wealthiest trading ports in Scotland, trading mainly in wool, grain and salmon. At one point, Berwick had its own mint making Scottish coins.

There was a mixture of holidaymakers standing at the station looking lost. *'Have they just arrived here or are they going?'* A large farmer person was at the ticket office working out a trip and his Range Rover hazard lights were flashing away in the car park. The name on the Range Rover was 'BIG GEM', *'but I apologise as he was probably a very successful lettuce farmer!.'*

As I made my way into the High Street I knocked on various B&B places, but they were all full. There was loads of construction work going on in the town. I went to the tourist office.

'They're all full here. Try over the river. They're usually cheaper there.'

'OK.'

Wow, what a bridge! The name is The Old Bridge and it was built in 1624. It has a 15 span sandstone arch, is 1,164 feet long and was built for

a cost of £15,000. It's not as old as St Charles' Bridge in Prague, or as long, but it's just as beautiful and doesn't have all those tatty people selling junk to tourists. It's also still a working bridge with a dignified modesty.

It seemed here that you were either a gentleman who fished the Tweed, or a worker, or on the dole. Berwick was a place of absolutely no eye contact, especially in the Spittle area. There were bald heads, tattoos, pit bull terriers and a 'someone else can pick up the dog shit' attitude.

I met Jim and Eileen who owned the Roxburgh Guest House. They gave me a huge double room all to myself. *'I am a happy boy.'*

I rested and washed and walked back to The Harrow for scampi and chips. Most of the people here were lorry drivers who had parked up at the lorry park. One man hauled white slag to the cement works. I found out all about them but they asked nothing about me, but it's always the same in local pubs. They live their cosy narrow lives, read *The Sun*, have a pint and half a tin of roll-ups and they're happy.

However, I did ask what Spittle was famous for. 'Fuck all' came the reply.

There was a big change in this between Edinburgh and Berwick. It had gone from 'Aye' to 'Like'.

I met Norman Fail when I was walking back from the pub. He was the highlight of the day. He was eighty-eight years old and an ex-submariner. I asked him about the history of the beautiful Berwick Bridge; he kept all facts about bridges in his wallet, but the zip was stuck so there I was trying to free it for him. I was sure that if anyone had looked they would have thought I was mugging him.

He told me that there was a 5% survival rate among submariners in his day.

'What was your biggest fright?'

'We were based in Australia and had to go to Burma to rescue American pilots who'd been shot down. Every time we went above water we were fired at by the Americans.'

I asked him what he thought about the young today. 'If yer don't work yer don't eat.' came the reply. He was in favour of the birch.

I asked, 'What's the secret of your long life?'

'Keep happy,' he said.

'Nice to meet you, Norman, and I want to thank you for what you did in the war to give us our freedom.'

'Oh, aye!'

He was a very fit man. He lifted his trousers to show me his bad knee. 'Got to keep walking to make it work.' And off he went.

What a pleasure it was to meet him and it brought a tear to my eye.

I hadn't slept at all well. I just catnapped all night. I met Roy and Brian at breakfast. They were up here on holiday and had done the west and done the south, so thought it was time to do the north. I told them about 'help yourself' accommodation at St Andrews and Stonehaven. 'I don't think we want to know that' was the response. They were a couple of dry old sticks and I wasn't sure if they were father and son.

As soon as I walked out of the house a bus came along and we went round the whole of Spittle picking up all and sundry. There was even a lurcher and the young lady let me take a photo.

'Hello, Marjorie.'

'Hello, Fred.'

I asked if they were just off to do their shopping and they said they were.

'Have you got a Tesco?'

'No, a Co-op. Tesco tried to build here but there was a lot of opposition.'

The bus driver chipped in and said that Tesco was turned down on appeal.

A lady got on the bus beside me with a load of bottles for the bottle bank.

'Had a good evening then?' I asked.

'Mind your own business.'

'Sorry, I was only joking!' *That's really put me in my place.'* When she got off the bus I felt like telling her that if she could find a shop selling 'sense of humour', to buy some, but I thought better of it.

I sat in a coffee shop and sent a card to the brand new 'Archie Burden'.

I caught the bus and we drove about and arrived at the very 'up-your-jumper' village of Bamburgh. *You don't let your dog on the grass here, let alone do anything else.'*

BAMBURGH CASTLE

It was the home of Lord Armstrong who lived from 1810 to 1900 and he was an engineer. He made the hydraulics for Tower Bridge. He had seen a steam driven machine whilst working in a quarry and thought he could do better than that.

The castle was built on a basalt outcrop and the location was previously the home fort of the native Britons known as Din Guarie, and may have been the capital for the British Kingdom from the Realm's foundation in roughly 420 AD until 547, when the first written reference to the castle was made. The citadel was captured by the Anglo-Saxon ruler Ida of Bernicia and became Ida's seat. The Britons briefly retook it from his son, Hussa, during the war of 590 before being relieved later the same year.

There was a machine for winding up crossbows and they had German matchlock muskets.

The castle's ex-laundry rooms feature the Armstrong and Aviation Artefacts Museum; with exhibits about the Victorian industrialist William Armstrong and Armstrong Whitworth, the manufacturing company he founded; as well as displays including engines, artillery, weaponry and aviation artefacts from the two wars.

The castle now has apartments, which help to bring in rent and people can get married here for £2,000.

I got a quote from a Welshman when I said I had been to Pontypridd. 'Oh yes,' he said, 'Pontypridd, where men are men and women are pleased to be women.'

One of the elderly ladies had fallen down and the castle guards came running. She was all right and probably enjoyed all the attention.

Outside the castle and across the fields is a dovecote, sometimes called a ducket. This is not on the tourist trail, so I had to hunt it down across several fields. It has a scruffy low doorway covered in nettles and when I poked my nose inside I got stung and covered in pigeon shit. A rabbit inside made me jump as I thought it was a rat. What a gem of a place this is.

I went to the Castle Hotel for lunch and Carl from Blackpool was there. He was a window cleaner, was nearly as nutty as me and was camping in a car. He looked like a stockbroker and apparently was brought up in Papua, New Guinea. We seemed to click. He probably owned a huge cleaning company.

It was now raining. When I'd been climbing on all fours into the dovecote I broke my glasses, so the lady in the pub kindly went and read the bus timetables for me. It was not long until the bus arrived and took me to Belford.

Mrs Stuffed Shirt was one of those sorts of women who terrify me, being very upright, well spoken, correct and to the point, with no humour. I couldn't make out why one so young had let her hair go so grey. She and two mates had walked from Land's End to John O' Groats and had done it two weeks at a time. It had taken seventy-eight days.

I was back in Berwick and had a long walk to my guest house. It was quiet back here and the wide streets gave it a feeling of space.

I had a rest before walking back into town on another long walk. I tried the Red Lion pub but it didn't do food, so I thought that having walked this far I might as well go over the bridge into town. I was hoping to see Norman as I hadn't got his photograph, but didn't.

I went up to a drunk who was talking to a taxi driver. 'What's that place like to eat at?'

'Depends how much money you have.'

'Not a lot. I was going to do the washing up for them.'

'You look like a chap not hard up for a bob or two' he said.

'Never judge a book by its cover.'

I had a huge meal and ate the lot, washed down with a couple of glasses of red wine. I watched the body language of a man and a woman. He was touching her and she was trying to get away. It reminded me of the prostitute at the Royal in Thurso.

I couldn't stand the idea of walking back to my room so took a taxi for £5.

BERWICK TO ALNWICK

At the bus stop it's always a good feeling when you find others going to the same place as you.

294

'Holy Island here we come!' And we're not alone. There were loads of coaches and tourists in sheep-like mode.

I took the Holy Island bus to get closer to the castle and the driver, who was an islander himself, was in good form.

'See the dark rocks over there? They're seals and they have salmon for breakfast, lunch and dinner.' He had an amazing accent, coming right from the front of the tongue.

The Lindisfarne Castle can only be reached at low tide and was built in 1550, around the time that the Lindisfarne Priory went out of use and stones from the Priory were used as building materials. Its position on the North Sea made it vulnerable to attack from the Scots and Norsemen. As time moved on it was used as a coastguard look-out and then became something of a tourist attraction.

Like sheep, we followed each other and were met by our shepherd from the National Trust, who was trying to sell membership. The National Trust is really the Tesco of 'Castleland'. There were signs everywhere so we really knew we were sheep!

'DO NOT TOUCH.'

'DO NOT SMOKE.'

'DO NOT SHAG THE SHEEP.'

I didn't hang about and didn't see the rest of the island. I really wanted to lose the rest of my flock.

I started walking off the island and got a lift straight away with Fred who worked for Scottish Power. 'For God's sake, don't tell anyone I've given you a lift or I'll get the sack.' It was a good but short lift as I wanted to be dropped off at the Barn at Beal.

Farmer Rod Smith had just opened his farmyard to the public. He had a café and information area, and a playground. It was all done well. I told him so and he was appreciative.

Apparently the castle has 600,000 visitors a year and he was hoping to cream off some of them.

The falconer, Mark, was erecting houses for his birds and told me of the different sorts of accommodation they each needed. He hoped to have it finished by the weekend.

'Walkabout' is full of the unexpected and after watching the workmen cutting the kerbstones I found another dovecote. It was in a very bad state of repair and overgrown with ivy.

I crossed over the railway line just before the lights started flashing.

It's always good news when you find a bus stop. I looked through all the timetables and we were hours away from any bus. I thought it would be hours before I got to Chillingham, but looked around and there was a bus.

David, the driver, was very helpful but had never heard of Chillingham Castle. He dropped me off in Belford and said, 'You've done well on that ticket. I thought you wanted dropping off earlier.'

I offered to pay more but he wasn't interested and just wanted to chat. He came from London years before and in six weeks was due to retire to Spain. He was really looking forward to it. I think he really enjoyed the chat as the other old girls on the bus looked as though they were on the way back from the crematorium! Perhaps they were on their way to it.

GET YOUR THUMB OUT DAY

I had a fair way to go so I walked out of Belford and was lucky enough to get a lift with Alan Lidyard. He'd just played a poor round of golf and had retired up here some time ago from the Hampshire Police Force. He was amazed that I knew Popham and Doug Ranger who used to service my plane. He went out of his way and dropped me outside the gates of Chillingham Castle.

I was feeling smug as I was here by 12.50pm. *'Didn't I do well?'*

After rain, snow, fog and mist, it was now a perfect day with no wind. In fact it was turning out to be a special day.

Sir Humphrey Wakefield owns this castle.

'A worker of miracles' (*Daily Telegraph*)

'Legendary restorer' (*The Field*)

This place felt more like a home than a National Trust type castle and it was stuffed full of interesting things. The reception area was full of old gun cases and cartridge boxes. Every corner of the castle was amazing and even in the tea room there was a fire that was constantly kept alight and had lovely ironwork. In addition, if you were in love you could get married here.

There was half an elk horn that had been found in an Irish bog and it must've been fifteen feet long. They had made another replica one to keep it company.

Sir Humphrey had spent a lifetime collecting bits and pieces for this place.

For over seven hundred years the Chillingham wild cattle have been contained within the park. They are the sole survivors of the ancient cattle that roamed Britain and are the only cattle in the world to have remained free from any human interference or breeding management. No outside blood has been introduced for many centuries. In spite of all that inbreeding they remain vigorous and viable; not at all what you might expect from traditional genetic science. They are truly wild and potentially dangerous. No other herd exists like this one anywhere in the world.

In 1344 the King of England gave permission for Chillingham Castle to be 'castellated and crenulated' and it might well have been that the herd was corralled for the purposes of food and hunting.

I cut short my visit to the castle for a 2pm appointment with Richard Marsh, the cattle warden – he used to be a prison warden – but now loves his work.

I was the only one there and Richard Marsh drove me into the park. It had seven miles of stone walls built in 1200 to surround the estate. Only 360 acres remain which have now been safeguarded.

The bulls are 'top dog' for about three and a half years and the DNA of them is identical. If a human touches one of these animals the rest of the herd will kill it. They have been here for seven hundred years and because of the foot and mouth scare one bull and two heifers were sent to Scotland, and now have a family of fourteen.

'This is the perfect situation to witness a piece of history. The sun is shining and the bulls are scratching themselves on a fallen walnut tree. Richard is standing there giving me the history and making sure the bulls don't get behind us. Mr Bull didn't like it much when I got down on my stomach to take a photograph.'

Richard's enthusiasm was such that it wasn't possible to put down all he said on paper. During the winter of 1947 the herd went down to just thirteen; the rest died in the snow drifts. They spread hay by helicopter, but when they were fed with cake they didn't know what it was and refused to eat it.

I said my farewells to Richard and paid my dues. I walked back across the fields back to the castle and saw a little bit more of this amazing part of the countryside. This place is a 'must' to visit.

Brian was my third lift of the day and his work was setting up musical equipment. He said it was a peaceful industry to work in.

The next lift was with John, a joiner. He was working about thirty miles from home on some stable conversions. He was looking forward to his retirement in three years' time. I asked him what he would do then. He said that like me he would get a rucksack and go travelling.

John was my last lift of the day and he dropped me off after a couple of miles on the outskirts of Alnwick. I enjoyed walking in the town. People were working in their gardens, and I was being as nosy as ever. I looked through a hole in the gate of the Duke of Northumberland's estate. The estate cottages all had matching paint just to let them know that they are common little tenants.

I popped into one hotel. 'Have you got a single room?'

'Yes.'

'How much?'

'£65.'

'I've got £40. Will you take it?'

'No.'

'Thank you.'

The miserable person running the hotel next door booked me in, but to be fair he seemed never to stop working. *'I wouldn't be surprised if his wife had buggered off.'*

My room was very small and the bathroom was as tired as I was. The shower door was hanging off and the basin taps were temperamental, but for £35 and right in the town centre what more could you expect?

I went next door to the Swan to eat and enjoyed watching the head waiter guy working the whole tourist restaurant. He had the whole place eating out of his hand.

I went to bed.

I couldn't stand the idea of staying in this room all day so I went and enquired at the King's Hotel. They wanted £70 and I offered £40, but it was 'no deal'. I went and found the Bailiff Gate where I'd been yesterday. I had a nice feeling about it and I booked in for £40. It was a bit like a miniature Court Lodge and the only thing was that the hall smelled a bit 'doggy'.

I went from pokey to lovely.

Hey guys! I slept in the same hotel as Charlie Dimmock. Maybe in the same bed.

I decided to stay another night in Alnwick, but when I got back I found a note saying: 'We're sorry, but we're fully booked.' In other words, *'On your way, mate.'*

I went back to the Tower Hotel for dinner. 'Could I have this wine, please?'

'Sorry, but we don't do that one by the glass.'

'I don't want a glass. I want a bottle.'

'Oh!'

I went to bed.

The next day was June 6th and it was the first time that I'd been up-to-date with *Walkabout* – I'd been up since about 4am.

At 9am I'd booked into The Georgian. It was right next door to the Tower and the castle.

ALNWICK CASTLE GARDENS

I arrived at the garden at 8.45am only to find that it didn't open until 10am, so I had a walk round the castle grounds and nobody hassled me. This was funny as I was trying to get out of the grounds on the other side and it said: 'Private – Keep Out', but I couldn't get over the gates. As I'd been a naughty boy I crept around the perimeter and met an amazed stonemason. He wondered what I was doing going through his site.

'Sorry, but I got lost. We're lucky to have craftsmen like you.'

He smiled and I cluttered off.

I sat in front of the gardens and watched everybody turning up for work. It was interesting and made me realise how much labour these places need. A larger than life lady was whipping everyone into action.

When the place opened I really enjoyed a privately conducted walk around the poison garden. Henbane gives off a nasty scent that can easily make you faint. Laurel leaves are used to kill insects and spurge produces a white sap that can badly affect the eyes. Opium, henbane and hemlock put you to sleep; also couch seed is poisonous.

Apparently a lady in Egypt wanted to kill herself so she experimented with her slaves. *'Whatever is wrong with that?!'*

I met a lovely looking girl called Susan, who was a cleaner and was totally dedicated. She told me that people just thought the place cleaned itself. I also met David, a very young gardener who certainly had fire in his belly.

There was a sign in the gardens saying: 'Only dead fish swim with the stream.'

I really don't know what to say about these gardens. They're different and contemporary with modern water features. It would be wrong to slag them off and maybe a change is not altogether a bad thing, but they're not for me – although I did love the poison garden.

Alnwick Castle is the second largest inhabited castle in England and has been the home of the Percy family, Earls and the Duke of Northumberland since 1309.

The castle was first restored, primarily as a fortress, by the first Lord Percy of Alnwick in the early 1300s and bits of the restoration remain to this day, including the Abbot's Tower, the Middle Gateway and the Constable's Tower.

In recent years the castle has been used in the making of the Harry Potter films.

To have your wedding at the castle would cost £1800 plus £35 per head if you wanted food which I thought was relatively cheap.

I went back into the Garden Centre and showed my concessionary card to a young man. 'What! You found that?'

'No, I didn't.' *'At least someone thought that I was a liar!'*

I had a piggy night's sleep and was glad to get back out on the road. I filled in the comment book: 'Love the ceiling mirror. I'll bring the girlfriend next time.'

ALNWICK TO LENHAM

The Friday night revellers had left Alnwick bus station looking more like a rubbish dump than a bus stop. An old boy at the bus station said the bus goes all the way to Newcastle.

Warkworth Castle imposes itself on the village. On the top of the bus I had a grand view of all the vegetable gardens round here.

Anne sat next to me and got chatting away. She worked in the laundry department of Morpeth mental hospital with a team of twenty-five. The other day only five of the team had turned up. The rest were lead-swinging, saying that they were ill.

'Do they get paid for that?' I asked.

'Oh yeah.'

At Morpeth the poor old bus driver got out for a cigarette and the inspector turned up and gave him a right dressing down in front of us all for not letting the passengers off first. Someone shouted that it wasn't right to tell him off in front of everyone. The inspector did apologise and carried on strutting about like a sergeant-major.

I caught the 9am train out of Newcastle having had a shitty breakfast at the station. The train was full and most people had booked. Every now and then I was bunked out of my seat. I met some fun people who liked talking: there was a couple off to take photos at a wedding; a lady who

told me all about her hitch-hiking experiences around Europe; and a funny middle-aged bachelor boy who worked in an insurance office doing administration and told us all about his holidays.

London was bulging at the seams with people. They had just closed the gates at King's Cross Underground because of overcrowding and the poor guy on the gates was getting some nasty abuse from some yobs.

Lynn Fletcher picked me up from Sittingbourne Station. 'Home Sweet Home!'

CHAPTER NINE

Newcastle to Boston

'What time is your train?' Valerie asked.

'6.52am.'

'It's now 6.15am.'

'Christ!' and the train's going from Headcorn.

At 6.45am Valerie was waving goodbye to me outside the railway station and I was well satisfied that with my checklist I had everything for my two weeks of rucksacking. However, when I got to Tunbridge Wells I realised that I'd left my toilet bag hanging on the bedroom wall.

The last time I came up here the train was so full and everyone had booked, so this time I did the same; a return ticket costing me £54.50. As soon as I had booked I knew it was a mistake, as it would tie me down to a date and a time, which later proved to be right. Once again the King's Cross train was full and some of the people on it I didn't fancy sitting next to for four hours, so I tried first class, which was nearly empty apart from some mouthy tennis player who asked the pretty conductress if she was 'all right'. The conductress replied that she was and asked the tennis player if he was all right, as if to say 'fuck you, too'. She then proceeded to chuck him out into standard class. It cost me another £25 but was worth every penny.

A few tractors were working the fine black soil on this Sunday morning near Peterborough, and the auto-cast planted rape looked its usual terrible self.

For my extra £25 I got free black coffee delivered whenever I wanted. The carriage had seventeen seats and I was the only one there, so I was enjoying the journey.

The train creaked its way out of Doncaster and went into cooling tower country.

Our 'no-mess' conductress was knackered and had a coffee. She said, 'I shouldn't moan as I'm on overtime.'

Once we got through York the land looked wetter and colder, and before we knew it we were passing the Angel of the North.

After just under four hours we arrived in Newcastle. I was surprised to see that the station information office was open. Before I got to it a friendly official asked if he could help me. He gave me a map and directions to the Westgate Road Hotel. He then asked if he could help in any other way. *'I think I'm going to like Newcastle.'*

I had half an hour's walk to the city centre and the Westgate Road Hotel, and I was warmly welcomed by the owners who were a Pakistani family. The place was simple, clean and cheap.

I showered and then caught the bus back into the city centre and discovered the Tyne Bridge, the Sage Gateshead and the Old Baltic Flour Mill, which had been turned into an exhibition centre at huge expense.

Newcastle used to be famous as an important wool centre and trading area, and it became a major coal mining place. The port developed in the 16th century along with shipbuilding and repairing. Most of this took place lower down the river. The industries have since declined and most have closed. Today the city is mostly concerned with business, culture and night life. The population is around 274,000 with a mixed race population of 25%.

Gateshead, on the south bank, has its own separate town and borough and is joined by a series of dramatic bridges, including the Tyne Bridge which was built in 1928. The high level bridge, constructed in 1849 was the first rail and road bridge to be built in the world.

The Sage Building cost seventy million in 2004. It drew me inside as it seemed the whole building had been wrapped in bubble wrap – it was like being in a cruise liner. I walked downstairs where it was all divided into small rooms with young people learning to play different instruments, or learning to write music. It was a real centre of learning and it was a breath of fresh air.

I had a look round the Old Baltic Flour Mill. It was a funny place and full of things I couldn't quite get my head round.

There was another great little bridge, the Gateshead Millennium Bridge, known by the locals as the 'Winking Eye' when it opens. It cost a mere twenty-eight million pounds.

Where the hotel was situated, just north of the Westgate Road, was interesting. It was the working-class area with people from all over the world, and shops to go with it. I saw produce the like of which I've never seen before.

'You get some interesting vegetables here,' I said.

'Oh yes, we have people from all over the world. You name a place and they're here.'

It was really fascinating. There was every spice imaginable and even a man cutting up meat in the back. You could buy fish and it was all rough and ready, but it worked. I settled for a tooth brush, tooth paste and some soap.

I caught the bus back into Newcastle and avoided all the fast food shops. I ended up eating in the Royal Station Hotel but the only fancy thing about the place was the name.

When I got back to my hotel the children on the estate were searching for conkers and screams of delight went up when they found one. I felt quite guilty with all the conkers that there are around our house.

Breakfast was a fairly simple 'help yourself' affair. The cornflakes were fed out of a hopper. The Pakistanis don't seem to do interior design, but at least you couldn't fall out with the staff because there were none this morning.

I decided to stay another night to give me time to discover Newcastle, only to be told that Newcastle was playing Manchester City and the only available room was a double one for £55.

'I'm sorry but someone will take the double room.' At this we both slapped hands and I took the room. I couldn't be bothered to hunt all over Newcastle looking for somewhere else.

I left the hotel at 9.15am and it started to rain, so I dashed into a school porch to put my leggings on. A coloured gentleman joined me.

'British weather!' he muttered.

'Yeah, you born in this country?'

'No, I came from the Congo.'

'Well,' I said, 'you might get wet over here but at least you won't get your head cut off!'

With this he roared out laughing and we went our separate ways.

I've never in my life been to a football match, so I took the hotel's advice and went to the football stadium at St James' Park. It was all very smart, but I hadn't a clue what I'd have to pay or whether I'd get a ticket at all.

'Do you want a stand or something else?'

'Sorry, but I'm not a football fan. What does that mean?'

'£30 or £35.'

'I'll take the £35.'

'Gates open at 6.30pm and the game is at 8.00pm.'

Whilst waiting for the open-top bus a little jerk threw his cigarette packet onto the clean pavement. I tried very hard not to say anything, and all the more so as there was a litter bin not fifteen feet away, which was advertising a sign saying that the fine for litter was £50!

As I was carrying £2,000 in cash and cards and I was in Newcastle I kept quiet. I was not happy with myself.

A young cheerful girl in *The Sun* red uniform was selling newspapers on the corner.

'Hello, are you paid on commission?'

'No, £7.50 an hour.'

'Are you a Geordie?'

'Nay, I'm a Maccam.'

'What's that?'

'I come from Sunderland.'

'Would you mind if I took your photograph? Your uniform will come out a treat.'

'Sure, and have a good day.'

'You're doing a great job. Keep it up. Are you going to the football match this evening?'

'Nay, I have to get up early to sell this newspaper. I need a good night's sleep.'

She was a plucky cheerful girl.

Two van loads of wheel clampers were getting ready for another day. They were big, fat, ugly and tattooed. They put a clamp on a car.

'How much will that cost them?'

'£90,' he replied, with a deadpan expression.

I jumped on an open-top sightseers bus. We passed St Mary's Catholic Church which was built in 1844 and we went past the football stadium for tonight's match. The stadium holds 52,000 people. The driver told us the names of all the bridges; the high level one opened in 1847 and the swing bridge in 1876. The Baltic Flour Mill cost forty-six million pounds to convert. The Millennium Bridge cost twenty-eight million and only uses £4 of electricity to open it. Gateshead has the largest shopping centre in the world and the Sage Music Centre has twenty-five rooms for learning and listening to music.

I had all my cold-weather clothes on and it was still cold. After an hour I jumped off the bus at St Andrew's Church. I left a message there congratulating all the cleaners on a good job.

A new hospital was being built.

Most of the city wall was knocked down in 1810; it had originally been built in the 13th century.

I went into a Pizza Hut for lunch and met Mrs Lard. She was about seventeen and had legs like an elephant and gold earrings about the size of a football. As for Mr Lard I'll leave that to your imagination; and yes, they had produced little Lard.

I moved my rucksack so that they could move to the next table with ease, but there was not as much as a nod, let alone thanks. They slumped into the seats.

I was wondering how many tubes of Bostick you could get out of this little family. When they got up to leave the table looked like a bomb site. It was obvious that they were both on Social Security and didn't even have the brains to take the two thirds they'd left home for supper.

I popped into the tourist office where they were very helpful. They told me I needed the pink bus for the Angel of the North and they also told me about the bus that I'd need for Hadrian's Wall the next day.

I went into St Nicholas' Church with its fancy ornate tower. As I crept through the door I was caught by a red-robed man who wanted to give me a conducted tour. I told him that he had a very nice church, but that I had a pink bus to catch at any minute and I would be back later.

Apparently the spire, which was built in 1448, was a navigation point for shipping, and it would be considered to be a daring construction if it had been built nowadays, let alone back then.

Waiting at the bus stop to go to the Angel of the North, (the numbers 21, 22 and 25 stop here) the 21 came and drove straight by so I shouted and it stopped some fifty yards up the road.

'Why didn't you stop at the bus stop?'

'Why didn't you flap your arms when I drove past?'

'Because a bus driver's job is to pick up passengers, isn't it?'

'There are hundreds of buses going past here. How do I know you want me?'

'That bus stop says that the number 21 stops here.' *'I can see his point, but he's still a f..k-head!'*

The Angel of the North took a year to build and it was finished in 1998. It's made of 200 tonnes of steel by Hartlepool Steel Fabrication; it's 65 feet high; and has a wingspan of 54 metres. One person every second sees it; that's 90,000 every day and 33 million every year. It must get a lot of wind pressure on it.

I was hoping I wouldn't get the same miserable driver on the way back.

A fuzzy-haired coloured guy joined me and I asked if he'd been born in this country. He told me he'd been born in Ethiopia. We had a good chat all the way to Gateshead. He was trained in IT and English and had been over here for three years, working and studying part-time. I don't think he could believe that a fellow bus passenger had been to his country.

This was my first football match. The Shearer bar, or bars, were organised to serve 50,000 drinkers. There were only plastic glasses and the beer cost £2.90 a pint. On every wall there was a screen blaring away.

I had to go through turnstile number 71 and it took a while to find my seat. I must've been the only one out of 50,000 who had never been to a football match before. I said that to the pie lady and she said, 'I wish it was mine.'

The pitch looked smaller than it seems on television and I was disappointed to see that the grass was artificial, only to be told that it was real and was re-laid every year.

Seat number 44GG was a cracking seat and I was in between two 'season' ticket holders; a lady on the right and a man on the left. Anne said it cost her £598 for nineteen home games and the supporters weren't happy with the owner, because Kevin Keegan had left. The supporters wouldn't put any money in his pocket.

At 7.30pm the stadium was only a quarter full but by 8.00pm it was nearly to capacity. The players were warming up and there was an advertisement for Northern Rock saying: 'True to our roots'.

A man with a little fork went round touching up.

'Who's going to win?' I asked.

'We're going to get beat,' came the reply.

It wasn't long until I realised that if you come back in another world, don't come back as a referee or a linesman. Nobody deserves this kind of abuse.

One of the Newcastle players got red-carded and that didn't go down at all well. Watching these professional players makes the £35 worthwhile. One of the Nigerian guys was built like a Formula One racing car and I was told that the two men warming up were Spaniards.

I think Newcastle were lucky not to lose as Manchester City had control of the ball for most of the game. 'You mustn't wink or you might miss a goal!' I said to my next door neighbour. 'This is my first match, you know.'

'I've been coming here since I was twelve. Used to have to stand on a sleeper then, and my father before me and his father before him.'

Some of the shouting at the players, the referee and the linesmen makes you realise the amount of passion there is in this game. I was sure the linesmen would need some sort of security on the way home.

It ended 2-2. I think the fans were pretty happy with the result and we all poured out of the ground. It was a strange feeling to be in a swarm and I had the impression they could stampede, but even walking home in this area I didn't feel threatened. There were few police about and none of the yob element I'd expected.

NEWCASTLE TO WHITLEY BAY VIA CARLISLE

I wanted to leave early and I was surprised to find the breakfast area open. I then wandered up the side streets and marvelled at the smart terraced houses. I noticed in Westgate Street that there were fifteen bike shops, mainly for motor bikes.

HADRIAN'S WALL

I bought an 'all-day' Rover ticket. I was going to enjoy this ride and what a ride it turned out to be. The sun was shining and it was a beautiful part of the world. Straw and hay stuck to the land like toothpaste refusing to dry. This countryside with its trees and animals unfolded like a film set.

It was good to get out of Newcastle and just like in the Lake District, I wasn't the only walker. *'These people are proper walkers. Damn it, it's much easier on the bus.'*

Heddon-on-the-Wall was the official starting point. We whizzed into the village and picked up a couple of people and then went to Corbridge, which is ruined by tourists. To prove it all it even had its own Orvis shop, which was a sure sign that it was 'up-its-own- jumper'.

Aydon Castle appeared on the skyline and looked down on us as if to say: 'Stop in the bus, sir!'

The driver shouted out, 'Chester's,' and was disappointed when no one got off.

Hexham has a huge wood processing plant and a cattle market.

HOUSESTEADS ROMAN FORT

Everyone got off the bus here, and the remains looked interesting so I joined the departure. I didn't realise how cold and windy it was when I'd been sitting in the bus, but at least the sun was shining.

Cumbria was hit hard by the 'foot and mouth' a few years back and the National Trust lady, who was also connected to farming, said it was eerie with no animals in the fields. She reckoned it was introduced by the government to get rid of excess meat in the area and I think she really meant it. Seeing ewes in lamb being taken off for slaughter was a sight she never wanted to see again. I asked her if she thought that many animals had been slaughtered unnecessarily and she said, 'Absolutely, and pedigree herds going back for generations had been taken off. It was a tragedy.'

Housesteads was built after the Wall in AD 124 by the Romans, and although there isn't much of it left now it is the most complete example of a Roman fort in Britain. The five acre area occupies a commanding position on the exposed escarpment. Looking north it is easy to imagine oneself at the limit of the Roman Empire which once stretched from here to the Arabian Desert.

It was one of the permanent forts built by the Emperor Hadrian in about AD 124 for the garrisons of his complex new frontier, now known as Hadrian's Wall. The visible remains include four imposing gates with curtain walls and interval towers, and examples of all the main buildings found in an auxiliary fort headquarters. There was a commander's house, barracks, granaries, a hospital and latrines. Part of the civilian settlement can be seen outside the South Gate, whilst in the valley to the east are the Knag Burn Gate and a fine length of wall. Housesteads Roman Fort is owned by the National Trust, but it is in the care of English Heritage and receives 100,000 visitors each year.

The bus stopped to pick up three pretty girls. This was rather needed on our old Saga bus.

This place is surely worth a visit some day.

'Have I got time to take a picture of that archway?'

'You got a minute and a half,' said Misery.

We passed through Brampton. I liked the look of it and it didn't look as 'touristy' as Corbridge. We wiggled our way through some beautiful countryside. Even the farmyard feed hoppers were camouflaged in green so that they would blend in.

I never thought I'd end up back in Carlisle. I found the railway station and was helped by a very kind Virgin Rail girl who had met Richard Branson and had even been to his home for a staff party in Oxfordshire. Apparently, he didn't have a huge television and it was quite ordinary and snug inside.

Both the Virgin train and ours pulled out at the same time. There was a sign saying: 'Don't put your feet on the seats and if you do, take your shoes off!'

Back in Newcastle I found the train to Whitley Bay. *'If we stuffed chickens in a cage like this we'd get locked up.'*

I had a horrible little man here eating ice-cream and sniffing every other spoonful. I felt like telling him to blow his f--king nose, or maybe I should've offered him a handkerchief.

WHITLEY BAY

'There must be life around here, judging by the amount of dog shit. I don't think they do doggie bags here.'

Whitley Station had loads of Victorian character and there were lots of B&B places as well.

I rang the Chedburgh. It said: 'Contractors Welcome – Quality Accommodation.'

'Could you tell me if you have a room for the night and how much for a single?'

'You're lucky. I had a cancellation. £25.'

'Is it en-suite?'

'Yes.'

'I've only just arrived. Can I phone you back?'

'Can I have your name?'

Experience shows that you shouldn't do things in a hurry, because you usually find something better round the corner, and I did. Right on the sea front I found the Rex Hotel. When I asked at reception if my room faced the sea she said, 'For £32, you must be joking!' She was right and it even had frosted glass so I had no view at all. It had low voltage light bulbs, but it was all offset by the polite and helpful staff. Nothing was too much trouble.

'What's Whitley famous for?'

'Spanish City.'

Apparently this is the amusement park!

We were asked in the dining room if we minded if one of the guests brought a dog in, and in it came. It was a funny little thing with bulging eyes, as though you had your foot on its neck. It had been found in Greece, quarantined in Germany for six months, and now, with its new owners had come up from London for a few days to get away from the congestion. Its name was Jim. 'Cost us a fortune.'

Today, I'm going to Blackhall. I had breakfast with all the construction workers and then I walked to North Shields.

Usually everyone avoids eye contact with me and gives me a five-metre berth, but Peter and Ken welcomed me with open arms and we chatted away. They asked if I believed in God and so on, and I told them it's the single families that need help. Peter told me that I was obviously a thinker and after a leaflet and a handshake off they went.

'Does God really care about us?

Will war and suffering ever end?

What happens to us when we die?

Is there any hope for the dead?

How can I pray and be heard by God?

How can I find happiness in God?'

I got locked out of the Parish Church of St George. I found out that Lord Cuthbert Collingwood, who was a modest, wise and brave man, had been Nelson's second-in-command and had looked out from here to the Tyne. The Black Midden rocks claimed five ships in three days in the blizzard of November 1864 and thirty-four passengers and crew perished within sight of the shore.

I noticed that there was plenty of dog shit, but on the whole the area was clean and had a nice feel about it.

I had a chat with Joan Chatwin who was taking her dog for a walk. She'd lost her husband a few years before and she was glad of the rest after having had to nurse him for many years. They had met at Glasgow University. She and her husband had done a teaching degree, and she thought that half of them shouldn't have been there.

One pound and five minutes was what it took to get from North Shields to South Shields on the Pride of the Tyne ferry. After a short walk I was in the old town centre with the Old Town House which was built in 1768. It was the only building to have survived the bombing and it had been used as a film set on occasions.

Whilst waiting for the bus to Sunderland I met Bernie Hunter. He was a fit-looking seventy-six-year-old and had been a ship's plumber and welder. He was neither a smoker nor a drinker, liked his own home and cycled regularly. His father was also in the dockyard after coming out of the army. He had served in the Indian cavalry and was a disciplinarian. He would have to get up at 4am and would tell Bernie that if his dad was up then he should be up as well!

Bernie jumped up and helped a young mother with her pram.

'Well done,' I said, 'I sometimes do that.'

'Aye,' he replied, 'I always do.'

He'd started work at the age of fourteen and earned seventeen shillings a week. He worked seven days a week and served an apprenticeship of seven years. He was paid a bonus if the job was done on time and it gave him enormous pride to see a ship launched.

'Mind you, my knees have gone, I've had major heart surgery and I've had tinnitus since a welding spark went down my ear.'

When they shut the Swan Hunter Shipyard they sold the contract to the Koreans. Then he told me the story about the Geordies and Maccams. Apparently they would never eat or drink at the same table in the workplace and hated each other's guts. They took it out of each other on the football pitch.

'Unlike you, I've spent my entire working life in enclosed spaces and I got all the awkward jobs as I was small. We had some nasty accidents.'

I showed him my foot just to let him know that we farmers get injured as well.

He told me that when he was young they had gangs and they would decide that the following night at 8pm they would go for a punch-up.

He'd been married for fifty-two years, still loved his wife and had two daughters and a son.

We arrived at a very smart Sunderland bus station. After chatting to Bernie on the last ride I didn't want to talk on this trip and being crammed in the bus my neighbours seemed to feel the same way.

'Going to Durham?'

'No.'

And that was it, thank goodness, and I was only being polite.

The bus driver dropped me off in Durham and said that he'd been in the job for seventeen years and was stuck in a rut. I noticed that the buses were full of cameras because of 'fraudulent claims'.

'What do you think of Maggie Thatcher?'

'I wouldn't have been able to buy my council house if it hadn't been for her. I paid £18,000 for it a few years ago.'

The Cathedral costs £60,000 per week to maintain, or £3 million a year. I walked up the 218 feet high tower, all 325 steps of it. It's an amazing building and was built in 1093. A lady helper said that if, as in York, people had to pay to pray, she couldn't handle the job.

I chased the bus through town and caught up with it. I showed the driver my 'all-day' ticket, which he wasn't going to have, and stood with all the school children.

Houses and industry was the name of the game here.

The bus driver asked where I wanted to go and I hadn't got a clue. I ended up in the middle of Blackhall. It was getting rather late and there were rows and rows of houses but no hotels. I asked an old boy if there were any hotels and he gave me a look of total astonishment. 'I don't know. There used to be masses of them but I think they're all closed now.'

Anyway there was a recently renovated hotel just round the corner. I had a bit of luck stumbling on this one. I got a double room with a double and single bed, and it was light and brand new. It was a good hotel with good food and I said to the girl, 'Something's got to go wrong!'

She replied, 'No it won't.' But it did, because at breakfast the next morning no one was around and the milk had gone off.

I went through and tried to have a chat with the locals. There were only two in there and they were friendly enough, but with their strong accents and with the television blaring away I had a job to understand them. I asked about the closure of the mines and how it had affected them. They looked at me in amusement as they couldn't even remember the mines. Then I realised that they'd been shut down in 1981 and these guys were only about twenty-three years old.

'What, you just passing through?'

'Yeah.'

'Bet you're glad about that.'

Another man recognised my Graghopper clothes and said he worked for them.

I had a superb meal and then went for a smoke outside the Navy Club.

'Do you have to be a member to have a drink here?'

'No, bingo tonight.'

'All right if I go in?'

'Aye.'

I couldn't stand the idea of drinking any more beer and felt a bit of a prick asking for a red wine. I don't think anyone had ever asked for a wine before – it was served in a half pint beer glass!

The old person I was talking to had spent many years looking after his disabled wife, and I could see that he was getting fed up with me firing questions at him – I couldn't understand him anyway.

I left at 10pm: other people were still arriving and the bingo hadn't even started. I didn't realise that most people around here are not working so they didn't have to worry about getting up in the morning.

To bed.

The lollipop lady gave me the run down on the history of Blackhall. The pit had been sunk in 1909, opened in 1913 and closed in 1981.

As I walked I noticed all the hotels in the area. The old miner last night must've been blind.

I walked out of town and found my way down to the coast under the railway and met Bill, who was walking his two retired labrador guide dogs.

'Do you know who the MP for this area is?'

'I don't know. They're all the same to me. You don't see them until they want your vote – a thieving lot of bastards. The world would be a lot better without religion or politics. See that cliff over there? It's where they filmed Michael Caine in *Get Carter*.'

A few of the wild flowers were saying goodbye before the winter set in and I even found harebells, and some others I couldn't identify. The knapweed had shut up shop until the spring. It wasn't the best beach in the world because of the steep cliffs.

After walking around dog shit all morning I was going to give the next dog walker a wide berth, but he looked interesting and I wanted to find out more about the old coal mining area.

Tony Davies had been a coal-face worker for thirty years, mining nine miles out in the North Sea. It was one of the wettest mines in the country with several hundred pumps getting rid of the water. When he started the pit ponies were just on the way out and he used to shovel coal into the trucks. Some of the tunnels were so narrow that if the trucks came off the rails it was a struggle to get past them.

He'd found several fossils including ferns. The water that was pumped out of the mine was four times the concentration of sea water. They were going to pump it to Scarborough for a firm to extract the magnesium, but neither party could agree on who would pay for the pipeline so it was never built.

'Who's the MP for this area?'

'MP? If you put this dog up for election it would get in!'

'What do you think of Maggie Thatcher?'

'Not much at the time. When Blackhall closed I was working somewhere else and then that mine shut and I haven't worked since.'

I told him that I'd met a miner from Wales and he'd said that Maggie Thatcher had 'done good by closing the mines', or his children would still be going down them.

He thought for a while and then said, 'I suppose I would've been dead by now, or buggered up.'

'You look fit now.'

'Aye, I walk fifteen miles a day with the dog.'

'What's your name?'

'Tony Davies.'

He had to repeat the 'Davies' four times for me as I couldn't understand his accent.

This is why 'walkabout' is so good. I'd never have met him if I hadn't been walking.

I left the coastal path, went under the railway line again and back out onto the main drag to Hartlepool. Inside, on the bus shelter wall someone had scribbled: 'Hartlepool are shit!' and another message said, 'If you remove this you're gay!'

LET'S GO FARMING

I saw a farmer drilling wheat, so I squeezed through the hedge only to see him disappearing into his farm building with the tractor and drill. I walked across the field and found he was drilling wheat and leaving a lot of seed uncovered. Otherwise it was going well. I caught up with him and he looked a bit surprised to see someone walking through his yard.

'Good morning. I'm a farmer from Kent and I was just watching what you were up to.'

He was quite a character. He was sixty-three years old, had a really ragged waistcoat and was a very keen farmer. He said he was going to keep going until he dropped. His son was away selling property, but one day this would all be his.

'I can't imagine that he'd be that easy to work with.'

After a while chatting I think he began to realise that perhaps I wasn't quite the prat that he first thought I was, and he was keen to learn. 'You can't get enough education. Come and have a look at my Vaderstad drill. It doesn't work too well in the wet and those back wheels pan it down. What do you think?'

He was a funny mixture, old Georgie. He'd been farming all these years and still left the seed on top. But he was keen to learn and kept picking my brains.

I asked him if he was going to do any more operations in the fields and he said, 'No, just slug pellets. My seed rate is two hundredweight to the acre, winter kill you know.' He said he'd bought a combine from Haynes years ago and asked what he should do with his headlands and whether we drill before or after. He'd had a bugger of a harvest and it had never stopped raining and the wheat had no bushel weight.

His family had bought the farm from the local estate when the owners had had to sell it to pay death duties. Georgie came down from the North. He also had a 100-cow suckler herd.

I gave him my card and said that if he was ever in Kent he could call in. I also got a photograph and he looked rather tickled with the card.

He said, 'You won't recognise me because I won't be in these clothes.'

I'd walked thirty yards past the bus stop when the bus came, so I went running back and he f..ked off. I gave him two fingers. I had my lunch and another bus turned up soon after, with another Mr Misery as driver.

Hartlepool was founded in the 17th century around the Northumbrian monastery of Hartlepool Abbey. The village grew through the Middle Ages and developed a harbour which served as the official port of the county palatine of Durham. Hartlepool was a target for the German navy at the beginning of the First World War. A bombardment of 1150 shells on December 16th resulted in the death of 117 people. A severe decline in heavy industry and shipbuilding following the Second World War caused high unemployment until the 1990s when major investment projects and the redevelopment of the docks area into a marina saw a rise in the town's prospects.

My first stop was at Asda for a drink and a write-up. What a fantastic store. It was clean and light and I felt quite guilty about the mud coming off my boots. You could get a Sunday lunch for next to nothing. There was even a place to put my rucksack.

By the way, the Hartlepool mascot is a monkey and according to legend it was the only survivor from a wrecked French warship and had been washed ashore. The locals thought it was a spy so hanged it!

I didn't have the energy to go round the shipyard so I went round the excellent museum.

I asked a lady working in the museum if Peter Mandelson was good for Hartlepool. She replied that he was always good to himself, always had been and always would be. Mr Mandelson was the MP for Hartlepool from 1992 to 2004.

I caught the train to Middlesbrough. For such a big town the railway station looked more like something in the middle of Africa. I arrived and walked into a rough old railway pub.

'What's Middlebrough famous for?' I asked.

'Good bar staff.'

There were some real old drinkers and smokers here.

I went for a walk in 'down town' Middlesbrough and stumbled across Seffort, who was trying to make safe a fairly new housing estate that had fallen into dereliction. All the manhole covers had been stolen.

'What do you think of our bridge?'

I thought he was joking as he pointed to what looked like a container loader in the distance. When I got closer I discovered Middlesbrough Transport Passenger Bridge.

Wow! This really is Fred Dibnah country and there's even an unmanned Visitor Centre which was opened by Fred in 2000.

I met an old boy with his daughter; he used to go over it for a halfpenny and you had to hold onto the halfpenny to get back. The bridge had been fully operational since 1911 and provided a regular quarter-hourly service between Middlesbrough and Port

Clarence for eighteen hours a day. It remains the largest transporter bridge operating world-wide. It provides a valuable public transport service and the river is crossed in two minutes.

Apparently the Sydney Harbour Bridge materials were made in Middlesbrough and shipped out.

I went to the tourist office to ask about accommodation and they told me to go to Marton Street. They said it was miles away and I would need a taxi, but it wasn't that far. I walked there and kept phoning different B&Bs and hotels. Earlier, I'd been into the Thistle Hotel in the middle of town. They could fit me in for £97. I offered £45 but they refused.

I found a contractors' hotel behind a grilled door and a hard-looking woman showed me a room, or maybe it was a cupboard, for £20. *'Surely, a man as important as me, a huge landowner from Kent, deserves better than this!'* I kept phoning around and they all asked £55-£65 per night. I offered them £45, but there were no takers.

I eventually booked in at a B&B for £30. There were two single beds in a nice room, but with a shabby bathroom and smelly towels. *'Beggars can't be choosers.'* It was good enough. The landlord was a bit of a misery and everything downstairs was in football style.

I went to the Baltimore Hotel opposite. In the bar, David told me that when he went down the mine, in one part you got rock salt and in another, potash. Apparently, the Cleveland potash mine, just out of Whitby, is the deepest in Europe.

MIDDLESBROUGH TO WHITBY

I wasn't sleeping well so decided to have a steady day.

I went into a café and asked a very cheerful girl where I would find the Newport Bridge. First she said she didn't know and then she said it was miles away and I would need a taxi. So I went across to the tourist office and they said it was about a ten minute walk up the road. They were right.

'Tanning machines aren't needed round here! Why is it that so many people don't like coloured immigrants and yet spend their time going to tanning salons to get as brown as possible? And why don't human beings wear blinkers, like horses, so that they don't have to look down at the ground when they go past you? It's different if they have a dog – then they have a wide smile and you're immediately bosom friends.'

After a short walk I got to the bridge, which was another amazing piece of Victorian engineering, although it no longer lifts up.

I went back and stopped in the Sainsbury café for a rest and a write-up. A tramp-looking man was reading *The Times*. He had a thick beard and a rugged head of hair. I wondered what his story was, but would never find out.

I was going to take the train to Whitby but it was nearly two miles away so I decided to go by bus.

All this area is very built up and most of the villages looked sad.

Jane phoned to say that Valerie had buggered her back up and she wanted me to ring home.

SEAT BELTS IN BUSES

This is a very interesting subject and you laugh at your own expense. 10% of buses are fitted with seat belts and 99% of people are too proud to wear them. What happens in a coach accident is that it usually tips on its side and you go through the windows and are crushed by the bus. But if you're strapped in you're alive and the rest of the passengers are probably dead or badly injured.

Q. How much does it cost the government to give the over 60s a free ride?

A. Dunno!

Q. Do they appreciate it or take it for granted?

A. Take it for granted.

En route to Whitby I noticed that the farmers had some really late planted rape crops and some backward autumn cereal crops, but it got better the nearer we got to Whitby. There were little fields with thick hedges.

I rang up a few B&Bs from outside their houses to save them telling me to my face that they don't do singles. I settled for a £30 per night place outside St Hilda's Church and I was happy.

I had a chat to the bowlers. They were a friendly lot and played all year round. They told me about the different types of bowling: Top Crown and Finger. I decided to spend two nights in Whitby and it was a much bigger place than I'd imagined.

I was told that the place to eat fish and chips was the Magpie and when I got there at about 7.30pm there was a queue to get in. I went on to the Quayside next door and had the best fish and chips I'd ever eaten.

Next morning it was very cold and windy and breakfast was a hushed affair with people whispering about their plans and, of course, the weather.

'Has that wind dropped?'

'Forecast said there was a front coming in.'

'We might miss it.'

'Snow next week.'

'Any more sauce, love?'

I said 'good morning' to a chap in a camper van who was here for the Manchester/Whitby football match. Playing a smaller club only cost £6 entry as opposed to £75 for a game with Manchester United. He liked the smaller clubs because they were friendlier. At the big clubs you know nobody, whereas here it's like a real club and you know everyone.

'What's your name?'

'Frank. They call me 'Frank from Manchester'.' He followed his club every weekend.

The old lighthouse was built in stone in 1835 and the harbour was extended in 1919.

There was a chance of a boat ride. 'How long does it last?'

'25 minutes.'

'How much?'

'£2.' *'Why not?'*

I asked our captain what the name of a particular bird was and he didn't know but made out that he did.

'Can you tell me the name of that bridge?'

'Hasn't got one.'

And to his second in command, 'Can you tell me the name of that bridge?'

'Hasn't got a name.' *'All you have to say is, 'I don't know nuffink. I been watching Big Brother for the past ten years!.'*

Later on I walked across the bridge and there was a big brass plate saying: 'Whitby Bridge'.

We were now in tourist country and they were looking helpless, like sheep looking for grass and they didn't know what to do other than look in crap shops one after the other. This was the first time I'd come across them on this phase of my 'walkabout'.

ST MARY'S CHURCH

This is a little gem stuck on a hill next to an abbey and it reminded me of the one in Cromarty. It had had many alterations over the years. The tower had been lowered and the roof flattened, and I wasn't surprised as it was so exposed to the wind. I watched a film show all about the church and was joined by a lot of smart noisy wrinklies. As they left I said, 'I hope we're going to see you in church a bit more often!'

I heard a muttering and one of them saying, 'He needs to be a bit more careful what he says.' *'You have to stir the flock up a little or else I get no reaction or anything to put in Walkabout.'*

I walked up to Whitby Abbey. 'I'll be sixty tomorrow. Can I get a reduction?'

Mrs Frump replied, 'Seniors get this, that and the other and if I joined today I could visit the moon twice a week for sod all!'

'Tomorrow I'll be a senior which means that for the past fifty-nine years I've been a junior.'

She replied, 'It's my job to point it out to you.' She wasn't looking very happy with me.

'I was only joking,' I said.

I went past a tattoo shop, which charged £60 per hour and a minimum of £10.

'How much would it cost to have that one?'

'£70.'

'How long would it take?'

'About an hour.'

When could you do it?'

'Later this afternoon.'

'I'll think about it.'

There was a stupid girl in there looking at a design. She wanted this bit longer and that bit narrower and her mopey old father was looking on.

I went back to the hotel for a rest and, *'Yes, sir, I am going to the football match!'*

WHITBY FC v MANCHESTER

The attendance was over a thousand and the kick-off was at 3pm. It was a local game and everyone was enjoying themselves. It was a good-humoured afternoon, with no booked seats, so go where you like and fans intermingled.

I nearly froze in the gale force wind, even with all my clothes on, and when the goalkeeper kicked the ball it came back to him. When I mentioned this to one of the stewards, he told me that the other week the goalkeeper had kicked the ball, it had come back and gone into his own net and the referee had to allow the goal.

I'd now seen two types of football and understood what Frank meant. The final score was nil-nil.

After bathing and changing, I went to the Asian Restaurant where I had a rather ordinary and expensive meal, but they were very friendly and it was good 'man-watching' country. The foursome next to me had chips with some Pakistani food and two of them had nearly finished by the time the other two were served.

There was a young guy with a multicoloured Mohican hairdo and 'Never Mind Bollocks' on his T-shirt. His trousers were tartan with chains hanging every which way and I didn't have the nerve to take his picture.

I asked the owner if he was born in this country and he said, 'No, but I've worked in Whitby for forty-two years.' I asked him if it would be safe for a lone traveller to go around Pakistan. He looked surprised and said, 'Of course!'

He told me he was always busy and owned the shop next door. I thought it might have been a jewellers or a shop selling Pakistani food, but in fact it sold T-shirts. One of them had on it: 'Save a mouse, eat a pussy!' It wasn't quite what I'd expected this family to be selling.

WHITBY TO BRIDLINGTON

The next day I crept quietly out at 6.00am old time as the clocks had gone back, and had a chat to the lads clearing up after the drunks. The bus didn't leave until 8.30am and it was now 7.00am, so I started walking. I tried hitching a few cars but had no luck. At last the bus picked me up – I was really ready for it. The driver was in a good mood and didn't stop talking.

'Have you seen the state of this bus?' he asked.

A passenger replied, 'Now he tells me!'

'This is hanging off. That's hanging off.'

'Does the Explore ticket take me south of Scarborough?' I asked.

'Don't know,' replied the driver looking it up. 'No.'

It was great, at last, to see some real countryside in the North Yorkshire Moors National Park. The driver took a three minute cig break.

There was an advertisement in the bus saying: 'Instead of taking a bus have you ever thought of driving one?'

It kept saying fifteen miles to Scarborough and eventually we arrived at Britain's first seaside town. What is Scarborough famous for? Nothing!

A young waitress was outside a café having a fag, and when she came inside she didn't wash her hands and carried on serving food. She always had her fingers in her mouth and had no eye contact.

An old boy had taken his teeth out before eating his bun and he was just returning from the loo, doing his flies up as he walked through.

'Dear Sir,

On Sunday 26th October 2008 I came into your restaurant and noticed a young lady with fair hair and gold earrings. She kept putting her fingers in her mouth and then handled food plates.

Perhaps you would be kind enough to explain this to her as she more than likely is not aware of what she is doing. It is not very hygienic.

Yours sincerely,

Mr Knowall'

Scarborough Castle has a long and bloody history. It was built as a wooden structure in the 1130s and then rebuilt in stone by Henry II in about 1157. It was an important fortress as it guarded the Yorkshire coastline. Scarborough was famous for its wool trade, and as a result was attacked several times by enemy forces. During the First World War it was bombarded by two German warships and was used for propaganda purposes. The raid killed nineteen people and severely damaged the castle. In the 1940s it was used as a prison. Nowadays, it's only invaded by tourists.

SCARBOROUGH TO BRIDLINGTON

There's no doubt that I'm a complete idiot with timetables and I always take the easy option, so I asked a lady at the bus stop and we got chatting.

'Do you think the recession is biting?'

'Well, I went to Debenham's and it was empty, so I went to Maitland's and it was full!'

'Why's that?'

'Cheaper.'

We were now upstairs and on the B121. What a great view it was as we wound our way through all the seaside caravan parks, with my head almost hitting the roof each time we went over a speed ramp.

Suddenly there was an inspector; he was the first I'd ever seen on my 'walkabout'. One young lad said that he'd put his ticket in the bin.

'What happens if I haven't got a ticket?' I asked.

'I give you three choices. First, you can pay up; second, you can have a £30 fine; or third, I can chuck you off the bus!'

'What if I said I'd put it in the bin?'

'We'll find it then.'

'What about him in the back?'

'His father vouched for him.'

We passed the Blue Dolphin caravan site and then the Primrose one. They had notices saying: 'Come Back Soon!'

There was a dad with his inquisitive young son, who was looking out of the window and longing for his dad to tell him what was in the country, but his dad was texting all the way and never spoke to the boy once.

We arrived at Bridlington, another seaside town and I went to another guest house.

'Sorry, we only do doubles but we can give you the number of someone who does singles.'

'Thank you.'

I booked in for the night. It was a lovely little room and I would've given him 10/10 but he was a bit mean with the heating.

'You're lucky you didn't come last night. The whole town was full.'

'Why was that?'

'There was a scooter rally.'

'Would you like dinner tonight?' asked Janet. This was the first time I'd been offered an evening meal.

'I don't want to put you out.'

'We have family coming so we're cooking anyway.'

'Book me in!'

There are two advantages. The first is that there's more of a family atmosphere and the second is that it gives the lonely traveller someone to talk to.

I had a shower and then came down. The guests had arrived. *'Bloody hell, you have to see this to believe it!'* It isn't very easy to explain but this guy was big, very big. In fact he was obese and had an obese wife and an obese son.

I was trying to be nice, and not show any amazement, acting as though they were a normal-sized family who could feel at ease with me. I asked them how they'd got here and they said they'd come by taxi. I was surprised, but once again I acted normally. They had come from Dewsbury. *'Miles away!'*

I only realised a couple of days later that they wouldn't be able to get through the door of a bus or train, so then I knew why they'd had to take a taxi.

When he sat down to eat with his back to me the light level went down and I never did see James or Mrs Small. I couldn't see how much he ate as he blocked everything out. We had roast pork and mashed spuds. I tried to keep up with the Smalls but crashed out on the first course.

'Anyone for lemon cake?'

'I couldn't eat another thing, thanks.'

'Would you like some, Mr Small?'

'Yes, please.'

'Wow, man, you need a fork lift with a bucket on the front to feed this lot.'

I went out and discovered Bridlington. It was half-term and the amusement arcades were buzzing and everyone was having fun. Even I had a go – all those pennies just waiting for that final push. I put in 20p and got 6p back.

It wouldn't have been so bad if the machine hadn't been playing 'Old MacDonald had a farm', and the faster I put the pennies in the more it went, 'Baa, baa, black sheep'.

I returned to the guest house about an hour later. Mr Small had gone to bed and Mrs Small and James were playing dominoes with the landlady, and though it's hard to believe, there was a huge pile of sandwiches on the table.

I went to bed feeling fairly fit.

BRIDLINGTON TO HORNSEA

I left really early, just as it was getting light. The only people about were the rubbish cleaners and dog walkers. I always admire the people who clear up after the yobs.

I walked along the harbour where each fisherman had a lock-up garage; the door on one was slightly open, and being a nosy-parker I put my head round. Wow! Please meet Tom.

Tom was a big, good-looking man and had a tattoo written all over his face with a bone through his nose.

'Good morning, and how's the fishing going?'

Anyway, we chatted away about the fishing industry and this, that and the other, and then I said to him that he had quite some tattoo. Apparently, he'd got it in New Zealand. He had some interesting history; he'd been an Icelandic fisherman for many years. After a time chatting I asked if he would let me take a photograph of him and he agreed. I took a couple of pictures and when he took his woolly hat off he revealed a Mohican. I shook hands with him and left. I realised that I'd rather have Tom as a friend than as an enemy.

I didn't realise what a fast and nasty road for hiking this was. I saw the boys knocking the dew off the golf course greens, and walked past a big bunch of flowers tied to a tree. There was a picture of the girl who'd been killed and this message:

"Just the average family, we didn't ask for more
Then life was changed completely with that knock upon the door.
The awful thing had happened and none of us know why.
You were never coming back again and we didn't say goodbye.
The world just fell to pieces and we cried in disbelief.
We had to stick together to overcome our grief.

We'll never understand it all. It all seems so unfair.
We wish we'd hear that knock again and you'd be standing there."

I saw a farmer slug pelleting in the distance and went to find him. I went over the hedge and into the field. It made me laugh because he didn't stop, but went to the bottom of the field, stopped and waited there until I'd gone. Maybe he thought I was a safety officer.

At the end of the drive Mr Westcott had a sign with the farm's name and a cow on it. I couldn't resist the temptation to write him a letter when I got home.

Dear Mr Westcott,

As you can see, I am a farmer from Kent. On the 27th October I went into your field to see the man spreading slug pellets and he probably wondered who I was. Can you thank him for stopping?!

Yours faithfully,

Mr J Knowall.

P.S. You're always welcome in Kent and your crops looked well.

Paul, the hot dog man, appeared like a mirage for the lone walker. He was a friendly man and had just come back from a holiday in Morocco.

The credit crunch had affected his business because there weren't so many construction workers around.

The road was dangerous and fast, with few buses and no bus stops, so I carried on walking. I had to cross from one side of the road to the other to keep safe.

A garage loomed up and I was thinking about food and drink, but it was closed. A few yards further on was another eating place: La Dolce Vita Ristorante. That was closed as well, so I sat at a table outside to gather my thoughts and had a picnic lunch and a smoke.

Just across the road was Barmston Church with its own pond that was full to the brim.

One gravestone read: 'Don Marshall, a dearly loved husband, dad and grandad, died 17th January, 1995, aged 59. 'We sow the seeds of love and forever harvest the memories'.'

The door was locked so I walked out past the new tombstones that didn't look quite right. They looked like soldiers standing to attention for inspection.

Around here the land was heavy and tough and wet. Apparently West Yorkshire is better.

After ten or twelve miles of walking a bus came and I took the short trip to Skipsea.

The lady behind chatted away and gave me travel advice. Another old lady really gave me an evil look and it would have made a great photo, but I didn't push my luck.

By now I was starving and the pub was closed, but just on the outskirts I found Moo Café tucked onto some farm outbuildings. Stumbling on such places when you are tired and hungry is heaven.

Back on the road the grass verges were manicured like a lawn and it was the same all around here. The caravan site and the golf course were owned by Bourne Leisure and the golfers were lapping up the sun on their backs.

I met Ian who was spraying in the next door field. He was disturbing hares as he sprayed. He would never win the Farmer of the Year award, but he was good enough to stop and talk to me.

I also met David. He worked for the caravan park, cutting back branches from the footpath and feeding them into a compost stirrer. I kept worrying that as he was leaning up against the machine he might land up in the compost as well. We had a lot in common as we both came from a farming background.

I love buses and particularly when you're dead tired and the driver stops. Although it wasn't far from Hornsea the journey was very much appreciated.

I tumbled off the bus at Hornsea and met Rose and a colleague sitting on a bench enjoying the last of the afternoon sunshine.

'Hello.'

'Been travelling?'

'Yeah, I've done a lot of walking today.'

'I'm a traveller, too,' the lady said, 'and I've been all over the world. Really I am a gypsy, a Polish one. Sit down. It's nice to have someone fresh to talk to.'

Rose had been smuggled out of Auschwitz in a laundry basket and brought up by a German military family. I could hardly believe what I was hearing. She did say that she was picked up by Hitler and that when her mother said to put her daughter down, she was shot in the back. This was the only part of the story I took with a pinch of salt. As a child she could have mixed up the military personnel as she remembered the medals dangling from their uniforms. She realised after a while that the people bringing her up were the same people that had shot her parents and she then became a disruptive child. Consequently, when she was fifteen they were glad to see the back of her. She was married at about that age and had three husbands who were all lost at sea or something like that.

'I like a drop of Vodka.'

'Well, at your time of life, why not?'

'I don't drink now because of my medication. You see, I was beaten up in the past and had part of my head smashed in. It also hadn't helped that when she took a photograph of St Petersburg the police pulled the film out and threw the camera back in her face. 'I can't see anything through this part of my eye and I used to have fits, but I'm fine now and am well looked after in a convalescent home. All my family were shot.'

She kept talking about Amy Johnson. I couldn't understand if it was her real name or a relation.

Rose's English family had all been separated and she had been lied to and was desperate to find them.

'You might think I'm being very cheeky, but could I take your photograph?'

'You're not a reporter are you?'

'No, I'm just an old travelling farmer.'

'Well, I've been abused and lied to most of my life and I know who I can trust and you look like an honest man to me.'

I couldn't believe what I was hearing. I just sat there in stunned silence and listened.

'Thank you, Rose. It has been a real pleasure to meet you and we'll keep in touch.'

I walked on down the street with all Rose's stories flying through my head. A young group of girls and boys were coming the other way and as they passed a young girl slapped me on my backside.

'Hello, luv!' she said, and burst out laughing as they ran off. She meant well and let's face it, it's not very often that I get slapped on the backside by a teenager.

I booked in to a garage that had been converted into a B&B; it had a perfect sea view, and was nice and light with plenty of room.

I asked if they knew Rose and the landlord said, 'She tells a good story!'

After visiting three concentration camps, and having listened to Tibor's story, a friend who had escaped persecution in Hungary, I knew Rose's 'good story' was a true story.

I woke at 4.00am thinking of Rose, with tears rolling down my cheeks for an hour. I found out where she lived and when I got home I sent her a big bunch of flowers thanking her for her time and story.

As daylight broke I got the most amazing view looking across the North Sea, especially through the reflection in my bathroom mirror.

Nick, with the 'Jim Noble' type voice was getting ready for another day on maintenance on the gas works. We swapped stories and telephone numbers and left. He said to me, 'You seem to have life sussed.'

I decided to stay another day and to discover this area.

I went for a walk before breakfast and met Reg Anderson. He was an ex-soldier and was busy in the corner of the Co-op setting up his British Legion poppy stand.

'Hello, are you getting ready for a busy day?'

'Yes, I hope so.'

'I bet you've seen and been to many places.'

'Oh yes, but you know, we don't talk about it.'

He was eighty-six and when I said he looked well, he told me that he checked his blood pressure regularly and had an ulcer on his leg that wouldn't heal up. He said there were not many of his comrades left now.

'Young people today wouldn't understand what you went through, would they?'

'And thank God they don't, and I hope they never will.'

Although he never talked about himself, he got wound up by the lack of support for our troops in Afghanistan. I thanked him for all his work for our freedom and went back to the B&B.

After yesterday's long walk, today was going to be an easy day on the buses. At the bus stop a couple walked by with cock pheasant tail feathers sticking out of their caps, only for their dog to do a huge shit on the pavement and that is where it stayed.

I met Pat and Margaret at this shelter. 'Good morning.'

'Morning! Better than yesterday, isn't it? Where do you come from?'

'Kent.'

'I used to live in Chatham.'

'Have you got a bus pass?' asked her friend.

'No, not until next year.'

'I'm a witch,' said Pat, 'I have three nipples!'

'That could be interesting!' I said.

And that is how the conversation carried on until the bus arrived. Both were divorced; Pat after eighteen years and Mary after fifteen.

'Sounds like you both served life sentences,' I said.

It was a lovely way to see an area, on top of a double-decker bus. *'Go upstairs, put your feet up, spread your maps and notebook, and see the world.'*

This is gas country and I had no idea how huge the depots were. The gas is piped under the sea from Norway and then stored underground here in limestone caverns.

WITHERNSEA

The last of the summer holiday half-term was just coming to an end and these folk looked really poor. The amusement arcades were full of people eating the most revolting looking food I'd ever seen. I had a hot chocolate whilst waiting for the next bus to Easington. I went into a knitting wool type shop which also sold joke things and asked how the business was going. She said she was closing down the following week because of lack of trade.

EASINGTON

Never put your cigarette out or throw your coffee away when the bus arrives as sometimes it waits for ten minutes before leaving.

This is heavy old ground here and they were ploughing and slug pelleting on the backward rape crops. The newly planted wheat was just shooting through the soil.

A new gas pipeline from the coast to Hull had just been completed. A lady on the bus told me that armed police patrols were a regular sight, protecting the new refineries.

'What do you want to go to Easington for? There's nothing there.'

'That's what I want to go there for. What's it famous for?'

'Nothing, except the bird reserve.'

'How are you finding things in the recession?'

'My gas bill for the next quarter is going up by 25% and the price of food in the shops has shot up. It's not easy.'

This is a poor part of the UK.

PATRINGTON

Patrington church has an amazing spire and I decided to investigate it on the way back. An old boy on the bus was itching to tell me all about the area but got off at Easington.

When we went back to Patrington I stopped off and admired the highest spire on a village church in England. It had been affected by the earthquake in the spring and apparently they've got to take it down and rebuild it, but for the time being it's been strapped up.

There was a funeral service taking place. There were no cars or noise so I went round the corner where the undertakers were standing by the hearse. We had a longish chat and it was amazing that they'd already done about 120 funerals that year – it was now October – and there was strong competition.

I told one of them to stop looking at me and to put his tape measure away. I asked them if I could take their photograph and then left them to go and collect their customer.

I couldn't go to Hornsea directly so I had to go to Hull by bus. I sat with Jill and Ian in the front seat upstairs.

Ian looked a bit of a screwed-up case with a tired but sensible wife. He asked me if I was travelling and I said I was. He said he was a telly-man himself. *'I've never heard anyone describe themselves as a telly-man.'* He said he had a mate who went to Thailand every year and insured himself well. When he got to Thailand he said he'd been robbed and the payout he received paid for his holiday.

Both Jill and Ian were having a beer on the bus. They had a son serving in Iraq; he had bullets flying past him and all for £17,000 per year. He could've earned five times as much if he'd worked as a ~~missionary~~.* (When I met the army boys recruiting in Hull and related this story they said, 'Yeah, but when you get into trouble you got no back up.') He'd fathered a baby at the age of seventeen, but it had all gone tits up and there was the usual mental anguish that went with it all. Jill was hurt as she couldn't see her grandson.

'See that building over there? It's Hull prison and I was in there for two years.'

'It must put a shiver down your spine every time you go past,' I said.

'Not really, it's like home from home. I did get lonely and I ended up sharing a cell, which was better.'

* mercenary)

They came from Castleford, a town that never really got over the pit closures. She was thirteen when the miners came out on strike and she remembered how hard it was for her dad to put food on the table, and they only survived thanks to the soup kitchens. As they were on strike they couldn't claim unemployment benefit.

'How are people employed now?'

'They aren't. They're either taking drugs or dealing in them.'

Ian said that at one time they went to live by the sea because they'd had so many happy holidays there, but after a while they'd got sick of it. Every day when they were going down the streets they would see different people, whereas back home you got to know your neighbours.

GRAHAM STEWARD, THE TORY MP

Ian and Jill had nothing but praise for him. They said he worked hard trying to save hospitals and post offices and he really connected with the people.

Somehow Jamie Oliver came up in the conversation and I stirred Ian a little, to see what the reaction might be.

'He's just there for his own importance. He wants his MBE or knighthood. He makes another million and just fucks off again.' *'A bit ignorant is our Ian.'*

'Do you still keep in touch with any of your cellmates?'

'Yeah. Bit of a mistake that was. I picked one up from prison and he stayed with me for a while. Then he broke up my sister's long-term relationship and now that's all gone tits up. I feel a bit guilty really.'

We got to the amazing Hull bus station and said goodbye.

I caught the connecting bus back to Hornsea and asked the bus driver if he would wake me when we got there. He said he wasn't going any further so I would be locked in the bus depot with the bus.

There was a German family back at the B&B place. They were playing a stick game at the table. The children were lovely and confident with big sparkly faces and were a joy to watch, compared with English children who just watch the television.

HORNSEA TO CLEETHORPES

I said my goodbyes after an enjoyable couple of days at the Admiralty. Everybody was friendly, especially Mary-Anne, the cleaning lady.

I caught the early bus to Hull and again I marvelled at the bridges and the Paragon Interchange, where trains and buses met in the same place; and it was spotless.

I asked the girls on the bus what Hull was famous for and got no answer. They were more interested in the latest chocolate bar that had just come out.

Hull must be the ignoramus capital of the UK. First the bus driver asked where I was from and when I said, 'Kent,' he replied, 'Well, someone has to.' Then when I crossed in front of an invalid car, although there was plenty of room I shouted, 'Sorry!' and he shouted back, 'So you should be.'

I was watching a group of men changing a huge window at head height.

'Are we all right?' asked one of them. I think they mistook me for a traffic warden.

'Yeah. I usually charge £100, but as it's a nice day I'll take £50 in cash!'

They didn't seem amused and just carried on fitting the window.

I went down to the tourist office and asked, 'What's Hull famous for?'

'The friendly humour of the people.'

I just burst out laughing. 'Well, you might think so, but everyone I've met has been bloody rude!'

I asked a railway worker if the bridge was built by Brunel. 'Ain't got a clue, mate.'

I had a chat with some army men and they told me that they had difficulty recruiting young people. I couldn't believe it and thought that in a city like Hull, they would be queuing up.

'You ought to knock them over the head like the Press Gangs did and then they would wake up in Iraq.'

'I think you might get done for that!'

'Well, I can tell you, I wouldn't want to mess with you.'

'No, I'm just a pussy cat.'

'Talking about the Iraq war, do you think we should be there?'

'Without a doubt.'

'What's your biggest fear?'

'I went through a minefield without realising it, so now I just live every day and count my blessings.'

'Why don't people want to join the army?'

'They prefer to watch the television.'

I thanked them for all that they were doing and told them how much their work was appreciated.

Meet Dave, who was an ex-policeman and a pilot on a ship. He was also the ex-organiser of the Traders' Market. Like me he was walking along the harbour finding subjects to photograph for his fourteen-week photographic course. Having retired, he was enjoying his new hobby.

I managed to get his life history. He'd been the captain of a pilot ship and they used to guide larger ships into Hull. When I asked him what had been his biggest fright in his career he told me that it was when, in the fog, the SS Glasgow had a collision and sank. He really thought his number was up.

He also used to teach boxing in the police force and could always look after himself, but one day he had been knifed right across the face. He'd had his fair share of knives but no guns.

When some smooth looking characters sailed out of port, I shouted out to see if they had room for me. Dave muttered that they were all bloody rogues.

I met the church warden, who couldn't have been more helpful. I also met Sandra, from the Congo. Her mother lived in Ireland and she'd just completed a degree in Social Sciences. I congratulated her on all her hard work in obtaining it, but she wouldn't have any of it. I said straight away that I knew she was a special person as the tears were rolling down her cheeks; and I wasn't far off that either.

Holy Trinity is the largest parish church in the UK. The oldest part was built using brick and the rest was built in stone. Some of the stained glass windows were taken out as they were too heavy for the foundations.

HULL TO GRIMSBY

I couldn't get over this incredible train/bus station. It would cost £5 to travel by bus, and £27 to go by train. The girl at the station advised me to go by bus, so I did.

I really enjoyed going over the Humber Bridge and into Lincolnshire. Everyone said that the bridge was a bit of a Labour folly as it wasn't really used that much.

The land changed to chalky fields and at last I felt like a farmer again after all that industry. A few drills were working and sugar beet now was a feature.

We passed Humberside airport, and I thought to myself that I didn't know that was there when I flew to Yorkshire.

Before I knew it we were at Grimsby and it was beginning to drizzle. I asked someone about accommodation and they told me to take the bus to Cleethorpes.

A crowded bus dropped me off in B&B streets; after the second one that was fully booked I managed to book into a smoking room. I didn't think it would affect me but it really got up my nose and I thought that anyone who smokes in a bedroom needs to get a life. Still, I was tired and warm and I made myself a nice cup of tea and got myself organised. Having managed to accidentally lock myself in my bedroom, when the pretty landlady came and unlocked the door I said, 'Seems like something out of the *News of the World*!'

Cleethorpes is a pretty tough working-class town and the eating places served mainly fast food – and there were plenty of them. I went to one of the better looking restaurants. My first mistake was to tell the waitress that if my steak was overdone I wouldn't pay for it, so you can imagine how it came out. Chips and steak on a cold plate annoyed me straight away, so now after two glasses of wine I was starting to get a bit arsy.

'Is it your husband doing the cooking?'

'No, the boss.'

'How long has he been cooking for?'

'Forty years.'

'For fuck's sake, has this plonker really been putting hot food on cold plates for forty years? Would you tell him please?'

'Yes.'

Twenty minutes later. 'Did you tell him?'

'Yes.'

I had the feeling that she wasn't going to tell him, so on my way out I put my head through the serving hatch.

'Excuse me, is anybody there?'

All of a sudden a huge body builder type chef speaking italian, came around the corner. *'Steady on, JA.'*

'Hello, I thought I'd just let you know that the steak was on a cold plate.'

As he put his muscular arm across his chest I imagined him pulling my head off and then he said, *'I cookied that steeak from the bottom of my heaarter.'*

'Well, I think we've both learned a lesson. Put the steak on a hot plate and the salad on a cold one.'

We shook hands and I got the hell out of it.

CLEETHORPES TO MABLETHORPE

I couldn't get out of this bedroom fast enough; the stale smoke and a cold coming on was bad news.

I signed the book: 'Anyone who smokes in a bedroom needs to get a life!' I went off quickly before anyone came down and read the comment book.

If you wanted to see the rough side of life in the outskirts of a fishing town which had been shafted by the previous government's fishing policy, then you should have joined me at 6.30am on the bus back to Grimsby. The sadness on some of the faces after years of struggle will remain with me forever, but the girl behind me was very chatty.

Grimsby was bigger than I thought and I kept going round in a circle until I got to the fish markets. Before that I went and had a chat with some very friendly butchers who were preparing meat. It was now raining and I could see how the fishing industry had been affected. The old warehouses were falling down and only about twelve trawlers worked out of the port.

Grimsby really is just a processing place for fish from Iceland and Norway. The company, Young's, has a lot of office and processing space here from which it operates.

John Nicholson was working outside his factory and I asked him how things were. He said the fishing industry was 'fucked' and now they were just a processing outfit. He was a traveller himself and took off with his wife and toured the world. He was interested in what I was doing and was equally pleased that I was concerned about the fishing industry. Large boxes of fish and ice were being brought in here and they were all over the place, but there was a feeling of desolation everywhere. There was a little café for all the workers and not really for the likes of me. I was served and didn't even have any eye contact. They just serve you and take your money.

I had to ask the way back to the town centre and a lovely lady couldn't have been more helpful. I went over a bridge called the Weak Bridge and passed some high-rise flats into town. I tried to break a £20 note up but couldn't do so even after going into several shops. It gave me some idea of how tight things are here.

I found the bus going to Louth. The bus shelter was full of partially-sighted people with their guide dogs. After an hour on the bus we arrived. It was like arriving on another planet. The people were different and it was a nice Lincolnshire town. It was quite a shock after being in major industrial towns and it was like a breath of fresh air.

I asked a man for directions to the market and he left his wife in the butcher's shop and actually took me there. The contrast between him and the lady who couldn't even look me in the eye couldn't have been greater. I had a bread roll and some soup and shed my wet clothes into my rucksack. Everyone was worried about me as I chatted away to myself.

ST JAMES' CHURCH

Once more there was a friendly bunch of people helping tourists with advice and saying how wonderful their church was. They said their church had the tallest spire in the country, but everyone seems to say that.

There was a rich feeling about this place; a bit like Tenterden in Kent.

The Lincolnshire Rising began in St James' Church on the 1st October, 1536 and for his part in it the vicar was hanged, drawn and quartered at Tyburn on 25th March, 1537. It all began after evensong and shortly after the closure of Louth Abbey. The uprising was only against the attempt to suppress the religious houses, these being Catholic, and was not against the King himself. It quickly gained support in Horncastle, Market Rasen, Caistor and other nearby towns. Angry with the actions of commissioners, the protestors demanded the end to the collection of subsidies; the end of the Ten Articles; an end to the Dissolution; an end to taxes in peacetime; a purge of heretics in government; and the repeal of The Statute of Uses. With the support of the local gentry, a force occupied Lincoln Cathedral. They demanded the freedom to continue to worship as Catholics, and protection for the treasures of Lincolnshire churches. It was led by a monk and a shoemaker and involved 22,000 people.

After roughly an hour the bus got me to the seaside town of Mablethorpe. It was the last half-term weekend before the schools broke up. B&B places seemed few on the ground and one was full. The one and only hotel didn't answer the telephone and looked a dump.

The one guesthouse looked rougher than me, so I gave that a miss.

I walked right through the town until I got to the beach huts, with curved asbestos roofs which gave them real character.

In the end I had no choice and went back to the tired guest house and checked in. I nearly told the landlady to stuff her house; as when I was booking in I asked her about the smoking room and she said it had been cleaned, and I was in her way when I was booking in the register. 'Two funny buggers here together.'

When I got out of her way and had refrained from telling her where to go, she became quite pleasant and wanted to know what I was up to. Anyway, my stay there was great. It cost £20 per night including breakfast.

This place had character. I could see the floorboards through the carpet, but it was clean. Unlike most places the heating was on all night.

I came downstairs and the bar lady was so glued to the television that it was difficult to prise her away. There were no customers until a funny little lady came in with two crying ten-year-olds. She was staying the night

345

and had an onward train journey in the morning. She was saying that she was going to get pissed and with that I went in search of an eating house, which I thought would be a joke in this town.

I found a Chinese restaurant, but again the food was brought out on a cold plate, so I sent it straight back. It was expensive for what it was and the only nice thing was the very young and attractive, innocent girl who served it to me. I apologised to her if I'd snapped about the cold plate, but she agreed with me and it wasn't her fault anyway. We parted as friends. The youngsters eating behind me left half their food, not because they didn't like it but that's life around here.

The lady who said she was going to get pissed was slowly on her way; her girls were still crying.

I got chatting to Eileen and Richard. He was an ex-farm worker and they were lovely honest country people. Like me they were pleased to have someone to talk to and Richard said that nobody talks to each other nowadays. He had lost a finger in a farming accident and I told him about my toes. He knew his farm machinery and they were up here for a long weekend following the death of her mother.

MABLETHORPE TO BOSTON VIA SKEGNESS

I had an early morning walk round Mablethorpe which introduced me to all the dog walkers. We talked about dog shit and picking it up and 'don't touch him, he was abused before I had him', and where the other two dogs came from. In the summer months the beaches are closed to dogs, but now they're full of them.

I had another look at all the fascinating types of beach huts; some old and a few modern ones. They even have a competition for the most outrageous.

The funfair looked as though it had already packed up and gone home for the winter; all the seats were empty as they looked out to sea.

I couldn't make out why the butcher's shop was open on a Sunday and then I realised it was Friday.

Breakfast was an enjoyable affair, as I chatted away to Richard and Eileen, swapping names and addresses and taking photographs. I would've loved to have taken a photograph of our waiter, but he would have nothing to do with it. He said he wasn't at his best in the morning, and with his football shirt and baseball hat he looked like the kind of guy who needed a grease gun up his rear end in the morning to get him going. A few months later Richard looked us up when he was in Kent.

I killed some time whilst waiting for the bus by talking to Fred from the Salvation Army, and writing *Walkabout* in a café. The woman running this place was very strict-looking and made me nervous of occupying her seat, but as there weren't many people in the place I wasn't that worried.

At the next table was a mother with her young daughter and they had come in to warm up. They were spending the weekend in their caravan and said it was freezing. It was OK in the summer, but not at this time of the year.

My brother rang and I told him that I was in a public place and I would phone him back in fifteen minutes. Other people's phones were ringing, but no one was answering and they were all trying to switch them off.

I said, 'Good Morning,' to Fred of the Salvation Army.

'God bless,' he replied.

I met Mr Clever Dick. He worked as a sound and vision engineer and travelled all over the world making a fortune. He could earn about £300 per day. I asked him what he was going to do with the money. 'Pension fund, mate!' Modesty was never going to be his strong point and before he got on the bus I'd heard his entire life story, his marriages, children, holidays, the lot.

Things were now warming up; there was an air of excitement as we approached the famous Skegness holiday complex.

Mr Happy was a large, tall and good-looking man in his mid-sixties. He joined us upstairs in the bus before I got off, and was singing away. Because I smiled he made a bee-line for me. 'La-de-da-la-de-da,' he sang and told me it was the last day of the season and that he always went for a swim. 'La-de-da, March is short and June is long,' he sang. He told me that he used to know this area when it was all countryside. 'The sea is colder in May than October,' he continued. 'You know, things always happen in November: fireworks night, Remembrance Sunday and

'Children In Need'. When my mum was alive we didn't need her pension so we gave it all away to charity, but now she's not about I can't do that.'

'Did you hear that? What a lovely attitude.'

We jumped off at Skegness.

'Would you like to buy the same perfume as Victoria Beckham uses? Not for £3,000, not for £2,000, not for £1,000, but for a special bargain price of £250? You can buy the David Beckham deodorant for the same price.'

And the sad thing was that people were being sucked in by this rubbish.

GYPSY LADY

'Would you like me to read the gypsy gold and tell your fortune?'

'How much?'

'Don't worry, come on in.'

'How much?'

'Come on in and don't worry.'

'How much?' By now I was walking away.

'Ten pounds.'

'No thanks.'

'Oh fuck ya, I didn't want to do you anyway!'

Well, you can buy anything here; body studs, tattoos, T-shirts. A young family let me take their picture, and a young lady let me take one of her highly studded face. She was selling studs and was a bit reluctant to let me take it so I mustn't expose it.

Talking to various traders it was plain that they were pleased the season was over. They were all ready for a rest, especially the fish and chip shop. They were on their feet in the heat all day. A lot of these stall holders go to Spain for the winter and I reckon that they must make some real cash.

I went round another shop and said that I was looking, not buying.

'Yeah, short arms and long pockets, eh?!'

I had a walk round and took lots of cheeky photographs, really taking the mickey. There was a man on a hired mobility scooter with a big hire sign and I wanted a photograph. I chased after him going the other way and said that my disabled mother was coming at Easter and I asked him if I could get a picture of the name of the hire company.

'Oi, stop Albert. The man wants ya!'

'Thanks so much. Do you think I could take a photograph to save me writing the name of the place down?'

'OK, we got it from Chip Alley.'

'Chip Alley!'

Some of the food people eat here is really disgusting. I'm not a snob, but some of the food is not fit for pigs.

SKEGNESS TO BOSTON

A wet and steamed up bus took me into some of the richest vegetable producing country in the UK. It was a picture postcard of intensive agriculture.

All the churches were amazing and I decided to look them up on my return here in April. I continued to look at the countryside as everyone else was on their mobile phones texting and talking. We picked up some passengers from the hospital and I asked one of the passengers, a coloured man, 'Does this bus go to the train station?'

'No, it's a bus and it goes to the bus station.'

I was trying very hard not to burst out laughing. *'Tis a bus and it goes to the bus station!'*

It was late and wet and there was a taxi waiting. He booked up my B&B while I checked the train times for the next day.

Brad, the owner, was an ex-oil man from Canada and he showed me to my room and suggested where to eat. Gee, I was tired.

I had a shower and found the Hammer and Pincers pub. It was full of friendly local people who were enjoying Halloween night and the first local said to me, 'You know, they're pinching our jobs, the Eastern Europeans.'

I was too tired and it was too late to pick an argument. I had lamb shank and a large bottle of wine, and all for £10.50. I gave them £15 and told them what a friendly pub it was and that I'd come back again in March or April.

I had a job to find the right road home but got there in the end. *'What a pleasant end it was to my fortnight on the road.'*

BOSTON TO LENHAM

I had breakfast with an elderly gent and when I told him that I was travelling the UK on public transport he replied in a dry old voice that he couldn't be bothered with public transport. I burst out laughing.

Whilst waiting for the train I started picking up rubbish and with both hands full I asked the young lad, who had just dropped some, if he would mind opening the bin lid. As I dropped it in I said, 'Dirty bastards, aren't they?'

I had an interesting journey through the countryside of Lincolnshire. Winston was sitting opposite me and was from Hackney. His hood was over his head, his arms were folded and he peered out of his hood and asked if we were in Grantham yet. He had been to Skegness to visit his grandmother and was on his way back home. He really hated the countryside and couldn't even look at it.

'You know, Winston, we have completely different lifestyles and should swap one day.'

'No, man, I just hate the countryside.'

'Wow, that's some watch you have there.' It was about two inches tall and wide and was gold. 'How would I get on in Hackney with mine?'

'They'd run you out of town, man.'

GRANTHAM STATION

Here the fun started. I knew that when I booked my return ticket and reserved a seat at a certain place and at a certain time, it was a mistake. I tried to change it at Newcastle on the way up but it was non-refundable. I would try to bluff my way to London. When the train arrived I saw Winston jumping on and we caught each other's eye. So I caught up with him and we marched up through a very smart, fully booked carriage with only two spare seats.

'Winston, sit there.'

'No man, they're booked.'

'Doesn't matter, you don't know the tricks. Sit there!'

Well, we sat down in the reserved seats and Winston' hood went back up. 'Here man, have you got a ticket?' he asked.

'Yeah, here.' I slipped one of my many tickets and receipts to Winston as they don't always look at them that carefully. We might get away with it, but not with this girl.

The conductress came. 'Tickets, please.'

I said, 'Plenty of tickets here!'

She said, 'None of them is acceptable.'

By now, Winston had paid his £21. I think it may have been the first time he'd ever bought a ticket.

I said to the conductress, 'Come back in a minute and I'll find the right ticket.'

'OK.' She wasn't an ordinary conductress but was a beautiful young lady and very nice with it. Back she came.

'No, these tickets are for the wrong date, but I'm on the wrong train.'

I explained to Winston that I was now using every trick in the book and putting on my strongest Australian accent. But the conductress would have nothing to do with it.

'I'm not robbing you; I've already paid £54. It's him who should be robbing you,' I said whilst pointing to Winston who was now hidden under his hood. 'Come on, Winston, you should be giving me some backup.'

Now all the passengers in the carriage were starting to enjoy the ride.

'Welcome to England! What a nice welcome, ma'am! £54 now becomes £75! Welcome to England! You wait, ma'am. If you get stuck in Aussie, we'll get our own back. Welcome to England! What if I don't pay, which is a joke as I already have?'

'A policeman will be called and you'll be chucked off.'

'Welcome to England!'

A passenger behind me asked what part of Australia I came from.

'Sydney, south Sydney.'

'So do I, what part?' *'For Christ's sake, I'm in enough trouble without this. I muffed my way out of it.'*

The conductress asked, 'Does anyone want an underground ticket?'

'You mean to say that my £75 doesn't cover the underground?'

'That's right.'

'Welcome to England!'

'Single or return?'

'You mean you want to put me through this again?'

You can imagine the amusement this caused around us.

'Come on, Winston, let's go and have a hot chocolate. I'll treat you.'

Winston was now warming to me just a little and we shared a few stories.

'How does a black man get a gun?'

'No idea. Drugs, man, drugs.'

The worst are the new car dealers. The car salesman sells a new Ferrari to a customer, and then two months later he tells his contacts the address of the purchaser so that they can steal the car for a fee of fifteen grand. The car salesman has already got a customer abroad ready to buy it. Then, with any luck, the original customer goes back to the same car dealer with his insurance money and buys another new one.

Another trick is when a new car comes off the production line the bad boys slip a set of keys and papers in the wing mirror and a nod from someone with a screwdriver and you get a new car.

What a naïve little life I lead.

When we arrived at King's Cross I said goodbye and shook Winston's hand. 'Watch out, I've got your watch!'

At least the underground was open this time. Two female police officers were doing a survey. One said she worked in the last terrorist attack and would never want to go through that again.

It rained all the way from Victoria to Lenham. Three badly behaved girls had blocked up the loo and spat all the way to Maidstone, but apart from that it had been a very interesting couple of weeks.

CHAPTER TEN

Boston to Lenham

It was time to get back to Boston. 'Ticket to Boston, please.'

'Single or return?'

'What's the difference?'

'Return is £68.80 and a single is £67.80.'

'Sounds a bit strange.'

'Business strategy.'

It wasn't long before we were in London. We were told there were engineering works on and off all the way to Grantham and that buses were provided. A man sitting opposite me had MUFC tattooed on his knuckles – Manchester United Football Club. He asked me where I was going.

'Boston,' I replied.

'Wouldn't bother.'

Looking out of the window I could only admire the ability of horsey people to ruin the countryside. There were shanty towns made of old lorry containers, white electric fencing tape, jumps made out of old tyres and white plastic bags full of horse shit.

At least with a train you get from A to B fairly quickly, but with a bus it winds its way through every village and town looking for the odd passenger.

'What's Biggleswade famous for?'

'Don't know, mate. I don't come from here.'

We arrived in Peterborough and there was time to spare until the next form of transport, so I went up to the cathedral. The town was heaving with people and there was a heavy police presence. It seemed there was a football match going on and there were plenty of bald-headed men covered with tattoos and trying to look hard.

Two men from Starbucks were trying to erect a small tent on the pavement so that they could sell coffee, but they were told by street wardens that they couldn't put it up for commercial reasons. They quietly took it down.

I passed the PMP Recruitment Centre with a long queue of bedraggled-looking Eastern European workers all looking for jobs. It reminded me of the Mexicans in Arizona.

The RAF was again recruiting and I asked them if they'd got anyone, but the answer was 'No'. With all the unemployment around I thought their queue would be a mile long. I suppose it's just easier to keep drawing benefits.

At last I reached the cathedral and what a building it is. On the war memorial outside was written:

"THEY SHALL NOT GROW OLD AS WE THAT ARE LEFT GROW OLD. AGE SHALL NOT WEARY THEM NOR THE YEARS CONDEMN. AT THE GOING DOWN OF THE SUN AND IN THE MORNING WE WILL REMEMBER THEM."

The cathedral was built between 1118 AD and 1237 AD and is 147 metres long and 44 metres high. Like most cathedrals it's had its fair share of fires and vandalism from the Parliamentarian troops in the English Civil War. Extensive restoration work was undertaken especially during the 17th and 18th centuries.

Catherine of Aragon was buried here in 1536 as well as Mary Queen of Scots, following her execution; she was later removed to Westminster Abbey.

I had lunch in a nearby café. A beautiful coloured girl came in and I frantically cleared my table in the hope that she might come and sit opposite me, but I was out of luck. I did get a big smile though.

The rail officials had a fair job on their hands to cope with all the passengers and to direct them to the right buses. A big cheer went up when the man shouted, 'Passengers for Sleaford,' and we all clambered aboard a very smart coach.

Driving through the Fens, I could see Eastern Europeans who were harvesting daffodil bulbs. A few potatoes had been planted and the vegetables were all in beautiful straight lines with sticks flying bits of plastic to deter the pigeons. However, they seemed happy enough nibbling away underneath, taking no notice at all.

A new road was being built right through the middle of this prime agricultural land. What a crime. It's like putting a knife into it and letting it bleed to death.

Sleaford's run-down railway station could well be in the middle of Africa with the weeds growing between the lines and just a straggling of passengers waiting.

At last I arrived in windy Boston. It was late afternoon and I popped into St Botolph's Parish Church, which is also known as 'The Stump'. It boasts of being the largest parish church in the country. There was a fat couple having a wedding blessing and the church seemed more beautiful than they did. I didn't really think they were being serious – even the schoolchildren practising in the choir were much smarter.

MARKET TRADERS

I can never quite make these guys out and I wondered why the poor old shops were doing no trade at all, whilst having to pay the rates, rent and building costs. The stall holders turn up with no overheads and sell from prime positions right outside the shops.

I found my B&B and then went to the local pub where I had a lamb shank and a pint of bitter for less than £10.

They had four televisions going in the saloon bar with three different programmes, and it was filling with some hard-looking blonde women with large gold earrings. The man setting up the karaoke looked as though he'd had more smoke through him than Battersea Power Station. It was time to leave.

It was a Sunday and I started the day by setting off all the smoke alarms when I burned the toast. Brad had to open all the windows.

I was on the road by 9.00am and the sun was shining. I walked past an old boy who was gardening. 'Looks like you're putting your garden down to grass.'

'Yes, then I can forget it.'

It took me an hour and twenty minutes to get out of town on the A16. The idea was to do a triangle. I would go to Borough-in-the-Marsh, cut across the B1195, come down the A52 and go in to see some of the beautiful churches.

I passed the Pilgrim Hospital; a huge place which was blue in colour and twenty storeys tall and didn't exactly blend into the local landscape. At least in Kent our hospitals are kept fairly low.

This really was cauliflower country and the pigeons were enjoying themselves as much as me.

I passed Maud Foster windmill but it didn't open until midday. I learned later that in the wind one of the sails had come off and had gone through the roof of the house next door. Luckily nobody was hurt. I couldn't believe that they could have built such ugly retirement homes right next door..

My stomach wasn't feeling a hundred percent that morning and there were no bushes in sight. It was as flat as a pancake and every steep sloping ditch had been cut and cleaned out leaving no shelter, so I just had to hang on.

I went into a garden centre, but it had no loos or café. '*Well, we are in downtown Lincolnshire.*'

Three quarters of an hour later a garage loomed up, and I was still squeezing with every available muscle when I was met by a sign saying: 'NO PUBLIC TOILETS OR CAMIONS'.

'What does 'camions' mean?' I asked. 'Foreign lorries?'

I bought a bottle of water and some chewing gum and got the feeling that this was not the friendliest garage in the world.

At last I found a hedge and I managed to get shit all over my shirt and all over my hands. Luckily I had the water and a spare shirt and the farmer got a fertilised hedge.

Now in the little village of Sibsey there was a sign saying: 'Windmill Open' and it sold teacakes. So I thought, 'Why not?' I got lost going through a housing estate and found Fred Carnt who had just renovated a 1986 International tractor. He was polishing and cleaning it on his front drive and his mother was polishing an old Morris 1000 in the garage. It had taken Fred over a year to do the work and he'd worked until 11pm most nights. He said he would sell the tractor if he was offered enough money.

I went past a lovely old brick barn behind the housing estate and being a nosy-parker I opened the gate. When I saw a huge wooden barrel that had been turned into a dog kennel I didn't investigate! Next door was a shed with two County four wheel drive tractors in it. In Lincolnshire they love their old farm machinery and it's real farming country.

SIBSEY WINDMILL

I had a pot of tea and some soup in bone china crockery. The café was in a very small converted shed and inside it was lined with about twenty clocks all working and all for sale. I thought they were horrible and thank God I was in there at 1 o'clock and not midday. The windmill was built in 1877 and was still grinding corn and what amazed me was how quiet the sails were. You were allowed to climb right to the top.

Back on the road there was no way I was going to get where I wanted to and nobody was going to give me a lift. Also, no buses were running on a Sunday. I had a quick look at Sibsey Church which was amazing. I then walked along the B1184. I met a gentleman who'd just finished ploughing a field. The plough had huge mould boards on it. He worked for Staples and said he didn't know where all the produce went, but every day forty articulated lorries left, full of vegetables, for customers all over the UK. He called drains 'grips'. After talking to him for five minutes and getting his photograph I took off.

I didn't really expect such a mother of a walking day. Most of the cars that went by contained fat low-lifers anyway. To be honest I was glad they didn't stop.

I walked along the road and there was a huge Crowbridge dyke/ditch or whatever they're called. It must have been nearly fifty metres across. I also saw a barn owl.

There were loads of farmyards which were fairly tidy but dead looking, and all the gardens and houses in the rural areas looked very 'tweedy', with plants all tied up like soldiers in a straight line – all very boring.

In the middle of nowhere and hidden in a dyke there was a pigeon shooter. He had two shots: one dropped half a mile away and his labrador was looking for the other. The pigeons were plundering the rape as well as the cauliflowers.

I seemed to have been walking hard towards Boston and yet getting no closer. 'The Stump' is a landmark that stands out for miles. Unfortunately, the Pilgrim Hospital does the same. How could they have built such an ugly building and then painted it blue? Why not paint it bright pink and do the job properly?!

I passed a huge vegetable farmyard and poked my nose in a little but the farmer was working near the entrance and wasn't interested in me, so the feeling being mutual I carried on walking.

By now old grumpy-guts had been walking for seven hours and I thought that if I walked into the hospital grounds I might get a taxi, but all I saw was a nurse having a quiet smoke.

As I walked into town a car load of young people drove past slowly in heavy traffic and one gave me the 'wanker' sign. *'Could this be another Eastbourne?'* But after seven hours of walking I hadn't the energy for a confrontation and probably would've come off worse as the car had five louts in it.

Back in Boston I treated myself to a five-minute taxi ride back to my B&B.

'Has the recession affected you?' I asked the driver.

'Killed it dead. On Friday night I hired the taxi out and after twelve hours I'd only taken just £38.'

'What would you take normally?'

'£150.'

'Any of the taxi drivers packed it in?'

'No, they just hang on in there. It's now 5.30pm and I've been waiting here since 3pm and taken just £3.50.'

'No wonder they sit about doing nothing all day. If they weren't so expensive perhaps more people would use them,' But I was knackered and was pleased to give him the money.

I went back to the local pub for dinner and the man I'd met in November and who didn't like foreigners was still sitting there in the same place. The joke was that he now had an Eastern European girlfriend! On both nights she had her back to everyone and the conversation was very intense, but there was no touching. *'I don't think he really knew how to handle it.'*

I went to bed. Seven hours of walking had done me no good.

There was another cock-up at breakfast. I ordered two boiled eggs and Brad turned up with a fry-up as well. He must've thought that I was a greedy person. He left it on the table so I made sandwiches out of it for my lunch.

At Boston bus station there were loads of holidaymakers hanging around this dirty scratched bus shelter. There were no signs and nobody around to help.

Anyway, we found the bus. You couldn't go to King's Lynn direct but had to go to Spalding first. We waited whilst the cheerful lady driver had a pee and then off we went. I met another taxi driver on the bus.

'How's business?' I asked.

'Much the same. People still need lifts and there's no public transport in most places, and it's not safe to walk at night.'

'You've got a lot of Eastern Europeans up here.'

'Yeah, we have two working for us.'

'I bet they're damned good.'

'They're all right but they drive like idiots.'

It was a nice sunny March morning and all the farmers were out either planting vegetables or ploughing, or drilling seed barley. Life was returning to the fields.

I couldn't get over these amazing churches. They're like mini-cathedrals and must have been built as a result of all the wool money years ago.

Holbeach, Long Sutton, Sutton Bridge and Torrington St Clements all flashed by on the way to King's Lynn. The bus filled up with young mums with babies and all the clobber that goes with them – the pushchair department was full.

At King's Lynn I helped a lady to take her pushchair off the bus and I found a town which the planners hadn't decimated. 'I'm enjoying my stroll.'

'What's King's Lynn famous for?' I asked.

'Nothing!'

St Margaret's Church suffers from flooding and had the high water marks etched on the sides. The mark from 1978 was the highest.

There were unspoiled harbour buildings and a grand square and again it was unspoiled.

I found an old warehouse that used to store wine and wool and now had been converted into a restaurant.

I met Jenny, who was doing a crossword puzzle and asked if I could help. I told her I was useless at that sort of thing. She was in the middle of her second divorce and vowed never to get married again. She was worried that she might lose her house. She was a beauty therapist and worked from home, mainly getting rid of unwanted hair. I asked her if she could do anything for me, but she just laughed.

She was fifty-six and would really have liked to live in a convent and get away from it all. She had a twenty-eight-year-old son whom she loved; he'd just got engaged to a lovely girl and they lived in Norwich.

Jenny liked gardening. She felt she'd been really mucked about by clients in the last few weeks. She envied me just being able to bugger off and reckoned I probably didn't have a mortgage to pay. I told her that she might be on 'a low' and to remember always that she did have good health.

I was trying to eat my homemade sandwiches without the staff noticing.

I wandered around the rest of the town and found the High Street which was a bit of a let-down, with the usual young fat mothers waddling along spending their benefits.

KING'S LYNN TO HUNSTANTON (PLEASE MEET MR MISERY)

'Can you drop me off at Castle Rising?'

'No, this bus goes the hospital route.'

As it turned out Mr Misery drove the double-decker bus right past the lay-by for the castle.

I had a really lovely view, passing Sandringham Road, Dersingham, Snettisham and Heacham. All the houses were built of sandstone.

On one side were the fens and on the other almost pure sand.

We went past Mountbatten Road and through real old Norfolk countryside.

'I'm off to see the Queen!'

We arrived at Hunstanton and I thought I would wind the bus driver up – and it worked.

'Excuse me, but I can't see any reason why you couldn't have stopped for me at Castle Rising.'

'No official bus stop.'

'Well, there was a huge lay-by.'

'Bus doesn't go to the castle anyway.'

'But you could've dropped me off and I would've walked. Don't forget that we passengers are paying your wages.'

This got him going and Mr Misery was now in full swing telling me what an ignoramus I was and all that sort of thing. He was still going strong when I walked off the bus.

The next thing I knew he was chasing me up the street. 'Don't walk away when I'm talking to you. I ain't finished with you yet!'

'Well, I'm not listening to you. You called me ignorant.'

'Where does a train stop?' he asked.

'At a train station.'

'There you go. A bus stops at a bus stop. You *are* ignorant.'

Now he was so close to me that I could smell his horrible garlicky breath. I said, 'You know, I thought Maggie Thatcher had got rid of most people like you, but you obviously slipped through the net.'

'Know-all bugger' and off he went.

You know, I really rather enjoyed that.

I wasn't sure if I'd done the right thing by coming here. It was a sea of caravans; in fact, at first sight I thought that it was the sea.

There was one very smart hotel: the Golden Lion Hotel.

'Good afternoon. Would you tell me how much it is for a single room?'

'We do short breaks.'

The rather dull blonde handed me a leaflet and never did tell me the price. When I looked at the leaflet all the rooms were over £100, so I walked out.

GAIL'S GUEST HOUSE

I phoned and asked if they had a room for the night and they said they had a 'single' for £35, or if that was an issue, £30. 'I'll take it!'

When I arrived there a man with long flowing hair took me to a lovely room and I was a happy boy.

It was only 4pm so it gave me time to have a shower and write *Walkabout*.

Richard recommended the Waterfront as a place to eat and it lived up to expectations. I went for a beer in the Golden Lion Hotel and met Claude. He was an eighty-five-year-old ex-window dresser who'd driven down from Carlisle that day and was returning here after fifty years. He was pretty lame and said the company he'd worked for was Timpson's shoemakers. He'd worked for them for forty-five years doing their window displays.

As soon as he sat down he sized me up and said, 'I must go and see if they've got my dinner ready.' I've found this with old people before. They very quickly exit without as much as a word.

I called it a day.

HUNSTANTON TO NORTH WALSHAM

It was March 9th and it was cold and dry. Even though I'd taken a sleeping pill the night before I still hadn't slept well, but at least I got the diary fairly well updated before a 9.00am breakfast.

Richard, the landlord, barked at me saying that I hadn't signed in the book to say that I would have breakfast.

I found out the bus times and bought a friend his birthday present. It was a Bill Clinton corkscrew and you can imagine what the cork screw was! I also bought some Hilary Clinton nutcrackers!

I met an old boy at the bus station who lived locally. He said he liked the summer because the town came alive. Another old boy told me that Hunstanton was the only seaside town on the east coast facing west and when you look at the map that's about right.

For £5 I was on the bus and I could jump on and off wherever I liked. At Titchwell the March carrot harvest was in full swing. I always wanted to see this so I jumped off. This must be a pheasant and hare paradise with a blanket of straw to keep them warm, and of course, the carrots. It was an impressive operation. The straw and plastic is all taken off mechanically by friendly Eastern European tractor drivers. That's more than I can say for the smug English Barbour-clad bosses sitting up in the harvester with the driver. They couldn't even smile, wave or tell me to bugger off their land. *Every time I see two carrots I know where I have a home for them.*

I met the couple who'd been staying at the Golden Lion Hotel the previous night. They'd walked out here and were walking back. We talked about old

Claude driving down from Carlisle, as they'd eavesdropped on our whole conversation.

The countryside was lovely and it was a relaxing way to see it, sitting in the bus. Along the top here the land was very sandy and the farming looked battered. Some of the land was wet and the rape had been trashed by the pigeons.

We passed Burnham Market and I was tempted to get off the bus here, but instead I got off at the entrance to Holkham Hall.

All the signs here said: 'Closed' and that made it more interesting to walk in. The gates weren't closed and no one told me to go away.

Holkham has an avenue of evergreen oaks which leads you into the parkland. There were some lovely old sweet chestnuts and it seemed sad that there had been very little recent tree planting. I walked through the deer park and cars kept driving past, but no one said the place was closed so I walked up to the big house.

I was met by Hector, a funny little dog that belonged to the staff and had a mind of his own. He was later caught by one of the staff after he'd peed up against every sign and tree there was.

I didn't see any point in stopping around here and it looked dull and uninteresting from the outside at this time of year. No doubt when the sun is shining it comes alive.

Cley Marshes is part of The Norfolk Wildlife Trust which is the oldest of all the trusts and has four hundred acres of reed beds and wet grassland.

We reached the twitchers' paradise and there were hundreds of sad middle-aged men with rucksacks running about like me, but they were more intense. I never could quite understand why people go bird watching in yellow anoraks, when I would've thought that they would wear camouflage. The place was full of geese and ducks in the long reeds.

We passed a little village called Kelling and then passed Sheringham Golf Club. I tried to recognise some of the greens where Valerie and I had played years ago.

Sheringham town was freezing as the North Sea wind ripped through it. The High Street was heaving with people but the shops were empty. I really couldn't think how people in the retail business made a living.

The whole place seemed to be like an old people's home with the inmates let loose.

I went into a café and a man walked out of the loo without flushing it, which rather put me off going in. He then went and sat down and had his soup with his flies undone. I felt like going up to him and asking him if he'd finished in the loo, the dirty sod. I think he was a half-bred tramp.

Thirty minutes was enough time spent here so it was off to Cromer. I showed the Indian driver my Coasthopper ticket that had run out at Sheringham, but he wasn't that stupid and charged me £1.40.

The man in front of me was on his mobile. 'Yeah, yeah, yeah! Right, yes! Yeah, all right! Yeah, all right, mate! Yeah, yeah, yeah, all right, mate! Yeah, all the best!'

I gave Cromer a miss as I couldn't recognise anything here from a previous visit, and I couldn't bring myself to get off the bus. It was another sad seaside town. I went down to the driver to offer my extended fare and he just said, 'Don't worry.' *'How different to Mr Misery.'*

We arrived in North Walsham and after a quick look round the church I booked in at the local hotel. It was right in the middle of the town and I had a choice of bath or shower. The bathroom was bigger than the bedroom, but not luxurious. I scouted around the town and there were only Chinese or one Indian restaurant – they looked smart but were empty. I didn't fancy sitting there on my own, so I went back to the hotel which was busy, mainly with heavy drinkers.

I had a huge helping of school-dinner food with an extra mug of gravy. It was pretty plain and I was getting fed up with this type of food four days running.

It was St Patrick's Day so everyone was drinking Guinness.

The big fat drinker who came in at 5.30pm was still at the bar at 10pm going on about how we should've kept the Commonwealth and how they all love us and how we raped India and 'fucking this and fucking that'. It was really old-fashioned talk and I didn't think such people existed anymore.

I met John, originally from Carlisle, who used to go to Ramsgate as a child and loved it there. He currently worked at the Bacton gas works and knew the gas trade inside out. The gas came from Norway to Easington and was also exported back to Europe all in a forty-inch pipe. John had been an aero-turbine engineer on aircraft for twenty-five years and had been stationed mainly in the Middle East. Because of this experience he got the job using the same aero equipment to push gas under the North Sea. I asked him what fuel the pumps worked on. 'Gas!' *'Oh dear, what a stupid question.'*

I went to bed.

I had a very basic breakfast and I was the only one there. I was given scant attention and my cheese on toast was slapped onto the plate. The eggs looked as though they'd been served with a builder's trowel. The girl doing the cleaning looked as though she preferred eating pussy than spotted Dick! *'It's time to get out of here.'*

The first man I asked about buses was a bit of a dry old stick. He produced a laminated bus timetable out of his shopping bag and then gave me precise directions.

I caught the bus and made my way to Great Yarmouth.

The spring crops looked well and again there was a scattering of lovely churches.

I said to the driver, 'I seem to be the only one giving you any money.'

'It's the same, day in, day out.'

For the first time in my life I saw the Broads with all the fancy, horrible boats cluttering up the rivers. It was off-season and nobody was using them. It was as if all the owners had died. Some boats were in dry dock or completely shrink-wrapped.

We passed through Potter Heigham, Rollesby, Ormesby and Caister-on-Sea. The passengers came and went but they all seemed rather ancient. The only time they smiled was when they flashed their OAP passes at the driver, so getting their free bus ride. Sitting behind them I was aware of a smell of cheap perfume and old flesh. But the good thing was that having been in the same shirt for four days I didn't know what I smelled like.

We arrived in Great Yarmouth. It was great not to be here in the summer, with all the junk shops selling cheap seaside souvenirs.

After wandering through the streets I found myself at the quayside, and met two pipe welders having a lunch break. They were working on a ship and were quite pleased to have a chat when they realised I was taking an interest.

I noticed Bunn's fertiliser yard over on the other side of the river, and as we had done a little business with them through Tim Boxall, I went to look them up. I kept looking through the gate like a gorilla that wouldn't go away and eventually they opened it.

Paul gave me a run-down on the plant. I asked why they put the price of fertiliser up when the price of wheat went up – he just smiled.

I went back to the railway station. You can only go to Lowestoft by going to Norwich.

What a lovely ride it was through the flat marshes of the Norfolk Broads. On the way I saw seven windmills all at the same time and some didn't have sails. There were also men thatching with reeds.

The train had just two carriages. I asked the driver if he worked this line every day. 'No, I generally do the main line.'

'Bit of a doddle this one, isn't it?'

'Bit cool, yeah,' he replied.

Norwich Cathedral has dominated the skyline for nine hundred years and is surrounded by forty-four acres of real estate mostly owned by the church. It will need all the rents to keep up with the huge maintenance costs. Since 1990 every Anglican cathedral has been required to have its own archaeologist.

I teased some of the church staff by talking about the fact that they charged people to come in. I said there was a fine line between those praying and the tourists.

One person said, 'I have a friend in Ely Cathedral and they charge £10 entry and they're full. Here we don't charge and we're empty.'

'If they do that here I'm having nothing to do with churches.' I asked how much money they got from donations and they hadn't a clue.

Diana said, 'If you pray hard enough the money always comes in.'
'Must try that one!'

£3,700 a day running costs wouldn't go far on this building. One small job outside was costing seven million pounds.

Norwich Cathedral has the second highest spire in the country, after Ely.

I had a cup of tea in yet another converted church where there were religious books and candles for sale.

NORWICH TO LOWESTOFT

The station had lovely freshly painted Victorian steelwork and was nice and clean. The only bad thing about this trip was that all the schoolchildren were on their way home. I noticed that the young person sitting next to me was a bit mouthy and seemed to have a bit of an 'attitude face', but he went to a smart school. What with the train noise and his accent, I had a job to understand him. Anyway, I decided I didn't like him so didn't bother. I had an idea the feeling was mutual.

I walked over the bridge and found accommodation. There were loads to choose from so I went by the appearance of the outsides and the gardens and for £39 I reckoned I had picked the right one. I asked, 'Is business good?'

The owner, Sue, said they'd had a good season and that the money was good.

'What has been your worst experience doing this?'

'Someone once pinched a television and a kettle. He was charming and he also conned me out of two weeks' board. He even got me to iron his shirts for him!'

I thought that really didn't seem too bad in twenty-two years. Sue recommended the Gourmet's Chinese Restaurant as I couldn't stand the thought of another ordinary English meal.

The service was lovely and done by the owner's daughter who had a delightful smile. She and her brother ran the place. The food was not the tastiest, but the service was 100 %.

As I walked back home I was surprised how quiet the streets were for 8.30pm and how many fast food outlets there were.

LOWESTOFT TO ALDEBURGH

It was March 19th and it was cold and dry and turned out to be a special day.

I asked an old boy what there was to see in Lowestoft and he told me that that depended on what you wanted. He then changed the conversation and told me his life story. These old boys always like talking if you take an interest in them, and one thing for certain is that they never ask about you.

I had nothing planned and I had no idea where I was going. All I wanted was to go inland and see the villages, and jump on and off the buses at will.

I couldn't really get my head around Lowestoft and asked a grumpy bus driver the best way to Halesworth.

'Don't do that route.'

'Not even for me?'

Not a flicker of humour. 'Anglian does it, over there,' he said.

I had five bus rides and I could jump on and off whenever I pleased. It was good to get out of the urban sprawl of Pizza Huts, Morrisons, Homebase and suchlike, and good to find the Suffolk countryside.

My first stop was at Wangford. When the bus stopped a very old lady fell onto the floor and I helped to lift her up. What had happened was that when she'd stood up the seat had flipped up behind her. But she didn't complain and was very grateful.

The driver asked if she wanted to make an 'Incident Report'.

'No, I'm all right.'

WANGFORD

It had a beautiful church and this seduced me off the bus.

 I met Eric Stockdale who was driving through the village on his vintage tractor. I waved at him and he stopped for a chat. He was eighty-one and had spent most of his life working on a local estate. When he was fifty-nine he got a job working in a quarry and he'd got the job because the other man had wanted to be a gamekeeper at the weekends.

I asked him if he took his tractor to the shows and he said he did and that he'd been a finalist in the National Ploughing Championships. He had competed in the Championship in Marden, Kent.

'That's near where I live.'

'Small world!'

He told me that the estate of two thousand acres had now been put down to grass and rented out.

'Lovely church you have there,' I said.

'You're not a millionaire are you, because we need to do it up?'

'Afraid not.'

'I've just been up there trying to hook my roller on but couldn't do it.'

'Would you like me to give you a hand?'

'No, that's all right. You can see it up there. I made it myself from bits of scrap from a quarry.' In fact it was made from a forty-gallon oil drum.

He told me all about the sheaves of wheat and how the knots had to face inwards to help the rain run off.

I said goodbye to that big honest countryman.

BLYTHBURGH

'I can't believe this. I'm not a religious man, but the architecture of these churches is so mind-blowing that I wonder why all these people go to the Costa del Sol when they have this on their doorsteps – as well as such beautiful countryside. Well, come to think of it maybe it's just as well they do!'

I rang the bus bell and got off. I thought that this must be the most windowed church in the UK. I also took a photograph of this nasty note in the visitors' book:

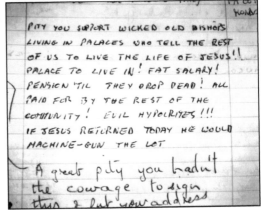

'Pity you support wicked old bishops living in palaces who tell the rest of us to live the life of Jesus. Palace to live in! Fat salary. Pension 'til they drop dead. All paid for by the rest of the community. Evil hypocrites. If Jesus returned today he would machine-gun the lot.'

The bus came past here every hour so you knew exactly how long you had to wait.

'Where does the bus go after Halesworth?'

'Don't know, mate.'

Past Lynsford there was a huge barn with a galvanised roof. I was tempted to jump off but decided to leave it for another day.

HALESWORTH TO LEISTON

I met a lady picking up rubbish at the bus stop.

'I'm eighty-one you know. I had a bit of luck the other day. I found a £10 note and I needed it.'

I thanked her for tidying up.

I was going to stay the night in Leiston but decided against it. I killed time in a little café and got chatting to a mum who had an eighteen-year-old son with autism. He now had a job in a supermarket for three days a week and was enjoying it and making friends. He'd been bullied at school and had been very overweight. A few days earlier someone had 'mouthed' him so he'd pushed the person and had got into more trouble.

The mother had also been very overweight, but was now pulling herself together and keeping fit. She used to suffer from depression, but started to get lots of hobbies and was now enjoying life.

I arrived at Aldeburgh and wondered if this 'up-your-jumper' town had got the Black Death as there was no one around. It was really eerie, although the Mill Hotel was full. I went into the Wentworth but it was a bit pricey. I said I would think about it. The White Lion had a room for £67, but that was again too expensive.

I then tried a guest house on the seafront. The husband opened the door and said, '£70 per night, but we'd be a bit expensive for you. I'll ask my wife.'

She peered round the window and gave me a look that suggested that I'd just trodden in a lump of dog shit. With this he said, 'Try number 55. It's cheaper.'

I laughed all the way to number 55 only to find that it wasn't a B&B!

I went back to the Wentworth trying not to look like a dog with its tail between its legs and was greeted with a big smile by Jana, the German girl at the reception.

'Well, how much do you want to pay?' *You know, I like that kind of attitude.'*

We did a deal with dinner included and I found that I'd landed on my feet. *'Wow, man, I have a ten foot wide bed with cushions on it. Luxury! I have the lot. There's a hair dryer, soap, shampoo, skin lotion, tissues, shoe-shining stuff and a shower hat! Lying in the bath with bubbles overflowing, I feel like Crocodile Dundee.'*

When I went down for dinner I'd expected the place to be empty, but it was full of mainly elderly folk in ties and jackets. I felt really scruffy, but had made myself as smart as I could. I had saddle of lamb that melted in my mouth. A group of very smart people were eating next to me. It made a nice change from yobs. What's the difference between 'posh' and 'yobs'? Answer: the author.

This is a family hotel. Kathy had worked here for twenty-two years and the waiter, whose night off it was had been here for forty-two years. Jana, the German girl at reception, had worked here for three years. She was lovely to talk to and would have no trouble getting your custom.

I mustn't be nasty about Aldeburgh as Penny in the tourist office couldn't do enough for me. I had asked a lady how to get to the tourist office only to be told that I was standing outside it.

Some middle-aged ramblers have not got the best sense of humour in the world. Perhaps it would help if they smiled and acknowledged you when they walked past you in the fields, and perhaps they could pick up a little litter, and whilst they were at it take the secateurs and cut a few brambles off around the stiles. (I've since been taken to task over this comment by a friend who belongs to the Ramblers' Association – sorry!)

And a big thank you to the dog walkers, the ones who give us the free fertiliser!

I had a dream the other night that a regular walker gave me a bottle of whisky for Christmas, for keeping the paths open, and providing a dog toilet with a view. Then, suddenly I woke up feeling really guilty that the government pays us all these subsidies to do just that.

Sorry, I forgot it's your right and our responsibility. (Do I sound arrogant?)

IPSWICH

At the bus stop I asked the way to the town centre.

'First right and then left.'

'What's your badge?'

'Royal Air Force.'

'I bet you've seen some terrible things.'

'Yes, and lived through them.'

374

'Our generation owes you a lot. Thank you very much.'

A man in a wheelchair was getting himself down the street and dropped something. I was watching as someone came up to him and asked if he was all right and put his arm round him – just an act of kindness. Mind you, he was a heavy smoker and drunk, but it was still very kind.

I went into 'Subway' to get a cheap salad and a drink. There were just as many pigs down here as me and when they finished their food they just left everything like a battlefield. It amused me when the young girl walked in and seemed totally unconcerned at the crumbiness and happily ordered her food and carried on eating amongst all the mess.

Ipswich was swarming with people and I went in to see the herb man. 'Have you got a sleeping pill?'

'Yes, try these. £8.50.'

'That's a little expensive. How about a fiver?'

'£8.00.'

I was now the proud owner of wild jujube seed!

The Chinese man had studied medicine for five years. I asked him what would happen if I took two of his pills and he said that the recommended dose was one. (They were useless!)

IPSWICH TO HARWICH

With the benefit of hindsight I realised that this was probably not the wisest decision in the world, but I was off to sunny Harwich on the train and I had to change at Manningtree. There was a huge wind farm. It took me a while to find my way out of Harwich International Ferry Terminal to Holland. I got fed up with waiting for a bus so I walked into town and caught a bus there, which duly took me back to where I'd started.

'Thanks for stopping.'

'No bother, mate. Have you got a bus pass?' *'Damn me, do I look that old?!'*

To kill time waiting for a bus to Clacton, I went to a Turkish café run by a father and son who were so gentle and polite it was refreshing to watch.

'What's the best thing about this country?'

'You can run a business with no hassle.'

'And the worst?'

'Broken family life of the English.'

For the first time I was seeing some good farming with early drilled wheat and no rabbit damage. Fowton Farm and Little Oakley Hall Farm were two fine examples.

There was a converted church that had been painted pink and to completely mess it up, they'd put skylights in the roof.

The bus dropped me off at Clacton railway station. I booked in at a B&B, which looked better from the outside than it was on the inside. The Aldeburgh Wentworth room seemed a million years away and I was back down to earth.

I ate a rather expensive dinner for what it was and I was put off more by the big, fat, dirty chef.

My nephew, Mark, has an old college friend who farms around here and he said I should look him up. I wasn't sure if Ben had better things to do than waste time on an old 'has-been' farmer, but I was glad we'd arranged to meet the next morning.

I went for an early morning walk along the seafront that was once a paradise for London holidaymakers. Nowadays, it's so quaint and old-fashioned it must be close to having a preservation order placed on it. No doubt they'll knock it all down and replace it with a Tesco or something just as ugly.

The name Clacton dates back to 500 AD when the Saxons settled in the area. The original name was Claccingaton, which means 'the village of Clacc's people'. It took off as a holiday resort in about 1871. This was the same year in which they built the pier. In 1893 they extended it to 360 metres. The heyday years were in the 1950s to the 1970s. It has a population of fifty thousand and all but three are over ninety years old, or so it seems.

Ben Parker joined me for breakfast and we then got the hell out of it and went farming.

My first stop was to see the Fairley family. John is a larger-than-life character and he was covered in grease and was about to calibrate the drill for pea planting. He was talking not in kilograms or hundredweights but in stones. He admitted to a few foul-ups in the past with calibrations but today he was determined to get it right.

Mr Fairley is well-known in the area as a first class farmer and has a dislike of any machinery not made in Britain. He was a bit edgy as the forecast wasn't good and he wanted to get on with drilling. His pet terrier that went with him everywhere was already in the cab. Don't tell Doe's but he ate through all the wiring the other day. He told them it was a warranty job.

John's brother joined us for coffee and he's just about as bad as him.

Mrs Fairley was nursing a nasty broken shoulder.

'Is he making a good nurse?' I asked.

'No different.'

My next stop was the Nursery and Garden Centre. Ben said, in a modest way, that this was where they made the real money. It was the day before Mothering Sunday and Ben, his mother and father and brothers and sister were all flat out, but they found the time to say 'hello' and made me feel welcome.

The place was heaving with people and they even had a male guitarist. The whole place had a club atmosphere and was a good spot to come to for a chat and a cup of tea (in bone china!), and to spend a bit of dough.

I had to laugh when I saw a sign on the wall advertising the 'Hedgehog Hospital'.

The Parker family have built up an amazing business here and are very unassuming about it.

We then went round Ben's wheat and oilseed rape crops and saw the next door farmer planting potatoes. After a very interesting morning Ben dropped me off at Clacton rail station.

Colchester bus station was bustling with people and buses were coming and going every minute. I was sick of towns and couldn't get out of the place fast enough. Burnham here we come! We would see rural Essex, or so I thought, but in fact I found the overspill from London and the travellers had done their best to urbanise it. They had bath tubs, muddy starving horses and caravans. There was no shortage of new 4X4s parked up. I asked the driver to take me back to Maldon.

I liked Maldon. I agree it had loads of fast food places, but St Mary the Virgin was a beautiful church. I had some difficulty finding a hotel. In the end I found one and not cheap. The room was dirty and I even found an old teabag in the teapot, and old shit and stale urine in the loo. I continued to look for filth and there was no shortage of it. It was late and I couldn't be bothered to look elsewhere.

I had breakfast and paid my bill and took 'Fancy Pants', the owner, to my room to show him the dirt. He didn't seem worried and didn't apologise. He said they had a new cleaner and he rated her highly. *'She leaves shit and piss on the loo and he rates her highly!'*

The next day on the way out of town I popped into St Mary's where there was a service in full swing. It's nearly always impossible to open a church door quietly. It was Mothering Sunday and the singing sounded beautiful.

Not many buses came so I started walking and met some real old travellers who had a fifty-six-year-old vintage Bedford lorry with the bonnet up.

'Do you take it to the shows?'

'Yeah, some of them.'

'What about Barleylands?'

'No, some of them are a bit snobby and charge £10.'

'They should pay you for entering!' I showed an interest, half hoping that they would offer me a lift but no such luck.

The A414 was a busy road and after a long walk I managed to hitch a lift. It was the first and only one since Newcastle. It turned out to be the last on my 'walkabout'. The driver was Mike Robson, who was a part-time gamekeeper and had been doing it for forty years. He was a keen photographer and liked walking – he was a true countryman.

I told him he had a deal for giving me a lift and I would give him a day's shooting. He dropped me off at Danbury where I waited thirty minutes for a bus. I kept on walking and walking and said to myself that I would give it until 1.15pm and believe it or not it turned up on the dot.

It wasn't long before we were in busy Chelmsford.

I chatted away to a Nigerian who had such a strong accent that I couldn't understand him. He talked in whispers as if the KGB might have been listening. He said that oil had brought more problems to Nigeria than good; then all of a sudden, Edward, who was sitting opposite, chipped in to talk about corrupt business people. He said his father owned an estate in Wiltshire and had told him to get a proper living. He said that he used to love it when he helped a gamekeeper, but he hated working with rich people to make them richer.

On the way to London we passed many buildings. 'What's that?' I asked.

'Building for the Olympics.'

London was full to the brim and it didn't help with the Victoria Line being out of service. The whole city seemed to be bulging with people. Two young gay lads sat opposite, hand in hand.

By now my ticket was crumpled and wouldn't open the gate, so a lovely Muslim girl swiped the gate for me.

With half a minute to spare I was on the train and once again there were engineering works all the way to Faversham. It seemed built-up the whole way.

I booked in to the Shepherd Neame Sun Inn which is very smart. The only place open on a Sunday night was the Spice Lounge which meant two Bangladeshi meals on the trot. I asked what they thought best about living here and they said it was the freedom to go anywhere and to run a business. The worst thing was the culture and I think they meant that they were worried that their children would grow into yobs. It was an excellent meal and they were very hospitable.

FAVERSHAM TO HERNE BAY

I had an early morning walk around the town and although living nearby I'd never realised what a beautiful town it is. Faversham is home to the Shepherd Neame Brewery; the oldest brewery in Britain. It was founded in 1698 and is still going strong. They own most of Faversham and nearly all the pubs in the area. It's a pity another brewery let Tesco creep in right in the middle of the brewery's historic warehousing.

HERE LIVED MICHAEL GREENWOOD, MARINER (1731/2 – 1812), WHO WAS PRESS – GANGED IN 1748, WRECKED OFF THE COAST OF MOROCCO IN 1768, AND THEN ENSLAVED BY THE MOORS FOR 17 MONTHS, AFTER BEING RANSOMED, HE RETURNED TO FAVERSHAM.

'And if you think you are having a bad day think of Michael.'

Faversham was also famous for its shipbuilding and from 1916 until 1969 it built 1200 ships. It was also the heart of the UK explosives industry. The first plant was established in the 16th century. In 1916 a huge explosion killed 105 people when 200 tons of TNT ignited. Apparently there was another 3000 tons that didn't go off. All the dead were buried in a mass grave in Faversham cemetery. The munitions industry no longer exists, but there is a museum open in the summer months.

There were masses of plaques on buildings telling you their history.

After breakfast I had another walk and went to the creek with the idea that I might be able to walk along the sea wall to Whitstable, but I couldn't get to it because of the boatyards, and anyway there was a strong north wind. I chuckled at the different coloured wheelie bins. *'How can you have purple wheelie bins in a town like this?!'*

I caught the wrong train and ended up en route to Canterbury. I sat next to a disabled gentleman and made an effort to talk to him. He had a speech impediment, but soon I couldn't stop him talking. When the conductor came along he thought I was the carer and never asked to see my ticket.

CANTERBURY EAST

In the end I only had to wait for thirty minutes for the return train and I met a young soldier in desert uniform. He was a tall, blue-eyed and well-spoken, good-looking man.

'Are you just coming or going?'

'Just back from Iraq.'

'How are things going there?'

'We're making a lot of progress and things are going really well.'

'What's your equipment like?'

'Yeah, good. I'm in the tank regiment.'

'Have you lost many friends?'

'I've been lucky and only lost two and in a six month period that's pretty good.'

'It must be hard.'

'Yes, but you have to put it behind you and move on.'

'I bet that's easier said than done.'

'Yes.'

'What are the Americans like to work with?'

'Very friendly and yeah, good. Now and again they do a few silly things like blue on blue, but they're good.'

'Well, thank you very much for what you're doing.' I shook his hand and got the train back to Faversham.

As we stopped at Selling I noticed birch trees growing up straight through the redundant track.

Once more I got on the train only to be told that I had to move to the front half. I would've felt a real bloody idiot if I'd done the same again! I asked the station master what the smart train was on the other platform and he said it was the high speed train to London. 'Looks very smart,' I said.

'Bit like a cattle truck inside,' was the reply.

HERNE BAY TO RECULVER

I needed a walk and enjoyed walking along the beach dodging the dog shit. There was barely a soul about and when I was miles out of Herne Bay a man overtook me without a word. *'Good morning; nice day; lovely dog shit; no, nothing!'*

There were two lads in their late teens digging some steps into the sandy cliff and when I asked one of them what he was up to he got defensive. 'I'm just here with my mate!'

There was some scruffy old farming here but at least the golden plovers were enjoying the deep wheel ruts which gave them shelter.

I stumbled across another dear old pub.

'Still playing the fruit machines?'

'No, not like I used to.'

It even made me feel intelligent.

I walked up to Reculver Castle. The conservation worker was pointing the base and then the sky just opened up with 100mph winds and rain. All my clothes were in a bin liner in my rucksack so I went back to a little caravan café. I thought the whole place was about to take off. The owner said, 'Where the f.....g hell is this coming from?'

I passed the Blue Dolphin Carver Club. It was a beautiful Georgian house that had been completely messed up and I wiggled up the tiny lanes to Beltinge.

I couldn't find the Whitstable Road and there were no buses, but when I did run back to catch one he shut the doors in my face. I asked a girl who was getting off the bus what the problem was and she said it was the school bus. *'Plonker!'*

I saw some caravans for sale from £35,000-£85,000 and one even had a veranda. I kept asking the way to Margate and ended up back in Herne Bay. I couldn't believe I'd walked in a complete circle. You have to be able to laugh at yourself.

It was now 5pm and still cold and windy, so I decided to book in at the Bay View, which was a very smart family B&B. I had a long chat with the beautiful landlady with a Macedonian husband.

Tonight was my last dinner on 'walkabout' and what could be more suitable than fish and chips and mushy peas in windy, cold Herne Bay?

I went to bed.

I went for an early walk before breakfast and organised the best way to get to Margate. I was to go by train. The high winds had blown the streets clean and bins were everywhere overflowing with rubbish. I had a big hearty breakfast cooked by the husband in between getting his children ready for school.

Who said Margate was boring?

Margate was, once more, very windy and cold. A sign said about how the old town was being reborn. If this is reborn I don't know what it was like when it was dead!

The tourist office didn't open until 10am so a little café made a welcome shelter. All the construction workers were here reading *The Sun*.

I asked how far it was to North Foreland and was told it was about half an hour. About three hours later I found it! I never saw a bus and walked past golf courses, cliff tops and housing estates.

'Could you tell me the way to North Foreland?'

'Never heard of it!' a Cockney voice replied.

I wondered if I was pronouncing it correctly and got the map out to check. I showed them the map, but I don't think these stupid Londoners even knew where Kent was, let alone Margate. I couldn't believe I was only half a mile away.

I went past cauliflower fields and at last I saw the castle lighthouse. The castle was now a private estate with access only and covered by CCTV. The gate was locked and I thought better of creeping inside. I could just about make out the tip of Kent on the Isle of Thanet.

BIRCHINGTON

It was a funny part of the world and I hadn't seen a bus all morning. I walked into a shop with a real red telephone box outside and asked what the name of this place was. I was told it was Birchington. I went round the corner and it was full of young people eating fast food in the High Street. I found the bus stop and jumped onto the bus going to Ramsgate. Apparently they left every ten minutes. I hadn't seen one all day and now they go every ten minutes!

Somehow or other I'd lost my rail ticket, so at Ramsgate I bought my last £12.50's worth to get me back home. I felt that I really had to stop off at Dover to mentally finish my trip. I had a phone call from Jadwiga to say that Valerie was ill, but that she and Tom would meet me at Lenham.

Dreaming that the whole of Dover had turned out to greet me, including the Queen and the Mayor, tears of joy streamed down my cheeks. I wanted to jump and shout out about what a clever little shit I was and that I'd travelled all around the UK. I did tell the station master what I'd done.

'Yeah, that must've been very interesting.'

To kill time I popped out to the car park and saw a young lad giving a moony to his friends. I thought that this just about summed up the yob element of this trip.

For the first time on my 'walkabout' we had two rail enforcement officers who were keeping the peace. I must say I've been very impressed with the whole of the UK transport system.

There was no one at the station to meet me and I walked back to Court Lodge. I was met by a very emotional brother, Thomas, who has Down's Syndrome and hates me for going away; he was also ill...

We grabbed a bottle of champagne and went to celebrate at Valerie's bedside, only for Tom to spew up. 'I think I'd better get you home!'

As he got out of the car he was ill again. 'OK, Tom, we'd better get you in the shower.'

Transport around the UK

Buses	211	
Trains	104	
Hitches	94	
Ferrys	22	
Plane	3	
Private lifts	17	
Taxi	21	

114	Days over three and a half years		
93	B & Bs		
Cost	£8850	Per Day	£77.63